DILEMMAS IN DEVELOPMENT

Journeys of an Agricultural Economist

GEORGE GWYER

authorHOUSE®

AuthorHouse™ UK
1663 Liberty Drive
Bloomington, IN 47403 USA
www.authorhouse.co.uk
Phone: 0800.197.4150

Published by AuthorHouse 02/27/2016

ISBN: 978-1-5049-9796-6 (sc)
ISBN: 978-1-5049-9798-0 (e)

Print information available on the last page.

Any people depicted in stock imagery provided by Thinkstock are models, and such images are being used for illustrative purposes only. Certain stock imagery © Thinkstock.

This book is printed on acid-free paper.

Contents

Dramatis Personae

Abe, Christopher Columbus, Minister of Finance, Solomon Islands

Allen, George Fellow of St Edmund Hall, Oxford University

Anthony, Kenny Prime Minister of St Lucia

Anthony Browne, Laura National Authorising Officer of the EDF and Director of Planning in St Vincent

Apiyo, Timothy Head of Planning Division, Ministry of Agriculture, Tanzania, subsequently Permanent Secretary, President's Office

Arrowsmith, Keith Colonial Civil Servant in Nigeria, subsequently official of DG Agriculture, European Commission

Arthur, Owen Prime Minister of Barbados

Aziz, Aslam Desk officer for Sudan, European Commission, subsequently Head of Pacific Unit

Baker, Gordon British High Commissioner, Barbados

Beckett, Veronica First Secretary (Development), British High Commission, New Delhi, subsequently UK Ambassador to Ireland

Belshaw, Deryke Lecturer in Economics at Makerere University, subsequently Emeritus Professor, School of International Development, University of East Anglia

Bridger, Gordon Director of Geographical Economists, ODA, subsequently Mayor of Guildford

Bryceson, Derek Minister of Agriculture, Tanzania

Bunting, Hugh Professor of Agricultural Development Overseas, University of Reading

Carrington, Edwin Secretary-General of ACP Group, subsequently Secretary-General of the Caribbean Community

Carruthers, Ian Lecturer, and subsequently Professor of Agrarian Development, at Wye College, University of London

Chambers, Robert Research fellow at IDS Nairobi, subsequently Professor at IDS Sussex

Cheetham, Russell Leader of NEDA Regional Planning Team in the Philippines, subsequently World Bank Vice President for Asia and the Pacific

Clark, Colin Director of the Agricultural Economics Research Institute, Oxford University

Coulson, Andrew Economist, Ministry of Agriculture, Tanzania, subsequently Lecturer in Economics at the University of Dar es Salaam

Cunningham, Bob Chief Natural Resources Adviser, Overseas Development Administration, London

Cunningham, Jack Cabinet Minister, subsequently member of the House of Lords

Curtin, Tim UNDP adviser to the Ministry of Finance and Planning, Papua New Guinea, formerly economic adviser in the EC Delegation in Kenya

Dass, Sant Managing Director, NABARD, India

Denton-Thompson, Aubrey Secretary of TASMA Tanzania and subsequently senior agricultural adviser to UNDP in Indonesia

Dhua, S P General Manager, Hindustan Fertilizer Corporation, Calcutta

Douglas, Denzil Prime Minister of St Kitts and Nevis

Elkan, Walter Professor of Economics at Durham University

Falkowski, Christian Director, DG Development, European Commission

Foulkes, George Parliamentary Under-Secretary at the Department for International Development, subsequently member of the House of Lords

Frisch, Dieter Director General for Development, European Commission, subsequently Senior Adviser, Transparency International

Gadgil, M V Head of Evaluation, NABARD, India

Ghai, Dharam Director of the Institute for Development Studies at the University of Narobi, subsequently Director of the United Nations Research Institute for Social Research

Granell, Francesco Director, DG Development, European Commission

Green, Reginald Adviser to the Treasury in Tanzania, subsequently Professorial Fellow at the Institute of Development Studies, University of Sussex

Greenidge, Carl Deputy Secretary-General of ACP Group, formerly Minister of Finance, Guyana

Hamburger, Friedrich Director, DG for Development, subsequently EU Ambassador to Thailand

Heyer, Judith Lecturer in Economics, University of Nairobi subsequently Emeritus Fellow of Somerville College

Holder, Jean Secretary-General of the Caribbean Tourism Organisation

Hunt, Rex Governor of the Falkland Islands

James, Edison Prime Minister of Dominica

Jay, Michael First Secretary (Development), British High Commission, New Delhi, subsequently Permanent Under Secretary for Foreign Affairs, and later member of the House of Lords

Jolly, Richard Leader of the ILO Employment Mission to Kenya, Director of the Institute of Development Studies, University of Sussex, subsequently coordinator of the UNDP Human Development Report

Jones, Ray British High Commissioner, Solomon Islands

Joseph, Andrew UNDP Resident Representative, Indonesia, subsequently Associate Administrator, UNDP

Kabui, Joseph Premier of Bougainville Province, PNG, subsequently President of the Autonomous Region of Bougainville

Kauona, Sam Commander of the Bougainville Revolutionary Army

Kiernan, Bob Desk officer for India, Overseas Development Administration

Kim, Jim President of the World Bank

Kinnock, Glenys Member of the European Parliament's Development and Cooperation Committee, subsequently member of the House of Lords

Kurien, Verghese Chairman, National Dairy Development Board, India

La Corbiniere, Bernard National authorising officer of the EDF in St Lucia, subsequently Chairman of the Caribbean Development Fund

Lawas, Joe Regional Director of National Economic and Development Authority, Philippines

Lewis, Vaughan Prime Minister of St Lucia

Lipton, Michael Professorial Fellow at the Institute of Development Studies, University of Sussex

Lowe, Philip Director General for Development, European Commission

McNamara, Robert President of the World Bank

Marin, Manuel EC Commissioner for Development

Maxwell, Simon Agricultural economist to the British Tropical Agriculture Mission in Bolivia, and subsequently Director of the Overseas Development Institute, London

Meade, Reuben Chief Minister, Montserrat

Mellor, John Director of the International Food Policy Research Institute, Washington DC

Miller, Billie Deputy Prime Minister, Barbados

Mitchell, James Prime Minister of St Vincent

Mitchell, Keith Prime Minister of Grenada

Momis, John Minister for Provincial Affairs, PNG, subsequently President of the Autonomous Region of Bougainville

Monck, Nicholas Senior Economist, Ministry of Agriculture, Tanzania, subsequently Second Permanent Secretary in the UK Treasury

Morris, John NR Economist, subsequently Head of Evaluation, ODA

Moti, Julian Adviser to the Minister of Finance, Solomon Islands, subsequently Professor of Law at the University of Fiji

Natali, Lorenzo EC Commissioner for Development

Nicholls, Neville President of the Caribbean Development Bank

Nielson, Poul EU Commissioner for Development

Osman, Mekki Deputy NAO, Sudan, subsequently Counsellor, Sudan Embassy in Brussels

Patten, Chris EU Commissioner for External Affairs, subsequently member of the House of Lords

Perryman, Chong Managing Director of Winban

Pepson, Gabriel PNG Ambassador in Brussels

Peters, George Lecturer, and subsequently Director of the Agricultural Economics Research Institute, Oxford University

Pinheiro, Jao de Deus EU Commissioner for Development

Porter, R S Chief Economist, Overseas Development Administration

Pugh, Frank Tenant farmer at Grove Farm, Kinton, Shropshire

Rini, Snyder Permanent Secretary, Ministry of Natural Resources, subsequently Minister of Finance, Solomon Islands

Rolls, Maurice Director of the Agricultural Extension and Rural Development Centre, University of Reading

Ruigu, George Research Assistant, IDS Nairobi, subsequently Senior Lecturer in Economics, University of Nairobi

Savage, Frank Governor of Montserrat

Short, Clare Secretary of State for International Development

Singer, Hans Professor, Institute of Development Studies, Sussex University

Skilbeck, Dunstan Principal of Wye College, University of London, and sometime Master of the East Kent Hunt

Smith, Lawrence Leader of the Glasgow Team, IDS Nairobi, subsequently Chairman of the Centre for Development Studies, Glasgow University

Soeroso Director for Smallholder Plantation Crops, Indonesia

Soomer, Rodinald Deputy NAO, St Lucia

Soubestre, Philippe Deputy Director General for Development, European Commission

Stern, Ernie Vice President for Operations, World Bank

Stiglitz, Joseph Research fellow, IDS Nairobi, subsequently Chief Economist, World Bank

Stutley, Peter Ford Foundation adviser to the Ministry of Agriculture Tanzania, subsequently Principal Natural Resources Economics Adviser in the Ministry of Overseas Development

Swaminathan, M S Principal Secretary, Ministry of Agriculture, India, subsequently Director General of IRRI

Thomson, Brian Head of Caribbean Development Division, DFID

Togolo, Mel Provincial Secretary, North Solomons Province, subsequently Country Manager, Nautilus Minerals

Tolley, George Professor of Economics, North Carolina State University subsequently Professor Emeritus in Economics at the University of Chicago

Wibberley, Gerald Professor of Rural Economy, Wye College

Wilson, Thomas Adam Smith Professor of Political Economy, University of Glasgow

Wood, Rob Adviser to the Ministry of Industries, Tanzania Government, subsequently Director of the Overseas Development Institute, London

List of Illustrations

Coffee shambas on the slopes of Mount Kilimanjaro

Nicholas Monck and the General Manager of Amboni Sisal Estates

FAO Planning team visits Menado on coconuts mission

Smallholder rubber nursery in Kalimantan

The World Bank regional planning team in Manila

Visiting the Visayas with Domingo Raymundo and David Parbery

Natural Resources conference at Magdalene College

Villagers in Maharashtra during agricultural credit mission

Inspecting IBFEP block demonstrations with Dr Das

The Governor's residence in Port Stanley

Penguins

Monitoring EU food aid shipments in Port Sudan

EU Parliamentarians interview displaced people in Darfur

Christoper Abe and Victor Ngele with spouses in Honiara

EC Delegation staff and technical assistants in Solomons

Bougainvilleans during Commissioner Nielson's PNG mission

Prime Minister Kemakeza with Anthony Crasner

List of YouTube Videos

Readers familiar with YouTube may wish to view some videos of my field trips in Sudan, Papua New Guinea, Solomon Islands, and the Caribbean, which can be found in YouTube under George Gwyer/Playlists/ An Agricultural Economist's Journey

Delivering EU Food Aid to Sudan 1985-1989

New Ireland Cocoa and Oil Palm 1991

Bougainville January 1990

Porgera Gold Mine PNG 1990

Passam-Tuanumbu Road 1991

Solomon Islands Independence Day 1991

Solomon Islands Munda-Noro 1991

Solomon Islands Fisheries Tatamba 1991

Solomon Islands Temotu Province 1994

Solomon Islands Malaita Agriculture 1992

FFA Solomon Islands

Rural Training Centre Solomon Islands 1993

Stuyvenberg Rural Training Centre Makira 1994

Logging Guadalcanal 1993

SIPL Oil Palm Guadalcanal Solomons 1994

Rural Roads Solomon Islands

Rural Roads 2 Solomon Islands 1994

Makira Roads Solomons 1993

Rennell Solomons 1994

Rennell Roads 1995

Solomon Islands Small Malaita 1994

Morovo Lagoon Cocoa and Copra Farmers 1994

Ranongga Rural Health 1994

Ranongga 1994

Diplomatic Moments Solomon Islands

EU Delegation Barbados

St Vincent Bananas 1997

Montserrat Volcano 1997

Cariforum Meeting Georgetown Guyana October 1997

Glossary

ACP	African, Caribbean and Pacific Group of States
ADB	Asian Development Bank
AEC	Agency for Economic Cooperation (EC)
AERI	Agricultural Economics Research Institute, Oxford University
AERDC	Agricultural Extension and Rural Development Centre, Reading University
AICF	Action International Contre Le Faim
AIDCO	European Commission's Aid Delivery Directorate
APROSC	Agricultural Project Support Centre, Nepal
ARDC	Agricultural Refinance and Development Corporation, India
AUSAID	Australian Aid
BAPPENAS	Central Planning Agency, Indonesia
BDDC	British Development Division in the Caribbean, Barbados
BGA	Banana Growers Association (Windwards)
BRA	Bougainville Revolutionary Army
BWIs	Bretton Woods Institutions
CDB	Caribbean Development Bank
CDC	Commonwealth Development Corporation
CENICAFE	Centro Nacional de Investigaciones de Cafe, Colombia
CG	Consultative Group
CGIAR	Consultative Group on International Agricultural Research
CHOGM	Commonwealth Heads of Government Meeting

CIAE	Centre for Indian Agricultural Engineering
CIAT	International Centre for Tropical Agriculture, Cali, Colombia
CIMMYT	Centro Internacional de Mejoramiento de Maiz y Trigo (International Maize and Wheat Improvement Centre), Mexico
CNRA	Chief Natural Resources Adviser (ODA)
COPR	Centre for Overseas Pest Research, London
COTONOU	A Partnership Agreement for development and trade between ACP and the EU signed in Benin in 2000
CRA	Charles River Associates, an Australian Mining Company
CTVM	Centre for Tropical Veterinary Medicine, Edinburgh
DEVDIV	Development Division (ODA)
DFID	Department for International Development, London
DG	Director-General, Directorate-General
DG AGRIC	Directorate-General for Agriculture (EC)
DG DEV	Directorate-General for Development (EC)
DTW	Deep Tubewell
EC	European Commission, European Community
ECGD	Export Credits Guarantee Department
EDF	European Development Fund
EIHRD	European Initiative on Human Rights and Democracy
EOM	Electoral Observation Mission
ESCOR	Economic and Social Committee on Overseas Research (ODA)
EU	European Union
FAO	Food and Agriculture Organization, Rome
FCI	Fertilizer Corporation of India
FCO	Foreign and Commonwealth Office, London
FFA	Forum Fisheries Agency, Honiara, Solomon Islands

FIAC	Fertilizer Industry Advisory Committee of FAO
FMO	Framework of Mutual Obligations (EDF)
GOI	Government of India
GOL	Government of Liberia
HFC	Hindustan Fertilizer Corporation
HRS	Hydraulics Research Station, Wallingford
IBFEP	Indo-British Fertilizer Education Project
IBRD	International Bank for Reconstruction and Development
ICA	International Coffee Agreement
ICAR	Indian Council for Agricultural Research
ICO	International Coffee Organization
ICRA	International Centre for Development-Oriented Research in Agriculture
ICRAF	International Centre for Research on Agro-Forestry
ICRISAT	International Crops Research Institute for the Semi-Arid Tropics, India
IDS	Institute for Development Studies, University of Nairobi
IDS	Institute of Development Studies at Sussex University
IFAD	International Fund for Agricultural Development
IFC	International Finance Corporation
IFPRI	International Food Policy Research Institute
ILCA	International Livestock Centre for Africa
ILO	International Labour Organization
IMF	International Monetary Fund
IRRI	International Rice Research Institute, Los Banos, Philippines
JNKVV	Jawarlal Nehru Krishi Vishwa Vidyalaya University, Madhya Pradesh

KHARDEP	Kosi Hills Agriculture and Rural Development Programme, Nepal
KILIMO	Ministry of Agriculture, Tanzania
KNCU	Kilimanjaro Native Cooperative Union
KTDA	Kenya Tea Development Authority
LBOD	Left Bank Outfall Drain (Pakistan)
LOMÉ	The Lomé Convention a trade and aid agreement between the EC and 71 ACP countries signed in Togo in 1975
LRDC	Land Resources Development Centre, Tolworth
LSE	London School of Economics
MDGs	Millennium Development Goals
MEP	Member of the European Parliament
MIRDP	Malaita Integrated Rural Development Programme
MSF	Medicines sans Frontieres
NABARD	National Bank for Agriculture and Rural Development, India
NAO	National Authorising Officer of the European Development Fund
NBSS	National Bureau for Soil Science, India
NCAER	National Council for Applied Economic Research, India
NEDA	National Economic Development Authority, Philippines
NGO	Non-Governmental Organisation
NIAE	National Institute of Agricultural Engineering, Silsoe
NIP	National Indicative Programme (EDF)
NRSS	Natural Resources Studentship Scheme
NSSRDP	North Sumatra Smallholder Rubber Development Project
ODA	Overseas Development Administration, London

ODI	Overseas Development Institute, London
ODM	Ministry of Overseas Development, London
OECD	Organisation for Economic Cooperation and Development
OECS	Organisation of Eastern Caribbean States
OSAS	Overseas Service Assistance Scheme
PADI	Peoples Action for Development, India
PDIL	Projects and Development India Limited
PEC	Projects and Evaluation Committee (ODA)
PNG	Papua New Guinea
PMCU	Project Management and Coordination Unit (EDF)
RELEX	European Commission's Foreign Affairs Directorate
RRIM	Rubber Research Institute of Malaysia
RTA	Retrospective Terms Adjustment
SCARP	Salinity Control and Rehabilitation Project (Pakistan)
SCF	Save the Children Fund
SEADD	South East Asia Development Division (ODA)
SIDS	Small Island Developing States
SPC	South Pacific Commission, Noumea, New Caledonia
SRP	Smallholder Rubber Programme (Liberia)
STABEX	EDF Instrument for Compensating ACP Countries for Fluctuations in Agricultural Exports
SYSMIN	EDF Instrument for Compensating ACP Countries for Fluctuations in Mining Exports
TA	Technical Assistant
TCO	Technical Cooperation Officer
TANU	Tanganyika African National Union
TASMA	Tanganyika Sisal Marketing Association
TPI	Tropical Products Institute, London

UN	United Nations
UNDP	United Nations Development Programme
UP	Uttar Pradesh
UPNG	University of Papua New Guinea
USAID	United States Agency for International Development
USP	University of the South Pacific
UWI(T)	University of the West Indies, Trinidad
VSO	Voluntary Service Overseas
WAPDA	Water and Power Development Authority, Lahore, Pakistan
WARDA	West Africa Rice Development Association
WFP	World Food Programme
WIBDP	Windward Islands Banana Development Programme
WINBAN	Windward Islands Bananas Association
WTO	World Trade Organization

Acknowledgments

This book is in many ways a testament to those with whom I have worked over the last fifty years or so. It is an appreciation of their contributions to the cause of development. Many people have given me professional encouragement over the years, but I would like to record my sincere appreciation to my mentor, Professor Gerald Wibberley of Wye College. Not only did he help me to secure a place at Oxford, but he set up my PhD studies in North Carolina, and then offered me my first job!

This book has been a long time in the making. From time to time my wife asks me why I am not working on it, and I reply that like a good cheese (or red wine) my thoughts need time to mature (and in any case, the golf course beckons). I first put pen to paper in the year after my retirement from the European Commission, but twelve years later as I pass three score years and fifteen, I find that there is still some way to go. At the end of the day, my motivation in writing is driven by a sense of debt to family, especially my wife and four sons, who have had to bear my moods and absences while I have spent a disproportionate amount of time on work. To them at least I owe some return, and it is to them and my grandchildren (Katja, Toby, Ethan, and Woodrow) that this book is dedicated. I would like to mention especially the loving contribution of my wife Indu, who has given enormous support in good times and in bad, and who has worked tirelessly when the exigencies of my professional life required that we entertain, which was very often the case during our postings in Sudan, Solomon Islands, and Barbados. To this task, as to others, she gave unremitting effort and achieved no little success. She has been a spur to my writing, and a helpful critic as well.

I am very grateful to David Rudder for allowing me to include verses from his Banana Calypso in Chapter 21. Many thanks to my friend Kenrick Husbands for granting me permission to include one of his poems in

Chapter 20. I am indebted to Kathleen Hurley for going out of her way to put me in touch with David and Ken.

My son Julius has kindly kept me informed of World Bank seminars broadcast over the internet, which has helped to keep me current on development issues. He also encouraged me to pick up my pen again by introducing me to Voice Dream, so that I could listen to what I had written. My brother-in-law, Colonel Pavan Nair, and my son Nicholas, have taken the time and trouble to read though earlier drafts of this book, and provided valuable comments and suggestions, many of which I have taken on board. I am of course responsible for any factual errors that remain.

Pune, *March 2016*

Chapter 1.

BACKGROUND

Kinton is a remote hamlet in Shropshire near the Welsh border. It lies halfway between Shrewsbury and Oswestry, and in September 1958 seemed a long way from my parents' home in Surrey. At the age of seventeen, I started work as a farm pupil at Grove Farm, the smallest of three farms that made up Kinton. Mr Frank Pugh was the tenant of 60 acres of mixed farming land, which sustained some 30 dairy cows and their followers. The three or four churns of milk which I wheeled daily to the farm gate for collection by the milk marketing board, provided the Pugh family with their livelihood, as well as paying my modest wages of fifty shillings a week. One frosty November morning as I turned eighteen, I was an accomplice to the slaughter of Sam the pig, whose meat in one form or another comprised the main component of our meals for the rest of my stay at Grove Farm.

At interview in Wye three months earlier, the proud possessor of four A levels, I was delighted to accept the place offered to enrol in the BSc honours degree course starting in October 1959. Dunstan Skilbeck, the principal of Wye College, was a firm believer that students of agriculture should have a sound basis in practical farming. This experience I duly acquired, thanks to Mr Pugh. Starting with milking cows twice a day and harvesting sugar beet, I learned to drive the Ferguson tractor, to plough and harrow, to lug sacks of barley from the threshing machine to the barn, spread farm yard manure, and pitch hay bales. Saturday afternoon was my break which I spent in Shrewsbury, going to the cinema and learning ballroom dancing. A young farmers' certificate for proficiency in singling sugar beet was acquired. Most of all, I learned the satisfaction of a hard day's work in the fields. As I left Kinton in September 1959, Mr Pugh (a man of few words) told me that if I continued to apply myself to the task at hand I should have no problems in my future career. A few months later my farm diary won recognition from the professor of agriculture at Wye, William Holmes.

My seven years at Wimbledon College had passed without any great distinction. After dropping three catches in a match for the under thirteens, my hopes of making the cricket team subsided. I was no good at rugby. The Jesuits had done their best to teach me Latin and French, but I had mastered neither, and ended up in the sixth form studying geography, chemistry, zoology, and botany. With a love of the English countryside, I aspired to study forestry at university, but learned that physics was an essential prerequisite. And so I applied for agriculture.

The three years at Wye were my salad days. After a year of solitude in Shropshire it was refreshing to have the company of the student body, enriched by some who had completed their national service, along with some young colonials from Kenya and Rhodesia for good measure. The north downs provided a fine backdrop to the picturesque village of Wye, while the Kent countryside had some fine pubs and was a lovely place for walking and following the beagles. During the vacations I continued as a farm labourer, working with sheep in Kent, and bringing in the cereals harvest in Sussex and Wiltshire, and on a farm near Herford in Germany.

I chose to write my special study on the beta-degradation of fatty acids, a determinant of ketosis in cattle. This subject was close to the heart of Louis Wain, Wye's distinguished professor of biochemistry and fellow of the Royal Society, and he kindly awarded me a good mark which contributed towards an upper second in the final exams.

But it was the professor of agricultural economics, Gerald Wibberley to whom I owe most. Along with four other students, I was taken under his wing. We were invited to his home on Sunday afternoons for discussions on topics relating to the rural economy. Wibberley was an original thinker and eloquent speaker. Each summer he gave lectures at a number of universities in the United States. Through these contacts he was able to arrange for postgraduate placements for his students. And so it was that I went to North Carolina State University in September 1963, after a year at Oxford reading for a diploma in agricultural economics.

Looking back at my year at Oxford I regret that I did not study enough to gain the distinction that should have been within my grasp. Instead, I busied myself in social life, culminating in the summer ball at St Edmund Hall. I settled my student debts that summer from further farm work in Sussex. It was a rude shock to transfer from the glorious spires of Oxford to the more utilitarian buildings of the Raleigh campus.

My interest in development questions, although sparking from time to time during my studies at Wye and Oxford, really started at North Carolina State University in 1964 when I was invited by my tutor professor George Tolley to work with him on a paper concerning the role of agricultural trade in economic development. This joint effort, which was researched over several months, and put together in many sessions in Raleigh and Washington DC, eventually became a chapter in Southworth and Johnston's *Agricultural Development and Economic Growth*. This book provides a good summary of thinking on development at that time. Our chapter was favourably reviewed by Harry Johnson, but criticised by Sydney Hoos for being too negative on the role that expansion of agricultural exports should play in the economic growth of developing countries.

As the years went by, I increasingly recognised that Sydney Hoos had a point, and hope that our words written then were taken in the context of a longer term development strategy where agriculture will normally become secondary to other sectors as growth occurs. As the following chapters detail, I was to spend several years working with the agricultural export sectors of Tanzania and Indonesia, and more recently in the Caribbean, so I have had many opportunities to reflect on what we had earlier written.

Chapter 2.

BECOMING AN AGRICULTURAL ECONOMIST

The micro-economics of Marshall had been drilled into me at the Agricultural Economics Institute of Oxford University by George Peters and George Allen in 1962. The Institute, now defunct, was then under the direction of Colin Clark, the author of *Conditions of Economic Progress*, one of the first of such works on development, published in 1940. In North Carolina, Milton Friedman's difficult primer on micro-economics was our first text as I started my graduate studies there in 1963. I was duly schooled in the prevailing market philosophies of the sixties, according to the Chicago School, with its emphasis in macro-economics towards monetarist views rather than Keynesian.

George Tolley taught the advanced macro-economics course for PhD candidates. I was fortunate to become one of his research students. A distinguished scholar, Tolley had an incredible capacity for work combined with a passion for economics and utmost confidence in the power of the discipline. In 1965, Tolley was seconded to the US Department of Agriculture as director in the economics research service. This meant that he worked during the week in Washington DC, and flew down to Raleigh for the weekends in order to teach, and meet his research students. As I was the most junior of his several research students, my time with him would usually start on Saturday evenings, and continue on occasion to dawn the next day. Sometimes I had to travel to Washington DC to continue our work, where he introduced me to such Chicago luminaries as Arnold Harberger and Carl Christ at Johns Hopkins. George Tolley also encouraged me to make contact with IMF economists in Washington, including the monetarist Graeme Dorrance who graciously gave me an hour of his time to explain his latest rebuttal (in *IMF Staff Papers*) of the structuralist views of Seers and Prebisch.

At this time Friedman's thinking (and that of the Chicago School in general) was not much in fashion in UK thinking. Indeed, when I returned to England in 1967, it took me some while to adjust to the more socialist and (then) politically correct views of the pre-Thatcher era of the sixties and the seventies. UK development thinking was dominated by the likes of Dudley Seers and Paul Streeten, who adhered to central planning and structuralist (rather than monetarist) views of the developing world.

Another consequence of my training in the States was a fascination with quantification and statistical methodology, and a consequent search for data to which could be applied econometric methods to test hypotheses. I have never been a very able mathematician, and had to join undergraduate classes to come to terms with calculus, but multiple regression was a *sine qua non* of any PhD thesis, and mine was no exception. North Carolina State had an excellent department of statistics and I somehow managed to acquire a minor in this subject, to complement a major in economics and agricultural economics. This obsession to work with numbers stayed with me throughout my time in East Africa and South East Asia, and formed the basis of a number of articles published in professional journals whilst I retained the ambition of being an academic researcher.

Academic ambition gave way to more practical concerns. Eventually I derived the satisfaction of becoming a "hands on" aid administrator. I joined the British Ministry of Overseas Development (ODM) in 1977 and then moved on to the European Commission in 1985. With this transition came a better awareness of the importance of people as individuals rather than numbers. Towards the latter part of my career, new responsibilities required the skills of people management and diplomacy. However, it was not until 2001 that I was required to take a course in management. From being a "pure" agricultural economist at ODA, I succumbed to dealing with general economic questions when I joined the Commission. From being a "pure" economist, dealing with things as they were, I eventually became more of a political economist, recognising the importance of dialogue, negotiation, and compromise.

Over a period of forty years, I worked with colleagues from many countries (developing and developed), including many distinguished development practitioners (see *Dramatis Personae*). Several were inspiring for their hard work and commitment to development, and some have become good friends. As others have found, politicians are not always easy to deal with, especially when their short term agendas are at variance with longer term developmental objectives. Nonetheless I have kept faith in the worth of development assistance, when it is well administered, both as a means of promoting growth and of alleviating poverty. The good work that many NGOs and churches do to combat poverty and promote good governance has left a lasting impression on me.

Ad meiorem Dei gloriam

At a seminar on development at Wye College in 1970, I recall classifying those who worked overseas as missionaries, mercenaries, professionals, or academics. I suppose there has been an element of each of these in my motivation. My career in development has indeed been driven by a mix of factors. First and foremost, the need to earn a living and provide for my family. Professional ambition, a thirst for adventure, and a yen for travel, have also been driving forces. I must also acknowledge some missionary zeal, underpinned by seven years schooling from the Jesuits at Wimbledon College.

Paul VI wrote in his encyclical *Populorum Progressio* of 1967:

Each man must examine his conscience, which sounds a new call in our present times. Is he prepared to support, at his own expense, projects and undertakings designed to help the needy? Is he prepared to pay higher taxes so that public authorities may expand their efforts in the work of development? Is he prepared to pay more for imported goods, so that the foreign producer may make a fairer profit? Is he prepared to emigrate from his homeland if necessary and if he is young, in order to help the emerging nations?

It would be a sanctimonious person who would answer yes to these questions, but this text does convey something of the ideals to which many people of that era aspired. In those days flights were expensive, communications limited, and the social costs of living in the third world much higher.

It is pleasing today to observe how many people in India contribute to projects for the poor, how many consumers in the UK take the matter of Fair Trade seriously, the extent to which the coalition government is committing tax payers money to the aid programme, and the number of young people in Europe keen to spend their gap years working in third world villages or with NGOs in the front line of troubled areas. I took *More Help for the Poorest*, ODA's policy statement, very much to heart when I joined the Ministry in 1977. Today my development interests are sustained by observation of events in India, where the majority of the world's poor subsist, notwithstanding a remarkable transformation in the economy since my first professional encounter nearly forty years ago.

Transition from the Colonial period

I was young enough to have entered the third world in the years of post-independence, although if I had chosen in 1967 to go to Solomon Islands I would be able to claim some parity with those like my ODA boss Peter Stutley, who straddled the colonial era and the heady days of independence. Likewise, my friend Keith Arrowsmith was a colonial servant in West Africa. His book gives a vivid account of the work of a district officer in the 1950s, not dissimilar to the experiences in Ceylon at the beginning of the last century of Leonard Woolf.

Some colonial servants found the post-Independence adjustment difficult, and retired to the UK. Many continued their interests in development and found useful work in such institutions as the Centre for Overseas Pest Research (COPR), or the Land Resources Development Centre (LRDC). In fact, the post-colonial era led to a mushrooming of development-related specialist institutions in the UK, such as the Institute of Development Studies (IDS) at Sussex University, whose first director was Dudley Seers, former chief economist in the Ministry of Overseas Development. Some individuals relished the challenges and stayed on in the third world. Others may have become disillusioned and quit. A few became officials of FAO or the World Bank.

Aid Management

I consider myself fortunate for the insights I have gained from my training in agricultural economics, which gave me a particular focus in Tanzania, Kenya, Indonesia, and the Philippines. When I was appointed natural resources economist in the ODA, my interests broadened to include forestry, fisheries, and the environment. As time went by I found that my involvement in development transcended the natural resources sector as I became more involved in aid management. Indeed this was my principal concern and responsibility when I went to the Delegation in Solomon Islands. By the time I reached Barbados in 1995, the responsibilities of the job had broadened, requiring a more political role. Nonetheless, natural resources issues continued to dominate in these primary producing economies, as we sought to promote cocoa and coconuts for smallholders and conserve the forestry and fishery resources of the Pacific, and achieve competitiveness for the banana producers of the Windward Islands.

Dilemmas

There are many choices that need to be made in development strategy. The most fundamental of these concerns the debate as to whether more aid will actually speed development, or promote corruption (boost savings for private individuals rather than for the public good). It was Jesse Helms, the republican senator from North Carolina, who cynically referred to foreign aid as akin to stuffing dollar bills down a rat hole. Other dilemmas concern the balance between government led and private sector led growth: five year plans no longer seem to be so popular with the failure of centrally planned economies, although fifty years ago such models were taken very seriously by India and Tanzania. How much to invest in agriculture as opposed to industry, between agricultural extension and agricultural research, between large scale estate or smallholder production?

When I started out, little was written about the market in services, although technological change was coming into the theoretical picture. International travel by jet aircraft was in its infancy, and few thought of tourism as a leading sector for development, as it has become for many small island economies. Nor was it foreseen that aircraft would be the vehicle for fresh vegetables produced by African or Latin American farmers to be sold in

European supermarkets. We are now concerned at the environmental problems of carbon emissions as such fruits and vegetables collect air miles, and the consequences of cash crops supplanting food crops. Should scarce irrigation water be used to grow flowers for export or to increase food staples for domestic markets. How can one justify using such water for golf courses, even if these are needed to attract tourists or international investors like the German, Korean and Japanese car manufacturers in India.

MDGs

On returning to England for retirement, I found a renewed interest in development, symbolised on the one hand by the Millennium Development Goals (MDGs) and on the other by the slogan Make Poverty History. The G-8 summit in Gleneagles, Scotland in July 2005, spurred on by the Live Aid concerts, agreed further tranches of aid in support of Africa, alongside debt relief for some poor countries. The public in Europe has consistently shown itself to be responsive to photos of malnourished children in Ethiopia (1985), Sudan and Niger (2005), but many appear disillusioned by official aid with its seemingly disparate objectives. Few in the UK have little positive to say about Europe.

European Aid

The perennial debate within the UK about Britain's continued membership of the European Union continues. I believe there is a strong case for a European policy and programme in support of third world countries, to which the UK should continue to contribute. There are certain advantages in delivering development assistance in this way, even if there is scope for improvements in the ways that EU assistance is provided.

There is criticism of things European in the British media, much of which has a distinct anti-European bias. There is no doubt that the political agendas of the foreign-born press barons have had a disproportionate influence on the British public and British politics. Even among Ministers of the former Labour government, which was avowedly pro-European, there was a tendency to play to the gallery where matters European are concerned.

For example, Clare Short, in her critique of Blair's venture into Iraq, nonetheless repeated the DFID mantra that European aid is not very satisfactory, even while she tacitly applauds European foreign policy on Iraq. The former Secretary of State for Foreign Affairs, Jack Straw, before the Parliamentary Foreign Affairs Committee in May 2004 said *"You find all sorts of odd-bods from the EU running various sorts of offices around the world"* and *"We've got a lot of these people abroad and it is not entirely clear what they are doing".* Most of this criticism is based upon myths, and I feel that I may have some role to play in helping to dispel them. Having served in Papua New Guinea and Sudan, I was encouraged to read Chris Patten's response to Jack Straw's observations. His letter was robust, and is worth quoting.

I suppose it is safe to assume that in your comments you were referring overwhelmingly to the work of European Commission delegations around the world. These carry out wide-ranging and often challenging tasks in 123 countries, their staff working hard to carry out detailed trade and other negotiations, to support and help co-ordinate the work of the member states' own embassies, and to provide high-quality political and economic reporting, frequently from countries where not all member states are represented themselves. Perhaps most importantly, they deliver over € 5 billion of external and development assistance per year in support of the EU's agreed goals, and in support of the Union's policies, in places as far flung, and as difficult, as Afghanistan, Somalia, and New Guinea (sic).

Lessons of Experience

I hope that the lessons of experience recorded in these pages may be of interest to others who have trodden similar paths, including those with whom I have worked. They may also be of interest to younger students of development, who are at the beginning of their professional careers. Agricultural economists may find some of the accounts of land levelling in Sind and of dry land farming in India of value. Other readers may gain some insights into life in British and European administrations, and the complexities of identifying, appraising, and managing development programmes.

Chapter 3.

LECTURER IN DEVELOPMENT

After completing my studies at Raleigh, Gerald Wibberley invited me to apply for one of two new "home-based" lectureships in overseas development at Wye. In need of my first professional job, I took up the appointment, as Ian Carruthers did his, in September 1967. Ian and I had overlapped as undergraduates at Wye, and also at St Edmund Hall and the Institute of Agricultural Economics in Oxford. He had spent the previous four years working in Pakistan with Huntings on irrigation projects. Our appointments were linked to the launching of a MSc degree course in agrarian development overseas under the general supervision of Eric Clayton. Ian and I were responsible for the teaching of some twenty postgraduates from various parts of the developing world.

As a newly established PhD I started my part of the course with a series of lectures on development issues relating to the role of agriculture in the development process, drawing upon the literature of the day. In retrospect, I wonder whether these lectures were pitched at too academic a level, but some years later (in Trinidad) I was encouraged to hear Carl Greenidge (secretary-general of the ACP group) using some of the analytical framework that we discussed at Wye. Another course was on quantitative methods which Michael Boddington and I delivered together. After a couple of years, Ian and I were appointed recognised teachers of the University of London. Ian went on to become professor of development studies.

When I came back to Wye in 1967 as a lecturer in overseas development, it was apparent to many, including myself, that there was something of an anomaly in somebody lecturing on a subject in which they had no first hand knowledge, and who had indeed never set foot in a developing country. Fortunately the provisions of the "home-based" lectureship scheme were such that overseas experience was soon to be garnered. Those in London who were underwriting the scheme offered two possibilities: to be an agricultural economist doing field work in Solomon Islands (still a protectorate), or marketing officer in the Ministry of Agriculture in recently independent Tanzania. Having consulted the atlas, I opted for Tanzania. Solomon Islands was to call me some twenty three years later. The world seemed a much larger place in those days.

Chapter 4.

SISAL AND COFFEE IN TANZANIA

Harold Macmillan made his famous speech to the South Africa parliament in February 1960. *The wind of change is blowing through this continent and whether we like it or not, the growth of political consciousness is a political fact.*

Thus, in December 1961, Tanganyika became independent under the leadership of Julius Nyerere, and in 1964 merged with Zanzibar to become Tanzania. The Arusha Declaration was made by Nyerere in 1967, which set the country on course for a form of African socialism and self reliance.

Tanzania, in those days, was seen by many in the UK as an experimental ground for new approaches to development, inspired perhaps by British socialists. President Nyerere was a much respected leader, and his writings laid down many of the ground rules. He would drive around town in a small VW, unescorted by police, and sit with the congregation at Sunday Mass. Nyerere's modest life style and his reputation as a teacher (Mwalimu) commanded respect, domestically, and internationally. Out of this spirit of African socialism, came the Arusha Declaration in 1967. For the sisal industry, this meant nationalisation of most of the estates, and the formation of the Tanzania Sisal Corporation.

Ujamaa (working together) was another theme espoused by Nyerere, and led to the amalgamation of villages for the provision of services.

Nyerere wrote in his essay on *Socialism and Rural Development*:

Our agricultural organisation would be predominantly that of cooperative living and working for the good of all. This means that most of our farming would be done by groups of people who live as a community and work as a community. They would live together in a village; they would farm together; market together; and undertake the provision of local services and small local requirements as a community.

In some instances this had negative effects on smallholder production, as rural people were forced to live away from their farms.

Stopover in Uganda

Early in 1968 we travelled to Uganda, en route to Tanzania. Wye had built up a good working relationship with the department of agricultural economics at Makerere University. Deryke Belshaw led the department, with the support of Malcolm Hall (with whom I was later to work in Indonesia). They had a number of young students from East Africa in training, and an impressive list of papers on matters of agricultural policy significance. David Pudsey, a colleague from Oxford, was involved in the development of smallholder tea. It is sad to reflect that much of the institution building and training that was being carried out at Makerere was dissipated by Amin, who overthrew Milton Obote in 1970.

The first impressions of Africa will always stay with me. Flying on a BOAC VC-10 from London, I observed the arid scrub that characterises so much of the landscape around the Sahel. The contrast of the humid tropics of Kampala and the Makerere campus was striking. Loud laughter woke us in the morning as cheerful Ugandan women cleaned the guesthouse. Their gaiety, plus the warmth and humidity, the fragrance of frangipani blossom, and the vivid tropical greens and reds of the banana plants and flame trees, are lasting memories.

We arrived in Dar es Salaam three days later, after a bumpy flight in a Fokker Friendship that touched down en route in Nairobi, Mombasa, Tanga, and Zanzibar. No-one was there to meet us, and we had to find our own way to the New Africa hotel in the centre of town. The next morning

I turned up at Pamba House, the headquarters of Kilimo (Ministry of Agriculture), to find that the administrative officer to whom I reported had received no word of my coming. Tanzania had broken off diplomatic relations with the UK over Rhodesia. It was several days before the communication from London sent via the Canadian High Commission was unearthed.

Pamba House

My formal briefing began with the head of planning in Kilimo. Timothy Apiyo, a tall, serious and impressive personality came from the same district as President Nyerere. He spent an hour of his time to explain to me the functioning of the Ministry, and my expected future role in it. I was much impressed by Mr Apiyo, and was not surprised to learn later on that he had advanced to the highest levels of the Tanzanian civil service. Unlike the Kikuyu and Luo in Kenya, no particular tribe dominates in Tanzania (which may explain a greater tolerance towards the Brits and the Asians). The Asians tended to be treated as the commercial *wallahs* by both the Brits and the Africans, and although there was no *apartheid* as such in post-colonial East Africa, in those days the different racial groups tended to keep to themselves outside the office.

The marketing section of the planning division was led by Nicholas Monck, an old Etonian on secondment from the British treasury. Nick was a cheerful, energetic, and thoughtful personality who followed an empirical approach to problem solving. He was much given to calculations of the costs of production in order to determine the farmer prices that the Ministry should set for certain crops (cotton prices were announced annually). He also applied this methodology to assess the profits that the sisal estates were making. His relations with Minister Derek Bryceson were cordial. (Bryceson was the only white Minister in the Cabinet and the counterpart to Bruce Mackenzie, the formidable Minister of Agriculture in Kenya). However, Nicholas did not always see eye to eye with the principal secretary, David Mwakosya.

My colleagues and chums in marketing included Velji, an Ismaili, who was responsible for sugar and cotton, and Julius Semwaiko, an indigenous Tanzanian, who looked after tea. My responsibilities were coffee and sisal.

Other personalities in the planning division included Peter Stutley, a very experienced agricultural economist who had worked most recently in Zambia. Peter had started his career as assistant district officer in Lesotho, and was funded by the Ford Foundation. Andrew Coulson was a younger ODI fellow. OSAS officers like Andrew Lillie and myself worked in an established position, earning a local salary supplemented by a UK "topping up" allowance.

In those days, Kilimo still had many expatriates, mainly British, working alongside Tanzanians. This need for external assistance was a reflection of the somewhat precipitate way in which the country became independent in 1961, with only a handful of Tanzanian university graduates. Hence there was an important need for institution-building and on the job training for Tanzanian staff. Most of the expatriate staff showed a strong commitment to their work and to Tanzania's long term development goals. Many of us were inspired by the leadership of Julius Nyerere whose writings on *ujamaa* and the Arusha Declaration had a certain intuitive appeal, although the implementation of these ideas did not always meet the lofty aspirations.

Expatriate Advisers

Elsewhere in the Tanzanian Government service there were a number of experts advising ministers, or permanent secretaries. Brian van Arkadie, who displayed great confidence and certainty in all that he did, worked in development planning. Reginald Green, a somewhat eccentric American, wore a Muslim style cap. He worked in the Ministry of Finance. Reg was reputed to spend hours of reflection lying on the floor of his office. Rob Wood, a young Englishman of great presence, worked in the Ministry of Industries. Rob chaired a committee to define Tanzania's policies towards the recently founded East African Community. I had the rather dubious distinction of representing Kilimo on this committee, and often had to stretch my brain to decide where Tanzania's interests might lie. There were occasions when I wished that Rob did not ask me what Kilimo's position was on a particular issue.

Among the British expatriate community, there were some significant differences in outlook and attitude. Many who had started their careers in colonial times, and were engaged as engineers and technicians, resented the coming of Independence. They may have felt threatened that they might lose their jobs and easy life style. Some harboured negative racial attitudes, referring to Africans as lazy or incompetent. These attitudes were reciprocated by some of the Africans, who found these colonial types unsympathetic, arrogant and overbearing. Tanzania's party newspaper was written by locals many of whom were virulently anti-colonial and anti-apartheid. These were the days of the Cold War which found its own expression in Africa. It was still decades before Zimbabwe would emerge as an independent country, and South Africa would become a democratic country.

Racial tensions

Nyerere wrote in the Arusha Declaration:

We have been oppressed a great deal, we have been exploited a great deal, and we have been disregarded a great deal. It is our weakness that has led to our being oppressed, exploited and disregarded.

In any meeting with expatriates or Tanzanians, one quickly came to understand where an individual stood on matters of inter-racial tolerance or sympathy. There were certain places like the Yacht Club associated with strong colonial attitudes, where the tension between expatriate members and local staff was almost tangible. On the other hand, at the higher levels of Government and among senior advisers, there was mutual understanding and sense of common purpose.

Tanzania had its own special form of democracy which allowed only a single political party TANU to participate in elections. Among other things, this gave enormous influence to party members and the secretariat, which generally followed a hard leftist line.

The Asians, a mix of Ismailis, Gujaratis and Muslims, dominated in commerce and tended to keep a low profile in their rather shabby part of town, with blocks of flats rendered mildewed by the tropical sea air. Some Asians were prominent as sisal planters, and the Karimjee and Ralli estates were important producers. Jamal, an Asian, was Minister of Finance, and commanded much respect. Many a Tanzanian village would have an

Asian store which provided the necessities of life to local people (matches, candles, soap, tins of corned beef, cooking oil, bandages). Generally, there was a much greater tolerance towards Asians in Tanzania than in Uganda and Kenya.

I retain memories of stopping at Entebbe on an East African Airways Super VC-10 in 1972 and being instructed to move into first class by the British captain so as to make room for the Asians being expelled from Uganda by Idi Amin.

China in Tanzania

At this time of the Cold War, there was some concern among westerners by Tanzania's links with the People's Republic of China. British expatriates were much intrigued to observe the Red Chinese workers bathing in the sea at Oyster Bay on weekends. Even if language had not been a problem, there was no question of social contact with them. Nor do I recall a Chinese restaurant in Dar es Salaam where common ground might have been found.

A concrete expression of the Tanzania-PRC relationship was the construction of the Tan-Zam railway line. This transport link would bring Zambia's copper to the port of Dar es Salaam, instead of by trucks on the notorious Hell Run which crossed zones of black cotton soils and became virtually impassable during the rains.

Dress was often a good indicator of an expatriate's background, if not of attitudes. Long white socks, long white shorts, and a short-sleeved white shirt, had been the attire of the colonial civil servants. Those who belonged to the new wave of British advisers wore long trousers, and open necked, plain coloured shirts. Some like Peter Stutley, espoused khaki socks, shorts, and shirts. Safari suits were popular with some, notably the Asians, placing them in an intermediate category. For evening wear, colourful shirts were *de rigueur* for all, even if the Balinese batik style later popularised by Nelson Mandela had yet to arrive. Permanent secretaries might wear collar and tie, while some Ministers favoured collarless brown or dark coloured outfits in the Nyerere style, suggesting a more radical, even Marxist outlook.

My job was fascinating. I had a lot to learn, and there were frequent opportunities for travel by road or plane.

Sisal

One of my responsibilities was sisal, the principal export crop of Tanzania. Sisal had been introduced to Tanzania (then Tanganyika) from Florida and Mexico in German times, with the first plantation established in 1900. By 1952 exports had reached 158,000 tons, at which time the value of sisal exports exceeded that of all other products of vegetable, animal and mineral origin. By the late sixties, production was in excess of 200,000 tons.

Every three months or so, the Junior Minister, Nicholas Monck, and I would take the President's plane to Tanga for meetings with the Sisal Board, the Tanzania Sisal Corporation, and the marketing agency TASMA, where Aubrey Denton-Thomson was in charge. These meetings were usually followed by a good lunch. Our espousal of African socialism did not prevent us from dipping into the wine cellars of the Tanganyika Sisal Planters Association. The agenda would include such issues as the funding of sisal research at the Mlingano sisal research station (hybrid varieties had been developed there and were giving better yields), sisal diversification, management of the estates grouped under the Tanzania Sisal Corporation, sisal marketing matters, including increasing competition from synthetic fibres, and the FAO informal sisal agreement which required a reduction in overall sisal exports in order to boost world prices.

One modest contribution I made to sisal policy was to devise a formula for the allocation of Tanzania's national sisal quota among sisal estates. The formula favoured those estates which had maintained replanting in years of low prices, and penalised those that had not. The reasoning was that those who continued planting irrespective of prices had the intention of remaining in the industry for the longer term. A counter argument might be that the most efficient producers were those smaller Asian run enterprises who came into production when prices were high, and left production when prices fell. P T Bauer who wrote about Malaysian rubber producers under circumstances of fluctuating prices would almost certainly have supported such a thesis.

Sitting with Brian van Arkadie on the balcony of the rather run down Sea View hotel in Tanga one weekend afternoon in 1969, we pored over large spread sheets showing the planting records of the several scores of sisal estates. We made rapid decisions as to which would be allowed to continue in production and those which would receive a much reduced export quota. This system would allow sufficient market space for the highly efficient Swiss-owned Amboni estates, and of course the state owned Tanzania Sisal Corporation, a child of the Arusha Declaration.

Some of the smaller Asian planters may have suffered from this method of allocation, affecting their livelihood and funding for children's education. Such hardship cases were passed to the Junior Minister for Agriculture, whom I suspect had his own way of finding solutions. Some of the large estates which had escaped nationalisation and were owned by foreigners (Amboni, Ralli Brothers, Karimjee Estates) were more or less unaffected by the formula since their replanting rates were good. The Amboni estates had gone ahead with plantings of hybrid sisal varieties on a large scale. The Tanzania Sisal Corporation, run along the lines of a State farm, had large beef herds as well as sisal, and was exempted from the internal quota system.

Coffee

My other major concern was coffee, another very significant export earner for the country. Most of the production came from the arabica variety produced on the slopes of Mount Kilimanjaro and Mount Meru. Robusta coffee was grown in West Lake region. I attended meetings of the coffee board which were held in Arusha or Moshi. The coffee research station was based at Lyamungu on the slopes of Mount Kilimanjaro, and served both the estate sector (which survived but felt under threat from the Arusha Declaration), and the more significant smallholders producing arabica coffee under the auspices of the Kilimanjaro native cooperative union. A sub-station was located in Bukoba.

One of my contributions was to draft the national coffee diversification plan, a requirement resulting from Tanzania's membership of the international coffee agreement. In preparing this document I travelled with my colleagues from Kilimo around Mount Kilimanjaro to visit the exquisite smallholdings on the mountain side. The farming system combined arabica coffee as a cash crop, shade by bananas (for food and beer making), with stall-fed dairy cows. The hard working *Wachagga* were not always welcomed by the other tribes of Tanzania, and their enterprise did not seem to chime with the new ethos of *Ujamaa*.

Later we visited Bukoba, travelling via Mwanza, the capital of the cotton growing district on the shores of Lake Victoria. Our last port of call on this particular safari was Mbeya, the centre of the tea growing area in the south west, refuelling in Tabora the tobacco growing area of the west. The planes in use at that time included a fairly modern East African Airways Fokker Friendship, an aged Dakota, and for the crossing of Lake Victoria, a de Havilland Dragon Rapide, a pre-war veteran bi-plane made of wood. The Rapide seemed ill-equipped to encounter any thunder storms that had a disconcerting tendency to arise from the Lake during the afternoon.

Coffee growing in West Lake was of the robusta type, and smallholder tea was just starting up under CDC auspices, which was highlighted in the coffee plan as an excellent example of diversification. Ironically perhaps, Tanzania's desire to expand tea production ran contrary to the objectives of the informal tea agreement, whereby major producers like India and Sri Lanka sought to reduce the amount of tea coming on to world markets. One country's diversification crop is often another's mainstream export earner.

Derek Bryceson was quite shrewd in his dealings with the ICO and maintained that Tanzania's exports beyond its ICA quota to the so-called Annex B countries (countries where coffee consumption was low) did not enter the well known "tourist" coffee trade. Economists will recognise the difficulties of trying to keep separate markets for a single commodity.

ICO

With my colleague Julius Semwaiko, we represented the Tanzania government at a meeting of the international coffee organisation (ICO) in London in 1969. This multilateral organisation had the principal objective of acting quasi-monopolistically in the market. Coffee exporting countries' incomes would be boosted by restraining output in the face of a price inelastic demand for coffee. Of course, each country had to make much of its own efforts to restrain the growth of output, while hoping that the burden of adjustment would actually be undertaken by others. With some trepidation I made an intervention during the debates of this august body to highlight the measures that Tanzania was taking to hold its exports in check. The Kenya delegate (Nick Wallis) spoke with much greater assurance, with the benefit of some well-publicised press accounts of farmers uprooting coffee plants in one part of Nyeri. But at the end of the day, the Latin Americans, especially Brazil and Colombia, called the shots. The taste of strong Brazilian coffee (literally on tap) and the smoke filled conference room, are abiding memories. The powerful personalities of Mr Beltrao, the President, and Mr Van der Steene, one of his senior colleagues, left a lasting impression.

Back to Wye

My contract in Tanzania could have been extended for a further period of six months, but as a young person eager to build an impressive *curriculum vitae* I decided to leave after completing two years. Personal ambition won over loyalty to the government I was contracted to serve. Perhaps I had the impression that Tanzania was following a development path that would be hard to sustain. The photographs of vice-President Karume of Zanzibar which appeared in every office did not inspire much confidence. Beyond the impressive rhetoric of Nyerere, there were signs that nationalisation and *ujamaa* were not bringing the returns initially projected. There were even rumours that farmers were being forced from their land by TANU officials into centralised villages. And so I returned to Wye to reflect upon what I had learned.

The author views coffee shambas on the slopes of Mount Kilimanjaro
Nicholas Monck and the General Manager of Amboni Sisal Estates

Chapter 5.

WYE INTERLUDE

In returning to Wye I was keen to build on my experience in Tanzania, and augment my stock of human capital by extending my list of publications. As a young man I wanted to establish some kind of professional reputation, and for academics that was done through publications in the journals. *Publish or perish* was the academics watchword. The department of economics at Wye College had started a series of monographs. Ian Carruthers had already written a valuable piece on irrigation development planning based on his experience with the Lower Indus in Pakistan. On the basis of my Tanzania experience, I published three articles during the course of my second spell of lecturing at Wye during 1970. The Wye College monograph *Perennial Crop Supply Response: The Case of Tanzanian Sisal*, used an econometric analysis to demonstrate the strong responsiveness of sisal estate owners to price expectations in their planting behaviour. The multiple regression fit was strong, and the monograph won some professional acclaim. Moreover, the methodology was later taken on board and extended to Kenya by Enzo Grilli in a World Bank publication. While it may have satisfied my aspirations for a serious methodological work, and received a favourable review in the Tanganyika Sisal Journal, it did not turn out to be a bestseller!

An article in Oxford Agrarian Studies reflected on the disbenefits to Tanzania of the informal sisal agreement that had been launched by Szarf and Music in FAO. I was later berated in Rome by David Music for undermining the basis of this informal agreement, but I stood by my analysis and maintained that Tanzania gained little from the agreement in comparison to Brazil. During 1970, Ian Carruthers and I collaborated on an paper concerning East Pakistan's (shortly to become Bangladesh) prospects for tea development. I wrote an article on the shortcomings of

Three International Commodity Agreements, which was later published in Economic Development and Cultural Change.

Another positive experience during this year was part time employment as a consultant with the ICO in London to help in the review of the national coffee diversification plans for Uganda and Kenya. Here my experience as the *de facto* author of the Tanzania Coffee Plan stood me in good stead, and I enjoyed a cordial working relationship with Mr Van der Steene, a senior ICO official in Berners Street. In those days, the feeling that I could command a fee for my services outside teaching was a source of satisfaction. University lecturers then as now were not paid a great deal and it was accepted practice to seek additional sources of income during vacations. The status of being a consultant gave me a degree of professional confidence vis-a-vis my Wye colleagues, like Graham Donaldson, who was shortly to take off for a successful career in the World Bank.

During the summer of 1970, I attended a seminar at Nuffield College in Oxford. Professor Ian Little, the author of the definitive and highly mathematical work on cost-benefit analysis, led the discussion, along with Nick Stern. The Little-Mirrlees method of project appraisal was highly regarded in the economic literature of those days. However, it was a little too sophisticated and time consuming to be applied often in practice. These were the hey days of cost-benefit analysis when no development project could expect funding from the World Bank or the British government without demonstrating a satisfactory rate of return. Needless to say, the rate of return calculation was based upon assumptions. Factors like the rate of increase in crop yields in an irrigation project or the rate of uptake of a new technique by smallholder farmers could be quite difficult to assess, opening the door to subjective judgements.

On another occasion I was invited to attend a one day meeting in the Ministry of Overseas Development, chaired by the Minister Judith Hart. As at the Nuffield seminar, I remember feeling rather shy in the presence of such a distinguished gathering of development experts, but after a gin and tonic-charged lunch at Bob Porter's house in the shadows of Westminster Cathedral, felt comfortable to share my thoughts and experiences with others during the afternoon session.

As 1970 drew to an end, it became time to reflect on my next over-seas move under the home-based lectureship scheme. Responding to an advertisement in the Economist, I applied for the post of research fellow in the Glasgow team at the Institute for Development Studies in Kenya. Professor Tom Wilson called me for interview, which took place in the very grand and rather daunting buildings of the university of Glasgow. We had an excellent lunch with Alec Nove, the expert on Russia and I left Wye to join the Glasgow team in October 1970.

Chapter 6.

RURAL EMPLOYMENT IN KENYA

Unlike Tanzania, Kenya had been a colony where significant European settlement had taken place. The Happy Valley crowd in the so-called White Highlands had acquired significant farming land in the 1920s and 1930s. Unsurprisingly, this was the cause of resentment by Africans, particularly the Kikuyu, and was one of the reasons for the Mau Mau uprising from 1952 to 1960. Eventually in 1963, Kenya became Independent under the leadership of Jomo Kenyatta. Many of the Europeans left and their land was returned to African ownership under the Million Acre scheme. By the time I arrived in Nairobi in 1971, the number of European farmers had declined markedly, but some survivors could still be found in up-country clubs.

Kenya had a much more pragmatic attitude to economic policy than Tanzania. Its policy statement *African Socialism* espoused fine principles of equity, but these seemed to co-exist quite happily alongside a market economy where the Asians played a significant role. The numerical strength and influence of the so-called white farmers was much greater in Kenya than Tanzania, and this group had the ear of the President. Mzee Jomo Kenyatta had been imprisoned during the days of Mau Mau, and was above the kind of public criticism that is made today about Kenya's leaders.

IDS and the Glasgow Team

The Glasgow team was one group within the Institute for Development Studies. Dharam Ghai, a pleasant and soft-spoken East African Asian, was the Director. The IDS was seen by many development academics (including myself) as an ideal base for building one's development knowledge and extending one's reputation through research and publications. This somewhat selfish objective, which some might label as another form of neo-colonialism, was tempered by the opportunity of working with and training young Kenyan economists.

Lawrence Smith, with whom I had overlapped at Wye and Oxford, was the leader of the Glasgow team. Ian Hay, Walter Elkin, Martin Godfrey, and Michael Westlake were the other members, called to carry out policy based research of value to the Kenya authorities. Lawrence himself was engaged in questions relating to agricultural pricing policy. Walter focused on the benefits to the Kenyan economy of tourism. Martin was concerned with the operation of labour markets and trade unions. Michael worked on coffee and the International Coffee Agreement. I decided to work on the then fashionable theme of employment in agriculture, as this was seen as the basis for equitable economic growth.

George Ruigu, a young Kikuyu of undoubted ability, was assigned to carry out research with me. For several months we worked well together, travelling often to Mbere where I focused our field work. One day he told me that he was going to join another group working on agricultural extension led by Joe Ascroft and Neils Rollings. Joe was carrying out interesting work on rates of adoption of new farm practices by different categories of farmers, variously described as rapid adopters or laggards, and interesting data was being collected and analysed from different parts of rural Kenya. While I much regretted George's departure, I empathised with his decision since it was apparent that he would be joining a lively and structured research effort. George later went on to PhD studies in the USA. For my part, Joe was very helpful in showing me how to use the card sorting method for data analysis. This produced quicker results than the university's much-in-demand ICL computer, which sometimes delayed analysis by chewing up my laboriously punched data cards.

Eckhard Baum was a good friend and university lecturer, whom I had known from Tanzania days when he was working on a farming systems research project at Ifakara. Eckhard invited me to give lectures to undergraduates in the faculty of agriculture. This was an excellent opportunity to get to know some keen Kenyan undergraduates, and also to obtain their insights into life in the countryside.

Labour in Smallholder Faming

The chief government statistician Sergit Heyer, and his adviser Julian Exeter, kindly gave permission for me to use the Kenya Government's own data base on labour inputs in smallholder agriculture. This data base clearly had some weaknesses, but it did give some useful indicators of the labour intensiveness of different farming enterprises, and the seasonality of labour demand, as well as some interesting inter-district variations. I aimed to supplement this quantitative information in building up a picture of agricultural labour markets, by means of frequent field visits, and ad hoc farmer/farm labour interviews. I also learned a lot from essays written on the subject by the undergraduates I was teaching. Fellow IDS researcher and rural sociologist David Brokensha, an American based in California, had set his research base deep in the Mbere countryside, and was most hospitable and helpful. His own research was based on compiling rural songs, including one on honey collecting, an important economic activity in the drier parts of Mbere. Peter and Joyce Moock were most helpful when I visited them in Kakamega, one of the districts belonging to the Luhya tribe. The Moocks were researching the impact of hybrid maize on the rural economy, an innovation much promoted by USAID and the Rockefeller Foundation.

The Employment Mission

A major event during my time in Nairobi was the ILO/UNDP employment mission to Kenya. Hans Singer and Richard Jolly from IDS Sussex, and Louis Emmerij from ILO, were in charge. The mission became famous for the "discovery" of the *informal sector*, an important source of earnings for many poor people living in the urban slums of the Mathare valley, portrayed so dramatically in the film *The Constant Gardener*. A large number of people were involved, and many locally-based researchers (including myself) were keen to be associated with this high-profile mission, which included the likes of Frances Stewart. The mission lasted for six weeks. My own contributions included technical papers on *African Rural Incomes and Distribution of Agricultural Land, and Inter-District Variation in Crop Density and Seasonal Variation in the use of Labour in Small Scale Agriculture.* I was able to demonstrate that labour intensity on smallholder coffee farms compared favourably with that on large coffee estates, while tea harvesting provided fairly constant employment in comparison with the seasonal peaks of labour demand for planting, weeding and harvesting maize.

One of the sensitive issues that the mission had to address was the future of the white owned farms in the highlands. In point of fact, the issue (except in very general terms) was ducked. Perhaps there was a realisation that further land redistribution was a political minefield. Perhaps it was recognised that the white farmers did make an important contribution to food self-sufficiency, and in their way helped to sustain agricultural research, notably at the Kitale maize research station. Those mixed farms already transferred to African ownership had yet to prove fully productive. It has always seemed to me that Kenya dealt much more sensibly with the white farmer issue than in Zimbabwe, although recent revelations about abuses by the Colonial Government of alleged Mau Mau sympathisers reminds us of how difficult those times were.

On agriculture, the mission concluded:

Three major thrusts are proposed for an employment and income strategy for the agricultural sector:

   (a) the intensification of land use for both crop and livestock production with a concentration of effort directed to the poorer families in an attempt to raise their standard of living by comparison with that of the community as a whole,
   (b) a redistribution of land towards more labour intensive farm units, and
   (c) the settlement of unused or underutilised land.

Special Rural Development Programme

It was good experience for me to collaborate with Judith Heyer (wife of Sergit) on an evaluation of Kenya's special rural development programme (SRDP). I enjoyed working with Deryke Belshaw who was liaising closely with the head of administration in Mbere on district planning. Mbere district was part of Embu province which extended from the foothills of Mount Kenya to the arid bush of the plains. Lunch at the Isaac Walton overlooking a trout stream on the slopes of Mount Kenya was an attraction of visits to Embu. Robert Chambers' presence at IDS added a lot. His experience as a provincial administrator before independence gave him many valuable insights into rural development realities, even if his colonial past made him slightly suspect to some Kenyans. His reflections upon rural development tourism whereby the rural landscape is surveyed by donor missions from a passing car, with occasional stops to interview people who may be carrying loads along the roadside, are especially apposite. A common sight in East Africa is of a man walking along with an umbrella while his wife struggles behind carrying an enormous load of firewood.

Lawrence Smith showed some good management skills in bringing the Glasgow team together for lunch each day in the pleasant surroundings of the veranda of the Norfolk Hotel. However, the cohesion of the Glasgow team was not very strong, with recruitment to the team coming from different universities in the United Kingdom. I did my best when I became team leader to promote it, but I was still a young researcher trying to build a career, and my experience of personnel management did not extend much beyond organising cricket teams of commonwealth citizens in North Carolina. People like Walter Elkan with established reputations were keen to enjoy a sabbatical year or two, and academics by calling tend to be individualistic rather than team players.

Nobel Prizes

IDS attracted some big name researchers from the USA. While I was there, James Tobin and Joe Stiglitz (both Nobel Prize winners for economics) were my close neighbours in the rather simple wooden building which accommodated this Rockefeller-funded institute. In this rather rarefied atmosphere, I sometimes reflected on the limitations of my own research abilities. There used to be (perhaps still is) a rather competitive atmosphere among researchers in a university environment. Team players are a rare breed in academia. Even at the IDS, where the principles of equity and socialism are strongly espoused, researchers are aware that their marketability depends on the list of publications.

Moving East

At the end of my allotted time in Kenya, I decided to seek other areas of endeavour in the cause of development rather than continue in research.

I had been more comfortable in Tanzania working within a ministry of agriculture than in Kenya working in a university research environment. Thanks to my former colleague from Wye, Andrew Odero-Ogwell, who was working for FAO in Rome, I learned of a vacant post for an agricultural economist in a planning team in Indonesia. The person concerned should have a background in plantation crops. I duly applied, was successful, and after briefing in Rome, left for Jakarta.

Chapter 7.

COCONUTS AND CLOVES IN INDONESIA

After a rather pleasant few days of FAO briefing in Rome, staying in the Aventino close to the ancient church of Santa Sabina, we left for Indonesia. The KLM stretched DC-8 on which we travelled in October 1972 took a fairly leisurely route, stopping in Beirut, Karachi, Bangkok, and Singapore. By the time we arrived in Jakarta, some 20 hours later, I felt that I had journeyed to the ends of the earth. In those days, the cabin staff handed out certificates to passengers to record our crossing of the Equator!

At that time Indonesia was ruled by General Suharto, who had ousted Indonesia's first president Sukarno in 1967. Whereas Sukarno had flirted with Russia and communism, Suharto aligned the country with the west, and in the process attracted significant aid, notably from the World Bank. The Vietnamese war was still raging (although coming to its conclusion) and the western world was keen to see that Indonesia retained its allegiance. The UNDP had a large programme of technical assistance, which included support to agricultural planning, and to transmigration. The culture of Indonesia, my introduction to Asia, was also something quite different from Europe and Africa. In my first impression of Jakarta, I was struck by the strange Stalinist-type statues that marked the major road junctions (a relic of the Sukarno era), the urban poverty exemplified by the large number of *bejaks* (bicycle-drawn rickshaws) plying the streets, the number of prostitutes to suit all tastes on street corners, and the all pervading (and rather attractive) scent of clove-filled *kretek* cigarettes.

By contrast to the sweltering heat of Jakarta, the hills of Java rising above Bogor, with tea plantations and rice terraces partly hidden in the swirling mists, formed the background for some great weekend retreats. There was a slightly sinister feel, especially in travelling across darkened villages in western Java to view the residual flickers of fire that marked Krakatau in the sea channel separating Java from Sumatra. In field trips to villages in Sumatra, we witnessed Javanese transmigrants re-enact the *wayang* shadow plays using oil lamps and a special horse dance, acted out as a kind of masquerade.

As time went by I was able to appreciate better the depth of Indonesian culture, epitomised by the *Ramayana* performed over three days in Jogjakarta, and in the hauntingly beautiful sound of the gamelan orchestra in Bali, accompanying the famous welcome dance.

A transmigration programme was underway in order to alleviate population pressure on land in Java and Bali. This large scale resettlement scheme entailed the movement of people to Sumatra, Sulawesi, and Kalimantan. With the support of international donors, some four million people were resettled by 1990. Houses, land for farming, and primary schools were provided, mainly for young landless workers and their families. Planting rubber proved to be a key to economic viability for many transmigrants, many of whom found the transition from an irrigated rice culture to rain-fed food crops quite difficult. Intercropping of young rubber was often a way forward.

The Planning Team

The FAO planning team was situated in the planning bureau of the department of Agriculture. The team was led by Russell Shaw, an agricultural economist from Canada skilled in quantitative analysis. Other members included Uttam Chand, a senior statistician from Kashmir, Vidya Sagar, who had written on the comparative merits of the buffalo and cow, and Peter van der Goot, who contributed on irrigated rice. I was the plantation crops specialist. Paul Avontroodt and Gert Van Santen were young experts who gave important support. Malcolm Hall worked with us for a while, before joining the UNDP office in Jakarta as special assistant to the UNDP resident representative, Andrew Joseph, who came from Sri Lanka. So all in all, a good mix of nationalities, combining well as a team.

Our basic purpose was to strengthen the project planning and evaluation functions of the department of agriculture, working in close association with the central planning authority. Our immediate task was to contribute to the agriculture chapter of the national development plan *Repelita II*. Such was the urgency of this task that we were joined by our desk officer based in Rome, V D Stace, a New Zealander who had worked earlier for the central bank in Wellington. The planning volume was duly completed and bound in a rice green colour, and thus subsequently referred to as the *Green Book* .

Our team suffered something of an inferiority complex in comparison with the World Bank office in Jakarta, which was able to provide considerable sums of soft loans for many sectors, including agriculture. Our FAO planning team, like many other UNDP activities, was providing technical assistance, along with one or two cars and items of equipment, and some fellowships for overseas training of counterparts. The Indonesians provided office accommodation, albeit in somewhat cramped and stifling quarters. Russell Shaw chose not to fight battles with his counterparts over the provision of air conditioning. Wirismanto was our principal counterpart and a serious thinker, with whom I established a good rapport. The team might have been better located in the national planning agency where the major decisions on the workings of the economy were made.

Once the *Green Book* activity was accomplished, it was decided that I should be out-posted to the *Direktorat-Jenderal Perkebunan* which had its offices some way out of central Jakarta in a suburb called Slipi. I duly reported to the director for smallholder plantation crops (Perkebunan Rakyat), Mr Soeroso from central Java. He gave me a warm welcome. He was slightly bemused by my presence and somewhat perplexed as to how it might be that I could assist him and his team in their work. He sat in a large office which contained a long conference table. I was given a desk in this office. The only other occupant was a secretary Sri who responded to telephone calls, but did not type or take short hand. Unlike the British civil service, decision making did not involve much paper work. For some weeks I sat there, without any clear indication as to what I could usefully do. It was a difficult time in my career. Language was part of the barrier, but so too was a very different culture to those derived from British ways such as those I had encountered in east Africa. Happily I was able to build good relations with Mr Soeroso and some of the *Perkebunan Rakyat* colleagues by joining in their tennis games on Tuesday afternoons after work.

From time to time, Soeroso called meetings of the Cess Board, whose deliberations were always lengthy, arriving at decisions by a process of consensus. These meetings would become quite animated and invariably involved the smoking of large numbers of *kretek* cigarettes which filled the room with their fumes. As far as I could ascertain, there were no written records of these meetings, but the allocation of considerable sums of cess money was made (cloves prices were at high levels and generated considerable revenue for the Cess Board). Gradually, and thanks to lessons that Paul Avontroodt and I took with Madame Bang-Bang, my understanding of *Bahasa Indonesia* improved and I was able to make a more informed assessment of proceedings.

Coconuts

Fortunately, at the suggestion of Malcolm Hall who was now working in the UNDP Office, I was soon drawn into a UNDP/FAO mission on the rehabilitation of coconuts. Coconut palms were an important feature of the Indonesian landscape, a significant component of the national diet, and a major source of export earnings. Concern had been expressed for some time at declining earnings from coconut derived exports as growth in domestic consumption exceeded production growth from ageing stands of palms. Along with Cedric Fernandez from FAO in Rome, we travelled from Jakarta to Medan in North Sumatra, and then to Ujung Pandang and Menado in Sulawesi, to find out how the productivity of the area planted to coconuts could be improved.

At about that time, a Frenchman based in the Ivory Coast, Yves Fremond, was making considerable claims for the benefits from high yielding hybrid varieties resulting from West African talls crossed with Malaysian Yellow dwarfs. Yves came with glossy photos of fine looking hybrid coconuts. The research stations in Medan and Menado were potential centres for supervising the establishment of seed gardens. At the suggestion of the consultancy team, I developed a series of models demonstrating the respective benefits and costs of under-planting or replanting ageing tall varieties with the new hybrids, under varying assumptions of age-yield profiles.

One of the outstanding benefits of the hybrids was their early yield performance, coming into bearing at three or four years, compared to seven or eight years for the traditional talls. Another benefit was their relative ease of harvest, due to their low stature. We discovered that tall coconuts in Indonesia were harvested in a variety of often labour-intensive ways. In Bali by men climbing the palms, on plantations in Java by men with knives fixed to long bamboo poles, and in some other areas, by collecting the coconuts after they had fallen to the ground. In West Sumatra, some men use trained monkeys to do the climbing and detach the ripe coconuts. There is an optimum time of harvest if maximum oil is to be obtained, but some coconuts are harvested early so that consumers can drink the coconut water.

The director-general of *Perkebunan* became concerned about the rapid increases in the domestic price of coconut oil, the principal cooking oil in Indonesia, and requested an enquiry. Paul Avontroodt and I carried out a detailed investigation of the production and domestic and export markets for coconuts and coconut products. We sought to establish how much of the basic product was consumed as fresh nuts, how much was transformed into coconut oil and coconut cake, how much oil was consumed domestically or sold for export, and how much went into soap manufacture. The methodology we used was the construction of product disposition tables using a heuristic approach. We foresaw the emergence of a chronic domestic deficit of coconut oil so that palm oil and palm kernel oil would need to be diverted from export to meet consumption needs. We also noted that the long term supply position for coconuts and coconut oil was by no means secured. Efforts by the *Dinas Perkebunan Rakyat* to distribute improved seedlings were not yet on a sufficient scale to provide a rate of growth of output in the longer term commensurate with consumption growth. Our detailed findings were subsequently published in the Bulletin of Indonesian Economic Studies.

During the course of this exercise, Paul Avontroodt, Uttam Chand and I travelled with our counterparts to provinces in Sumatra and Sulawesi, in order to obtain data and review our preliminary results with the provincial authorities and private sector mills. Apart from the information gathering aspects of these trips, they were also a lot of fun. Not only did we explore some remote provinces in Indonesia like Bengkulu, West Sumatra, and Central Sulawesi, but we took our tennis racquets with us and would rise at dawn for an early morning game before breakfast in the provincial guest house.

Dr Lyanage from Sri Lanka came to Indonesia as a FAO consultant to set up seed gardens to produce hybrid coconuts. He travelled to Nias Island off the west coast of Sumatra (sadly devastated by an earthquake on 28 March 2005) to obtain dwarf varieties to cross with the Rennell Tall (from Solomon Islands). These would be much less costly than purchasing hybrids from Yves Fremond in Ivory Coast. The sea crossing to Nias was notoriously rough, but Dr Lyanage showed little concern. There was a lot of discussion within Indonesia as to whether the prolific and early bearing hybrid was really better suited to smallholders in Indonesia than the traditional Tall varieties. One farmer argued that dwarf coconuts had the disadvantage of being easy to steal. Others expressed doubts as to the longevity of hybrid palms.

Programmes for smallholder coconut rehabilitation were set up under Repelita II with Project Management Units to encourage improved husbandry, fertilizer use, copra quality improvement, mother palm selection, nurseries, intercropping, and the adoption of hybrid coconut varieties.

Smallholder Rubber

Next door to me in the *Direktorat-Jenderal Perkebunan* sat Brian Gray, a World Bank adviser responsible for administering the rehabilitation of many of the public sector owned rubber and oil palm estates in Java and Sumatra. It was Brian who introduced me to the North Sumatra Smallholder Rubber Development Project (NSSRDP), a World Bank financed project situated about three hours drive south west of Medan. The project had an Indonesian manager supported by a three man expatriate team led by John Greenwood, who lived on site in this fairly remote part of Sumatra. On one of my first field trips to Sumatra I was able to visit the NSSRDP, and following this, I proposed to director Soeroso and his chief of planning Koestono that we should seek to replicate the basic elements of the NSSRDP in other provinces, but without incurring the heavy overheads of employing and housing foreign experts. This idea was taken up, and later the directorate set up a series of seminars for the extension staff in several of the provinces of Sumatra and Kalimantan, all of which I attended. The seminars were successful in launching the assisted replanting programme which incorporated the provision of higher yielding clonal rubber material for smallholders, with the intensification of production from existing stands by new exploitation methods, and improvement in processing and marketing through the establishment of group coagulating centres. These smallholder replanting schemes later attracted the attention of World Bank finance.

Koestono and I also supported Brian Gray in his proposals for using some of the large Government owned plantations as nucleus estates to facilitate smallholder development of rubber and oil palm. Two types of schemes were identified: those which were based on existing estates, and those involving the creation of *ad hoc* nucleus estates on new land.

Cloves

Indonesia, home to the original Spice Islands, is still a major source of spices, notably cinnamon, nutmeg and mace, and of course cloves. One of the most stunning landscapes in the country is around Lake Maninjau in West Sumatra where all these species are grown and harvested. Indonesia occupies a unique position in the market for cloves being the largest producer, consumer, and importer of this spice. No-one who has lived in Indonesia can forget the special aroma of kretek cigarettes, which are made from a mixture of tobacco and cloves.

The clove tree is a perennial which comes into bearing at about six years, depending on husbandry conditions in early life. The product which is harvested is the flower bud picked at the time when it has reached a delicate pink colour. If harvesting is delayed, the cloves are over mature and have no value either as a spice or for oil extraction. Because harvesting has to be carried out quickly within a critical period of seven to ten days, this is a time of peak labour demand. A critical consideration in estimating future production of cloves is tree mortality at different stages of the tree's development. *Mati budjang* or sudden death of cloves is associated with the planting in unsuitable soil conditions. During my time in Indonesia there was a tremendous demand by farmers for clove seedlings as the price of cloves was very high. Clove seedlings were being distributed from *Perkebunan* nurseries financed by cess funds at a subsidized price. Following an analysis of the planting data, I made some projections of the future production of cloves in relation to domestic and foreign demand. From my calculations, I estimated that during the 1970s, domestic production fluctuated between 15,000 and 30,000 tons as a result of weather variation, while domestic consumption amounted to about 30,000 tons in 1975, rising to almost 50,000 tons by 1983. These findings were subsequently published in the Bulletin of Indonesian Economic Studies. I have not found any recent estimates of the balance between supply and demand, but according to one source, Indonesian consumption in 1999 was approximately 100,000 tons of cloves, with a production shortfall of about 30,000 tons.

Travelling in the Moluccas (Maluku) during the course of our copra market investigations, Paul Avontroodt and I climbed up some 200 metres to observe the oldest surviving clove tree in Indonesia. At some stage during the Dutch occupation the traders cornered the market in cloves, and to consolidate their position decreed that all clove trees in the archipelago should be cut down. The one that escaped we found on the side of the mountain that forms the island of Ternate. It was quite a climb on a hot and sticky day but it was well worth it. It was an enormous tree at least 200 years old with spreading branches and still bearing cloves. We left Ternate for Ambon in a Twin Otter in which the number of parrots perched at the rear of the aircraft exceeded the number of regular passengers. I fear that these birds were destined for export in clear contravention of CITES.

In 1975, the FAO planning team's work came to an end. Following consultations with Aubrey Denton-Thompson, senior agricultural adviser to the UNDP resident representative (and the former general manager of TASMA in Tanzania) I prepared a project to extend my services to the *Direktorat-Jenderal Perkebunan* for a further year. During this period, my work on encouraging smallholder schemes for rubber and coconuts continued, while four specialist consultants were brought to Indonesia to address specific topics.

Consultants

Bernard Zelazny made a most effective consultancy on combating Rhinocerous beetle, a serious pest of coconuts, through fostering viral infections. Leslie Fernie, former Head of the Coffee Research station in Tanzania, advised on coffee rehabilitation in Sumatra and Java. A programme of coffee stumping had been proposed in the Green Book following evidence from field trials in Lampung that significant yield increases could be obtained after stumping when combined with the judicious application of fertilizer. Eric Clayton advised on employment opportunities resulting from intensification of smallholder rubber production in Sumatra.

Dennis Murray from Trinidad advised on the cocoa moth, a serious pest of cocoa in Indonesia (and as it happened, the Philippines). Dennis and I made a memorable trip to Irian Jaya. Getting to Irian Jaya from Jakarta involved a five hour flight by Garuda DC-8 via Bali to the island of Biak, where there was an old second world war runway. There was then a shorter flight on an Islander to Manokwari on the main part of New Guinea. Dennis, who was getting on in years and like Leslie Fernie was a product of the colonial era, started to express doubts if he could reach the cocoa we had come all this way to inspect. In the event he had to be literally carried across a river in order to inspect a cocoa and coconut plantation which was found to be riddled with the cocoa moth. I was determined that having journeyed so far that Dennis would indeed inspect the plantation, and this he did.

All four consultants travelled extensively, and I joined them on most of their trips, during which I learned that consultants are not always easy to deal with and can be something of a mixed blessing. Not for the first time, my people management skills were put to the test. Of the four consultants, Bernard was the best and most technically competent. Leslie Fernie appeared unwilling to put his professional reputation on the line when it came to assessing the yield increments that could be expected from the recommended practice of coffee stumping, a drastic form of pruning, from which the straggling branches of Sumatran coffee trees would certainly have benefited. Dennis Murray brought his wife with him, who expected to be driven into town for her daily shopping in the project car.

Next Steps

At the beginning of 1976, I began to think about the next steps for my career in development. Having worked for nearly eight years in three developing countries, I felt I was ready now to work on development from a developed country base, not least for family reasons and the education of my children. Accordingly, I applied to the World Bank for a job in their new rural development and employment division in Washington.

The World Bank interview system in those days entailed a series of individual meetings with officials in their respective offices. Having travelled across the Pacific, I found the first day of eight one-on-one meetings quite exhausting. That evening I reflected that I had done reasonably well, but the next morning when I presented myself to the division head I detected a marked change in his manner of questioning. My last interview on the previous day had been with Ernie Stern, right hand man to Robert McNamara. Stern had most cordially discussed my perceptions of the World Bank over a cup of tea in his rather large and grand office. Imprudently I had said *en passant* that the World Bank might sometimes make mistakes. This was the time that the management of the World Bank was much incensed by a critical book *Aid as Imperialism* written by a former insider, Teresa Hayter. I did not receive an offer to join the rural development and employment division.

On this same job hunting trip around the world, I stopped over in Boston and was offered a post with the Harvard advisory team in Ethiopia. Unfortunately this fell away when the revolution took place in Addis Ababa. Nicholas Monck, now back in London at the Treasury, kindly invited me for lunch at the Gay Hussar to discuss job possibilities in the UK. At the IDS in Sussex I was interviewed by Michael Lipton and Scarlett Epstein for a field assignment in India, which did not seem very attractive at the time in view of my children's educational needs. I called in at the ODI in London, where I met the director, Rob Wood. A meeting with the Commonwealth Secretariat in London bore no fruit, as the post for which I was suited had just been filled. Thus I became reconciled to taking a further overseas assignment. The opportunity came in a telex from Washington to join a World Bank regional planning team working in the National Economic and Development Authority (NEDA) in the Philippines. While the Philippines was not top of my list of developing countries, I needed a job and so we went, *faute de mieux*.

FAO Planning team visits Menado on a coconuts mission

Smallholder rubber nursery in Kalimantan

Chapter 8.

HILLSIDES OF THE PHILIPPINES

My feelings about working in the Philippines were mixed. Ferdinand Marcos, and his flamboyant wife Imelda, ruled the country. Marcos had come to power in 1965, and in 1972 he declared martial law. The strategic importance of the Philippines in the Pacific and south east Asia was underlined by the American bases at Subic Bay (naval) and Clarke Air Force Base. The Asian Development Bank had its headquarters on Roxas Boulevard, bordering Manila Bay with its magnificent sunsets.

Compared to Indonesia, the Philippines seemed more compact and more developed. The cultural base was less fascinating if syncretic, as modified by periods of Spanish and then American domination. (Somehow the Dutch had been less able to influence Javanese or Balinese culture). However, English was the working language and my Filipino colleagues were good company, hard working and very supportive.

We flew to the Philippines via Washington DC and Hawaii. We arrived in Manila on 17 May 1976, two days before Typhoon Olga which left large parts of the city waist-deep in water.

The Regional Planning Team

Russell Cheetham, an Australian, was the leader of our planning team. He had recently written a book on the Philippines, and as staff member of the World Bank, he commanded a lot of respect from the Philippine authorities. He was one close terms with the Secretary of NEDA, Gerard Secat, and the Secretary for Finance, Jimmy Laya. Russell was also said to be well regarded by Marcos. Decision-making was highly centralised under the Marcos dictatorship, and although Jimmy Laya and Gerard Sicat were considered sound technocrats, at the end of the day it was Ferdinand and Imelda who called the shots. For the first time in my professional career I felt that my development instincts had been subordinated to other considerations in my choice of country in which to work.

Russell called in at the Hyatt Hotel for breakfast the night after we arrived and quickly impressed upon me the urgency of the tasks that the team had to accomplish. Although Russell was a hard working boss and good communicator, I wonder even now if the efforts of the regional planning team had a great impact on the future economic growth of the Philippines. At best it may have reminded central decision makers in Manila not to forget the poorer regions in the allocation of national resources.

We were a diverse bunch. Declan McIlraith was the transport specialist and deputy team leader. He came from Ireland, and at weekends would referee rugby matches. Declan went on to work for the World Bank in Washington. Audrey came from the USA, and specialised in sociology. It was her first overseas posting. Ben Zeevi came from Israel, a graduate of the LSE, and was a specialist in industrial estates. My immediate colleagues in the agricultural section of the regional planning division of NEDA were Domingo Raymundo, an experienced man close to retirement, and Romeo, a much younger person destined to go on to further studies in the USA.

Our office was initially located on Roxas Boulevard, looking over the bay of Manila, and with easy access to some pleasant places for lunch. Later, we moved into new purpose built offices in Quezon City, which was a desert as far as lunch places was concerned. Moreover, we had to endure a lengthy commute by office car through heavy traffic each day. Ben and I lived in Dasmarinas, one of the gated communities (or golden ghettos) surrounding metro-Manila.

Many young graduates were employed in NEDA and our task was to encourage them in regional planning. This meant examining the regional aspects of all the national programmes. Many beautiful maps were produced showing the differences between the dozen or so provinces that make up the archipelago. The relative prosperity of Luzon and the sugar producing

Visayas were contrasted with the typhoon prone regions of Mindanao, which were less well developed and subject to insecurity because of Muslim rebels. Other dissidents opposed to the Marcos regime were known to be active in the Cagayan Valley.

Cagayan Valley and Mindanao

It became clear to me at an early stage that it was important to travel in order to obtain a sound knowledge basis for our work. Accordingly I made trips by road through the Cagayan Valley, seen by Russell as having enormous potential for further agricultural development. On one occasion Domingo and I were warned not to enter a certain village as a rebel group was present.

Much of Mindanao was in the hands of Muslim rebels. In visiting Zamboanga, we travelled into the countryside with an armed police escort. Once Domingo and I visited a large plantation in Basilan, a small island in the archipelago that separates the Philippines from Kalimantan. In Davao City I attended an agricultural sector planning meeting, where those of us from regional planning liaised with colleagues from NEDA's mainstream planning division. The University of Manila had produced a number of well trained economists and NEDA's various offices provided useful work opportunities for them. Regional seminars of this kind would also bring together some influential people from the copra and the sugar and livestock sectors.

Rural Development

Rural development for the poor was very much in vogue. In the Visayas I identified a remote coastal village which I proposed as the focus for a special study for rehabilitation and economic rejuvenation. It is one thing to identify an area where poor people live. It is another to come up with ideas as to how their livelihoods can be transformed. The new team leader from the Bank, David Parbery, (who took over when Russell Cheetham was recalled to Washington) gave a courteous hearing to my proposals. These, as I reflect now, must have seemed rather naive in terms of their investment implications, which was David's main concern. He wanted the team to help prepare background studies that would be useful in defining projects for

World Bank financing, rather than indulge in endless planning exercises. Later on, David and I inspected pineapple estates and beef ranches in the north of Mindanao established on land recently cleared of forest. These seemed to offer much greater prospects for external investment.

Herd Simulations

The mid-seventies marked the advent of the programmable calculator. I was much taken with elementary programming, and its possible applications to agricultural economics. In Indonesia, my project provided a Hewlett Packard machine, which had some basic programming facility. In Manila, as part of our team's training responsibilities, the project supplied a number of Texas Instrument hand held machines, which I used to teach the elements of programming to NEDA's regional planning team, as well as basic rate of return calculations. It is amazing to reflect on the technical advances over the last thirty years as I write this book on a laptop capable of so much more computing power compared with the simple Texas instruments of yore.

Using these same calculators I ran a number of herd simulation models for the Philippines beef industry, and eventually a paper appeared in Oxford Agrarian Studies. On reading this article I can see how my fascination with numbers and the programmable calculator led to numerous projections, which might have seemed spurious at the time. However, on reviewing current levels of beef imports into the Philippines I find that my predictions of domestic demand and supply were not far off the mark.

Hillsides

From tours of the countryside, I became very conscious of the threat posed to rural livelihoods from maltreatment of the sloping lands inhabited by the rural poor. In an lead article published in Oxford Agrarian Studies, I wrote:

The principal problem confronting, but not yet adequately perceived by, agricultural planners in the Philippines is one that has not yet received sufficient attention in the literature of agricultural development or in terms of agricultural research effort. The problem arises from the coincidence of rural population pressures on land, steep slopes, and rainfall of high intensities. The problem is how best to use or rehabilitate hillsides in the interests of providing employment and income for rural people while making productive use of the land and conserving the environment.

I argued on the basis of the Philippine evidence that the development of farming systems appropriate to the hillsides which meet income and employment objectives for rural people, as well as ecological goals, was of pressing concern. The repeated mudslides burying whole villages in the typhoon-affected parts of the Philippines sadly bears this out.

Following an analysis which related existing farmland areas to land capability classes, it became clear that agriculture's boundaries had already spread onto hillsides. These farmers were among the rural poor. I concluded that more emphasis should be given to increasing the income and product of those obliged by population pressure to earn a living on marginal hilly land. Several suggestions were made as to how this might be accomplished, based upon on-going research in the Philippines, and my own field observations.

At one stage during my stay in Manila I was invited to join an FAO mission investigating prospects for further investment in smallholder coconut production in Indonesia. Understandably, Russell Cheetham felt it inappropriate for me to participate in such a mission, given my responsibilities to the World Bank project in the Philippines. I was disappointed. It would have been nice to have returned to Indonesia as a "coconuts expert".

Moving on

Instead I received an invitation to attend a job interview in London. Having travelled half way around the world, and thinking that I was in good time, I caught the train from Brighton to Victoria only to find a lengthy taxi queue. I decided to walk to Northumberland Avenue, but with limited geographical knowledge only reached the office with seconds to spare. Reassuringly, Peter Stutley, dressed in a smart suit, was on the interview panel.

At this juncture of my professional career, I was still thinking very much as an agricultural economist, and while recognising the dynamics of the rural employment situation, tended to look for solutions to rural problems within the agriculture sector rather than outside. The notion of rural livelihoods was still in its infancy at this time. This tendency to retain the specialism of an agricultural economist stayed with me throughout the following seven years after I left the Philippines to take up a position within the Ministry of Overseas Development as natural resources economic adviser.

Chapter 9.

AGRICULTURAL ECONOMISTS IN OVERSEAS DEVELOPMENT

It was in October 1977 that I signed on as a civil servant of the British government. This was my first permanent position after several short term contracts overseas. It was good to be in a position of responsibility, with some very specific development tasks to accomplish, after the rather whimsical nature of my work in the Philippines. Commuting by train to London (a journey time of four hours per day) was the price I was to pay for maintaining a house in Wye, and enjoying walks at the weekend on the North Downs in the heart of the Kentish countryside.

Working in the Ministry of Overseas Development (later the Overseas Development Administration) gave me professional satisfaction, and a renewal of missionary zeal particularly in addressing issues of poverty in India. The job gave considerable opportunities for travel with a consequent broadening of my development experience, to encompass the Indian sub-continent, and Latin America and the Caribbean as well. Trips to West Africa and the Falklands came along for good measure. As part of the job, I was able to build up a network of development contacts within the UK university scene, linked to agricultural economists working at the front line in third world countries.

On the other hand, I had to endure the pain of Thatcher-inspired cuts and reviews, and uncertainties about the future of the aid programme, which with the abolition of my senior colleague's post, effectively blocked any chances I might have had of promotion. I entered the civil service as economic adviser at the top of the principal grade, and when I left after seven years I was still there.

When I joined ODM, Judith Hart was Minister for Overseas Development, and a member of Jim Callaghan's cabinet. The policy thrust was well delineated in a White Paper entitled *More Help for the Poorest*, published in 1975. My appointment was to a new post which my boss, Peter Stutley, had gained on the basis that rural development was the key to dealing with poverty. In fact, a rural development department had recently been created.

The Ministry was structured along conventional geographical lines, with heads of department (assistant secretaries) responsible for the bilateral aid programmes in Africa, Asia, and Latin America, the Caribbean and the Pacific. Each significant country had its desk officer, usually with the rank of principal. Multilateral aid was channelled through the World Bank, regional banks, the European Community and the UN agencies. Decision making and financial administration were centralised in London, but there was some devolution of authority for project identification and monitoring to staff based in development divisions (DevDivs) located in Barbados, Bangkok, Suva, Nairobi and Lilongwe.

The Natural Resources Advisory Group

My rather ponderous job title *Natural Resources Economics and Management Adviser* meant that I belonged to two groups of Advisers within the Ministry: the *Natural Resources Group and the Economics Service.*

The chief natural resources adviser or CNRA, Bob Cunningham, had the rank of undersecretary. The natural resources advisers were a mature group of men, many of them with several years of African experience, garnered in part from colonial times. The only woman adviser at the time was Dr Terry Spens, a rural sociologist from Cambridge. The NR advisers shared the camaraderie and *esprit de corps* that comes with having experience on the ground in pursuit of development. There were senior advisers in forestry, fisheries, animal health, cooperatives, agriculture and agricultural economics. Many had close links with university departments for which they had helped to secure the funding. Thus the cooperative advisers had ties with Loughborough, and the agricultural advisers had an association with Reading University's agricultural extension and rural development centre. The veterinarians had common ground with the centre for tropical veterinary medicine in Edinburgh, and the foresters with the commonwealth forestry institute in Oxford.

Peter Stutley, appointed in 1972 as senior natural economics resources and management adviser, headed a small team comprising Martin Hebblethwaite and myself. We were ably supported by Beryl Castles, our secretary, who gave a lot of dedication to her tasks. This was before the era of word processing when secretaries had much to do in manual typing, and taking dictation. In her domestic life, Beryl had the care of two children from Cameroon. Beryl and Martin showed a lot of tolerance in dealing with the clouds of tobacco smoke coming from Peter's pipe (Gold Block) and mine (Balkan Sobranie). In those days, smoking in office meetings was accepted. We could even summon tea and biscuits for meetings with visitors.

The tasks of the natural resources economists were many, and thanks to Peter Stutley, ever expanding. On the one hand, we could engage in geographical work, advising on projects operating at country level. This was my first preference, and covered projects in Asia, the Caribbean and Latin America. During the course of our tours, we identified posts for agricultural economists to work overseas.

Briefing for ODA's position on matters relating to other development agencies such as the consultative group on international agricultural research (CGIAR), the European Development Fund (EDF), and the Food and Agriculture Organisation (FAO) was part of the job. Sometimes I joined appraisal and monitoring missions for projects we were co-financing with the World Bank. At the behest of the CNRA I attended the management committee meetings for the land resources development centre (LRDC), the tropical products institute (TPI), the centre for overseas pest research (COPR), the national institute of agricultural engineering (NIAE) overseas division, and the centre for tropical veterinary medicine (CTVM). I provided advice on natural resources research through periodic "projects assemblies" to decide on the merits of financing new research. I was the economist on the trypanosomiasis panel.

Each year we interviewed and recruited six or seven agricultural economists for MSc courses and overseas placements under the Natural

Resources Studentship Scheme (NRSS). Most students would go on to become TCOs. At any one time there were about fifty ODA agricultural economists working overseas, for whom we were professionally responsible. By way of comparison, Montague Yudelman claimed some 160 agricultural economists working for the World Bank, although many of these were Washington-based.

In sum, my working life in ODA was extremely busy and professionally satisfying. At the start, everything seemed to be going well for us: rural development was very much in vogue, the aid programme was expanding, and the focus on poverty meant a continuing interest in the rural sector. Unfortunately, things were to change after the winter of discontent of 1978.

Agricultural economists as TCOs

In recruiting agricultural economists to be trained or serve overseas, we would identify different kinds of roles that they might play.

Some would focus on understanding the *farming systems* of poor farmers, by means of interviews or farm surveys. Comprehending peasant farmer attitudes to risk and uncertainty was crucial. Assessing farm family labour constraints would help to determine whether new cash crops would be likely to find a place in diversifying farming production. Farm and crop budgets would illustrate times of cash, food or labour scarcity, which could be overcome by the timely provision of credit. Agricultural economists with this sort of farm management background would find employment in agricultural research stations advising on the appropriateness of new technologies or crop varieties. They would also play a critical role in multidisciplinary teams working in rural development programmes.

Other agricultural economists might specialise in project identification, preparation, implementation, monitoring, and evaluation. They would need skills in cost-benefit analysis, shadow pricing of farm labour and foreign exchange, farm modelling, and risk analysis. Such agricultural economists would find employment in development banks and aid agencies.

A third category of agricultural economist would become specialists in sector analysis. They would need skills in market analysis, agricultural pricing policy, terms of trade, demand forecasting, and production trends. Agricultural economists of this persuasion would find jobs in Ministries of Agriculture and Development Planning.

Some agricultural economists would go on to acquire experience and expertise in each of these fields, or specialise in forestry or fisheries economics.

We formed the core of an extensive development network in the UK and overseas. Peter Stutley was a member of the economic and social committee on overseas research (ESCOR), which funded *inter alia* much agricultural economics research. Peter had posted an agricultural economist (John Grindle) into CTVM, another into COPR, and a third at the NIAE at Silsoe. We had informal links with Doug Thornton at Reading's department of agricultural economics, Deryke Belshaw at the overseas development group in Norwich, Robert Chambers at the institute of development studies in Sussex, Professor Edwards at Bradford University's project planning centre, and Ian Carruthers at Wye.

When Peter Stutley left ODA, and Martin Hebblethwaite became senior economist at TPI, I became the principal focal point in the overseas network of agricultural economists (TCOs and NRSS students). At the suggestion of Michael Iles, an agricultural economist posted in Kathmandu, I started a newsletter which was sent every three months or so to those posted overseas. This was before the days of the internet and e-mail. As well as giving postal addresses to encourage contacts and exchanges of experience, I invited contributions from individuals working in different assignments. In order to keep young economists up to date with the latest thinking, summaries of recent journal articles and techniques were included, as well as news of recent postings and appointments under the studentship scheme. From time to time, I participated in seminars at the universities of Kent, Bath, Bradford, East Anglia, and Oxford, sharing experience of aid work with graduate students, many of them from third world countries. In March 1983 I was invited to join the overseas development group advisory panel.

Every month or so, the natural resources advisory group (NRAG) would meet under the chairmanship of Bob Cunningham. I once had the temerity to suggest to Bob that I might skip one of these meetings in favour of a meeting on India called by the desk officer. I received a fairly dusty reply and was left in no uncertainty as to which was the more important meeting. Rank counts for a lot in the civil service, which has a strong sense of hierarchy, akin to that of the Catholic church. Bob loved his NRAG meetings. His administrative assistant Ted Minns would herd us to the meeting like an anxious sheepdog. Bob had a rather sonorous and deliberate manner of delivery, with a pronounced Scottish accent, which Tony Peers would mimic, much to the amusement of those advisers who retained a schoolboy sense of humour. The meetings followed a standard format. The forty or so advisers as well as the heads of the scientific units would gather in a large conference room. Bob would commence with his own assessment of the state of the NR world. This would be followed by a *tour de table*, with senior advisers reporting on the activities of their sections.

Natural Resources Conference

One of the annual highlights of the NR year was a conference held to coincide with the Royal Agricultural Show. The justification for the conference was partly linked to the commercial aspects of aid delivery, and the occasion was used to invite a selected number of over-seas participants from the third world. I retain fond memories of the July 1980 conference which was held at Magdalene College in Cambridge. The theme of this conference was *Water Resources in Rural Development*, and the East Anglian water authority arranged a coach tour. As we passed a number of country pubs with free house signs, I was able to point out to our foreign visitors (including a representative from China) that the welfare state had advanced in the UK to the point that there was free beer for the workers! The closing dinner was addressed by the permanent secretary, Sir Crispin Tickell. He later went on to become UK ambassador to the United Nations, where he acquired acclaim for his advocacy of climate change.

Downsizing the Specialist Units

Under Thatcher, downsizing of the government was the order of the day, in which I somewhat reluctantly participated. In carrying out the Rayner review of the scientific units, I joined a small team reporting to the chief natural resources adviser, led by Ken Anthony, senior agricultural research adviser. Roger Smith, his deputy, and Michael Scott, animal health adviser, made up the team. Our brief in the words of Bob Cunningham was to review research programmes and the work of the scientific units, in order to identify those parts that were below the line. Bob believed that research work followed a normal distribution: some 25 per cent would be found to be excellent, 50 per cent, middling good, and 25 per cent would be below par. Our task was to identify activities in the last category. I put forward criteria for assessing the worth of research, which included the potential development impact, probability of success, and relevance to third world countries. Having worked with Ken Anthony on India, I had a good appreciation of his intellect and knowledge, and very rarely did we find ourselves in disagreement.

With Leonard Broadbent, Professor of Horticulture at Bath University, Ken and I carried out a review of pesticide application machinery, journeying to Imperial College's field station at Silwood Park, COPR's chemical control unit at Porton Down, Long Ashton Research Station in Bristol, and the National Institute of Agricultural Engineering at Silsoe. With Professor John Kennedy of Imperial College, Dr Braunholtz of ICI, and Dr Lewis of Rothamsted, we reviewed the programme and achievements of the Tropical Products Institute and the Centre for Overseas Pest Research, concerning the pheromones of insect pests of economic significance in developing countries. With Professor Michael Way of Imperial College, we carried out a review of the Tsetse Research Laboratory, reflecting on such arcane matters as the marketing and pricing of tsetse flies. With Professor Bunting and other scientists, I reviewed COPR's work on major migratory pests. With Ron Kemp, we carried out a review of the Commonwealth Forestry Institute in Oxford. With Tony Thorne and Michael Scott, we reviewed the work of the Centre for Tropical Veterinary Medicine at Edinburgh University. In the nature of things, it was not work that I particularly relished, although it was classic civil servant activity, but it did give me insights into much of the valuable scientific research that was being carried out in the UK.

CGIAR

The ODA also contributed a fair sum of money each year to the international centres for agricultural research. These included the International Rice Research Institute at Los Banos in the Philippines (IRRI), the International Maize and Wheat improvement centre (CIMMYT) in Mexico, and the international livestock centre for Africa (ILCA) in Ethiopia. In return, ODA advisers participated annually in Centres week, which was hosted in the autumn each year by the World Bank in Washington.

Bob Cunningham did not have a lot of time for rural development, but he did believe in the importance of agricultural research. His enthusiasm was shared by Ken Anthony, and the two of them would sally forth to present the ODA view to centres week. ODA in those days insisted on earmarking its funding for particular centres. Those regarded as making a strong contribution would receive a high proportion of funding, those who were not making such a good contribution would get less (or nothing). One can imagine the excitement generated in Washington meeting rooms before and during the Centres week, as Bob Cunningham and Ken Anthony compared their score cards with those of other donors.

Many research centres aspired to become part of this exclusive consultative group. The international food policy research institute (IFPRI) based in Washington DC achieved this status. It was the only centre with a specific agricultural economics mandate. The director was John Mellor, who had written a key chapter in *Agricultural Development and Economic Growth*. I called on him while in Washington one year, and he asked me when ODA was going to earmark some funds for IFPRI. I suggested that if he really wanted some money from ODA, he should pay a visit to London and give a seminar. The seminar was held in 1980, we gave him a lunch, and he made his presentation to a good sized audience of economists and agriculturalists. Subsequently ODA made its first contribution to IFPRI.

Natural Resources Conference at Magdalene College 1980

With villagers in Maharashtra during an agricultural credit mission

Chapter 10.

ECONOMISTS IN ODA

The chief economic adviser, Bob Porter, commanded some forty economic advisers, who were assigned to geographical, multilateral, and other tasks. With his cigarette holder in one hand, and the next cigarette in another, Bob Porter conveyed a sense of gravitas, interspersed on occasion with an infectious chuckle.

The economists were a different breed from the NR advisers. The economists regarded themselves (being part of the Government economic service) as the intellectual elite of ODA. They were a formidable bunch. Unlike the NR advisers, it was rare for economists to travel overseas together as this would mean doubling up. Hence there was not the same sense of *camaraderie* as existed among the NR advisers who often travelled together. Typically, they were younger men, many with first class degrees from the best UK universities. Some had gained their overseas experience as fellows of the overseas development institute, or in ODA's development divisions. Some had worked in other ministries, including the Treasury. As Bob Porter was fond of saying, the economists did make a difference. Senior economist for Asia, Barry Ireton, in reviewing the Mahaweli dam in Sri Lanka, suggested that the height of the dam be increased by a couple of metres or so. This had a dramatic effect on the cost-benefit ratio. Project design cannot be left to the engineers alone. On the other side of the coin, Mrs Thatcher's insistence on financing the Pergau dam in Malaysia (for commercial and political reasons), and contrary to the advice of the economists, proved to be something of a development disaster.

Economists were responsible for monitoring macro-economic trends in aid-worthy countries, which could have implications for the amount and forms of aid. They would contribute to briefing for IMF discussions, and

World Bank consultative group meetings. Economists gave advice on specific uses of the aid programme, and were often involved in project identification and appraisal, as well as monitoring on-going projects.

On Fridays, Gordon Bridger would call the geographical economists together at noon for meetings in his office. Gordon's office, with its ticking clock and an enormous hide from some hapless African antelope on one wall, had something of the atmosphere of an Oxford don's rooms. Gordon would brief us on the deliberations of the senior management meeting, and any events in Whitehall which would have an impact on the aid programme. John Roberts, senior economist for Africa, would enlighten us on the misdeeds of various African governments. Senior economist Jim Winpenny would pitch in with an Asian *tour d'horizon*. Jim also covered the Caribbean and the Pacific. At that time he was much taken with a particular ODA project to build an airport in Turks and Caicos, which would serve a private sector hotel development, to which he was firmly opposed. The Aid-Trade provision or *credit mixte* also came in for a lot of discussion. Prospects for proposals about to come before the projects and evaluation committee were considered. Later when Gordon was removed from the service by the Thatcher-inspired Hudson review, these briefings were done by J K Wright. As undersecretary, he brought to the meetings a strong sense of *Yes Minister*, as he spoke in solemn tones of Whitehall tales garnered from his luncheons at the Athenaeum with other senior civil servants.

On one occasion I agreed (naively perhaps) to chair a seminar on *Marxist Notions of Development*. This was inspired by a training course I had attended as a civil servant at the IDS Sussex, where at least one of the lecturers was an avowed Marxist. It was against this background that I sought a better understanding of how Marxist thinking on the development process differed from that of classical economists like Ricardo. At the ODA seminar, the speaker was Jim Moran, one of our former students who had gained experience in Pakistan at the Kamalia sugar factory. There was a very large audience. Many had come out of curiosity. There must have been speculation as to how soon the chair and the speaker would receive letters of dismissal from the Ministry. In the event it was not a very lively discussion. Jim's presentation was very brief, questions from the floor were stilted, and I was unable to raise the debate to any worthwhile level. Jim later went on to become director for China in the foreign service of the European Commission.

Economic Appraisal Methodology

One of Gordon's contributions to ODA was a series of appraisal manuals aimed to provide guidance to economists. I was assigned the responsibility of editing such a manual on appraising beef livestock projects, written by Morag Simpson from Leeds University. This proved a difficult and long-winded task in which I received much help from Brendan Galpin, a vet who had considerable on the ground experience from Kenya. John Grindle (CTVM) and Judy White (working also in Kenya) also had views to share. I believe today that very few outside interventions in the livestock enterprises of sub-saharan Africa (including those of the World Bank) have been successful. As I had found in the Philippines, it is quite simple to develop a herd model on paper showing how seemingly small improvements in livestock parameters (calving rates, calf survival rates, age at first calving) as a result of project activities (such as improvements in veterinary care/ feed/management) could lead to impressive increases in herd size. These improvements in coefficients are likely to be much more difficult to achieve on the ground. Later on Gordon Bridger and Jim Winpenny produced a more wide ranging book on Project Appraisal, which gives a good account of the state of the art at that time.

ODA economists placed great store on a project's economic rate of return . Thus the south Sudan tea project, which came before the EDF committee was opposed, because it only achieved a rate of 3 per cent. Looking at this project in broader terms, it could be argued that in such a remote area it could be difficult to justify any project on this basis. The tea project, and the Imatong forestry project, might well have been the best options for this part of Sudan.

The Projects Committee

The projects (and evaluation) committee was chaired by Bob Porter, although in later years Rex Browning, deputy permanent secretary, took over. The PEC, as it was called, was the decision making body for the approval of major projects for financing. Lesser projects could be approved at undersecretary level, or by the head of a department, and small matters like technical assistance by the desk officer. To present a proposal to PEC was, for an adviser, a major and sometimes rather daunting task. The individual concerned was asked to present his arguments in favour of the project before the committee, comprising five or six undersecretaries and the deputy secretary. Timing was significant. Proposals that came towards the end of the agenda might be whisked through as the chairman had his eye on the clock, and at 1.00 pm other duties called. I was the lead adviser for two proposals to the PEC for India (IBFEP and ARDC IV), but was in attendance for many others, including the Windward Islands banana development programme.

Tony Peers liked to recount a story about an agricultural adviser who was defending a project proposal for Pakistan to the projects committee. The adviser in question had given a very detailed introduction to the project, going on at some length about the expected improvements of yields in the local environment, as a result of the proposed project's activities. At a certain point, the chairman of the projects committee interrupted him and said *"You have visited Pakistan?"* The adviser replied "Actually, not". *"Please carry on"*, said the chairman, having effectively taken the wind out of his sails. I should point out that this was a rather rare occurrence. Most NR advisers travelled extensively, and I would notch up two to three months in overseas missions a year.

In countries for which the London-based economists overlapped with development division economists, an important operating principle was to avoid what was known as *double guessing*. The London based economists were responsible for taking projects to the PEC, and therefore retained the right to challenge material in PEC submissions that could meet a sticky passage. There were two specific areas of expertise where the London based economists were responsible, even in development division areas. One of these was in the economics of natural resources. The other was in manpower, where Professor Fyfe was the paramount chief. Reviews of country training programmes and technical assistance, mainly in the Pacific, Caribbean and British dependencies, were his responsibility.

ESCOR

Bob Porter chaired ESCOR (the economic and social committee on overseas research), which decided on the allocation of funds for development research in the social sciences. This quango brought together a number of distinguished academics, including the likes of Walter Elkan from Durham, Paul Howell from Cambridge, Ian Livingstone from East Anglia, Doug Thornton from Reading, Robert Chambers from Sussex, and latterly Ian Carruthers from Wye. Lord (Tommy) Balogh, former special adviser to Harold Wilson, would sometimes make an appearance. Once Peter Stutley left the service, I was invited by Bob Porter to join the ESCOR committee as the in-house agricultural economist, just as Terry Spens represented the sociologists. The agenda was set by senior economist Barry Ireton as secretary to the committee. Each proposal would receive an initial assessment from a designated specialist on the committee, followed by open discussion, after which Bob Porter would decide whether to reject or accept a proposal, or seek further information. The meetings were conducted with a marked degree of formality, which softened a little after the lunch, which comprised wine and sandwiches served in Bob Porter's spacious office.

ODA economists held the World Bank in great esteem. The bank's appraisal reports, with different coloured covers as they progressed towards financing decisions, were seen as models of their kind. Certainly, bank staff were very professional in their approach. Their systematic review of projects, including ex post evaluations and project completion reports, was in many ways exemplary.

European Development Fund (EDF)

The second Lomé Convention, which the UK ratified in 1980, came into force in 1981. The UK, having joined the European Community in 1973, participated in the first Lomé Convention. The earlier Yaoundé Conventions were mainly concerned with the former French colonies in Africa. There was a distinct antipathy towards European aid among ODA staff, partly because the UK allocation to the EDF was taken out of the aid programme, which meant that there was a corresponding reduction in the amount left for bilateral aid. I recall the shock when this announcement was made: some had optimistically assumed that our EDF contribution which was seen as having been negotiated by the "other wing" in the FCO would be funded from additional resources. This antipathy was re-enforced by a belief that EDF aid was inferior to ODA bilateral aid. ODA then, as today, had a superiority complex based upon the belief that the UK had a deeper understanding of the real problems of development than our European colleagues. Certainly our long experience as an imperial power found its expression in the wealth of expertise residing in the numerous UK based institutions to which I have referred earlier.

Hence when we received EDF proposals for comment we were expected to review them critically, so that our representatives to the EDF committee could in turn express reservations. Gordon Bridger was particularly vocal in this matter, and we felt like crusaders being sent off to Brussels. Accordingly, I would prepare comments on EDF proposals (which reached us late on a Friday) over the weekend, with comments to be sent off the following Monday in time for the EDF committee meeting on a Tuesday. Because of translation constraints, the EDF proposals often seemed too succinct in comparison with the World Bank appraisal reports.

Occasionally I was invited to join the UK delegation at the EDF committee meetings. Travelling to Brussels, in those pre-Eurostar days, involved an evening flight from Heathrow. The next morning, we would take the metro to the EDF committee room in the Berlaymont, and sit around the table with the member state representatives. Klaus Meyer chaired the meeting. He was fairly adept in dealing with hostile questions. My comments on such issues as internal rate of return assumptions or extent of poverty focus were termed "technical details", best sorted outside the meeting proper with the concerned Commission expert. On one occasion, having studied the agenda carefully, I left the meeting room briefly for a bathroom break, and on return found that the project for which I had prepared my comments had suddenly come up, as the two preceding items had been withdrawn from the agenda. My colleagues were in a state of consternation, but fortunately I was just in time to make my comments. I am glad my journey to Brussels was not in vain. In those days, the Commission did not share the "More Help for the Poorest" agenda to the extent that the UK did.

It was noteworthy from the questions raised that the Italian delegation was mostly concerned with the commercial aspects of projects, whereas the Danes, the Dutch, the Germans, and ourselves, were much more concerned with developmental considerations. In those days, the Irish, Greeks, and Belgians said very little.

FAO and IFAD

ODA tended to take a rather dim view of the FAO. David Evans, the senior agricultural adviser, went to Rome for the biennial world food conferences (much in the same way that Bob Cunningham went off to Washington for Centres week). These gatherings brought together representatives of all third world countries, as well as the richer western countries, to review the state of world food and agriculture. As in the UN general assembly, it was a question of one country, one vote, and the director-general knew how to play to the gallery.

Some of ODA's disillusionment with FAO may have sprung from the reign of Eduard Saouma as director-general. As a good bureaucrat he aspired to extend the influence of the organisation. When I worked for FAO in Indonesia, the FAO country representative was designated senior agricultural adviser to the UNDP representative. Later it was decided that FAO country representatives should have their own country offices, along with the traditional white Mercedes. This seemed to me an unnecessary extension of bureaucracy. Not surprisingly, the UNDP were not amused, and when it came to the allocation of UNDP funds, FAO found that it was no longer favoured as it had been in the past. So FAO had to create its own fund for technical assistance projects, which was very modest in size.

When the question of UK support to IFAD was raised, I argued in favour of a contribution, recognising on the one hand that there were political reasons for harnessing finance from the oil rich Arab world, and that IFAD's mandate to help the rural poor was in line with ODA's own goals.

Rural Development

Following McNamara's Nairobi speech in the early seventies, donors tended to rush into rural development projects, without checking to see if there was a viable technology to extend to farmers. In 1980, Bob Cunningham, CNRA, and David Evans, senior agricultural adviser, made a joint mission through a number of African countries to assess the status of rural development programmes in which ODA had been involved. Their findings were not encouraging: there was little evidence of sustainability.

It is unfortunate that the move into rural development programmes coincided with a period when, whatever agricultural research capacity the African country had possessed, had been run down in the post-Independence period. Countries like Tanzania sought to Africanise rapidly under situations of scarce trained manpower.

Nonetheless, the experience with the take up of hybrid maize in Kenya demonstrates that where sound agricultural research innovations had been developed they can take off on their own accord. They may not need special promotion through projects, as Uma Lele observed in her book on Rural Development Experiences in Africa. A World Bank policy paper showed that low income countries spend too small a proportion of their GNP on agricultural research, when returns to such investment are very high indeed.

The Rural Sociologists

Towards the end of my time in London, I felt that I was fighting a losing battle to sustain the voice of the agricultural economist within ODA, notwithstanding the support of Dr Charles Clift who became my staunch and able colleague. My colleague, Johnny Morris, moved to head up evaluation on promotion to senior economist. In 1984, I invited Sean Conlin, a rural sociologist, to join us on an IBFEP review. Given the poverty objectives of IBFEP, this gave Sean plenty of scope for analysis. Unlike agricultural economists, who tend to frame issues from a farm viewpoint, rural sociologists take a wider perspective and look at rural livelihoods. Once I left ODA for the European Commission, I observed a trend for the social development advisers to take over territory formerly occupied by the agricultural economists.

After the Hudson review, the agricultural economists were increasingly looked at as unnecessarily overspecialised. This perception coincided with other trends: disenchantment with rural development in the aid community at large, a squeeze on the bilateral aid programme, and the increasing influence of the sociologists within ODA. As many rural development projects had been designed and managed by agricultural economists, they had to suffer their share of responsibility for their perceived failure. The rural sociologists would claim that only they understood the complexities of rural societies, whereby official aid could be said to reach the rural poor. Unfortunately, when it came to recognising what makes for success in agricultural development, the rural sociologists did not have much to offer.

Chapter 11.

SHIFTS IN UK AID POLICY

My time in ODM/ODA was marked by a sense of commitment in trying to implement *More Help for the Poorest*. This policy, launched in 1975, was in some ways a response to McNamara's game-changing Nairobi speech of 1973. In January 1978 the Government announced that the aid programme would rise steadily in real terms by 6 per cent per year over the period 1978 to 1982. The intention was to make progress towards the UN target for official development assistance of 0.7 per cent of GDP, against a 1977 performance of 0.4 per cent.

Helping the poor

The World Bank had defined rural development as a strategy designed to improve the economic and social life of a specific group of people, the rural poor, which subsequently became the lower forty per cent of rural incomes. According to the World Development Report of 1978, there were 770 mn people in developing countries living in absolute poverty in 1975.

ODM's objectives were more modest:

The improvement of living conditions in rural areas through the increased production of agricultural and related enterprises and, if it is to benefit lower income groups, the equitable and fair distribution of the wealth so created, taking into account the need to maintain a balance between individual consumption, investment and improvements in communal social services.

There were different degrees of poverty-focus as envisaged by ODA's White Paper. First, aid to poor countries; secondly, aid to the rural sectors of poor countries (where most of the poor people live), and thirdly, aid to the poorer rural people in poor countries. One must probably acknowledge that reaching the very poorest people in the rural sectors of poor countries is a difficult task for official aid, and is better done by the voluntary agencies working on a small scale.

In 1978 ODA's concern was to build up disbursements of bilateral aid in implementing the *More Help for the Poorest* policy, in the hope that increases in the aid programme would become available in the years to come.

Other aid objectives

In May 1979, there was a change of Government. Mrs Thatcher and her Ministers decide to incorporate Overseas Development as a separate administration within the Foreign and Commonwealth Office. ODM became ODA. We then had a succession of aid Ministers who lacked cabinet authority, and were subservient to Secretaries of State (Lord Carrington, Francis Pym) for foreign affairs. An aid policy review completed in February 1980 concluded that:

It is right at the present time to give greater weight in the allocation of our aid to political, industrial, and commercial considerations alongside our basic developmental objectives.

As part of the overall reduction in public expenditure, the aid programme would fall in real terms by around 14 per cent. Because of substantial existing multilateral commitments, the proportion of UK aid which could be allocated to bilateral aid had to fall.

How different from today when there is cross party agreement that DFID's fast growing budget should be maintained even in times of economic recession.

When the permanent secretary Peter Preston left ODA on 29 July 1982, he wrote:

Inevitably the economic stringency of the last few years has been a cause of great disappointment to us all but I believe that we have succeeded in maintaining a substantial programme of high quality concentrated on areas where the need is greatest.

Preston was succeeded by Sir William Ryrie. Sir Crispin Tickell took over when Sir William went off to Washington to head up the international financial corporation wing of the World Bank.

Secretary of State Pym, who visited ODA on 1 November 1982, told us that:

Our aid programme is a vital arm of British foreign policy. It is also an important part of the international community's effort to create a more stable and peaceful world. I believe Britain has a special role to play in this by virtue of the breadth of our international contacts and the depth of our expertise. I know that the ODA and its staff have passed through a very difficult period in recent years, with administrative changes added to the unavoidable economies of the aid programme. I hope that the ODA and the rest of FCO can continue to work as closely as possible together to achieve our common objectives.

British aid has always had to be justified to the electorate. For the purists, like most aid officials in ODA, British aid was always for development and humanitarian purposes. However, British commercial interests had also to be satisfied, giving rise to such anomalies as aid being tied to the provision of British goods and services, and the Aid and Trade Provision to soften the terms of any loan for aid purposes. For the foreign office, aid was seen as a tool of foreign policy, a useful sweetener, which could be turned on and off according to political circumstances. The switch from a Labour to a Conservative administration brought these questions to the fore.

The dispersal of the ODA effort over a large number of countries was queried by Sir William Ryrie when he took up his appointment as Permanent Secretary in August 1982. The foreign office view was that aid should be spread widely in order to maximise our influence in foreign policy. Bilateral aid flows can help to influence votes in the United Nations. For the development specialist, concentrating aid in the poorest countries is a much better strategy.

The basic aid framework concerned the allocation of British bilateral aid among countries. As the paragraph below illustrates, British strategic and commercial interests, as well as historic ties left over from the days of empire, were paramount.

India was the largest aid recipient by far in 1981 (£168 mn), followed by Turkey (£ 32 mn), Sudan (£ 31 mn), Bangladesh (£ 30 mn), Kenya (£ 26 mn), Tanzania (£ 25mn), Sri Lanka (£ 25 mn), Pakistan (£ 21 mn), Zimbabwe (£17 mn), Zambia (£ 16 mn), Malawi (£ 12 mn), Morocco (£ 11 mn), Jamaica (£ 8 mn), Nepal (£ 8 mn), Botswana (£ 7 mn), Ghana (£ 7 mn), Solomon Islands (£ 7mn), Indonesia (£ 6 mn), Burma (£ 5 mn) Egypt(£ 5 mn), Lesotho (£ 5 mn) Kiribati (£ 5 mn), Jordan (£ 5 mn) Vanuatu (£ 5mn), Mozambique (£ 4 mn).

There were 65 programmes out of 120 of less than £ 1 mn. Three quarters of them consisted solely of technical cooperation.

Political parties in the UK have usually argued for a substantial aid programme based on three main pillars, humanitarian, commercial, and political. The first of these is sometimes called the moral argument, recognising our responsibility as a Christian nation to help those less fortunate than ourselves. But for some taxpayers this is not enough, and so the case is made that there are commercial benefits from aid. Thus in the early days of official aid, commodity aid took the form of shipments of fertiliser or tractors to India or Pakistan, goods which had been manufactured in the UK and paid for from the aid budget. Aid was tied to the purchase of UK goods and services. The latter could include consultancies to undertake feasibility studies for large projects, or the provision of technical cooperation to overcome skilled manpower constraints in the recipient countries. A refinement of the commercial case is that aid leading to development would lead to enhanced trade prospects for UK exporters.

The political case takes account of foreign policy considerations. The cold war gave rise to a spate of development aid to Africa and the subcontinent, often linked with military assistance, to retain allegiances to the USA or the USSR. Some of these transfers earned development aid a bad name, with suspicions that funds were being transferred into Swiss bank accounts, rather than being applied to genuine development.

Commodity Aid

Food aid is a form of commodity aid that was a convenient mechanism for disposing of food surpluses in the USA and the EU. The development literature is replete with the merits and demerits of food aid. Those who oppose food aid cite the deleterious effects on domestic production through lowering prices to farmers in the recipient country.

One of the pluses of commodity aid for donors is that it creates counterpart funds which can be applied to meet the local costs of development projects, as was the case for some of the earlier fertiliser shipments to India which helped to finance wells for poor villages. In Sudan we were able to use food aid counterpart funds for the transport of food to those in greatest need.

Cuts in the civil service

Mrs Thatcher was determined to reduce the size of the civil service. The Rayner exercise led to a review of the natural resources advisory group, in which the agricultural economists became a target for cuts. With the axing of Peter Stutley's post (as well as that of Gordon Bridger as director of the geographical economists) any prospects for promotion to senior economic adviser that I might have entertained were effectively demolished.

Of course, I was not alone in regretting these changes. Some, however, who were perhaps Conservatives at heart were quite keen to go along with the new approach. Bob Cunningham, as CNRA, suddenly found himself drawn into policy discussions from which he had hitherto been excluded. Although the civil service is ostensibly apolitical, Ministers and their staff have a sixth sense as to where political allegiances lie. Bob Cunningham found that his responsibilities were much in demand, particularly in trimming down the size and remits of the outside units, in which exercise I was instructed to participate. Others who had been closely identified with the Labour administration or were seen as liberals became something of a spent force. Bob Porter stepped down as chair of the Projects Committee. Gordon Bridger, with his Argentine background and scourge of the EDF committee, left the scene, and, after working as a consultant for the Crown Agents, became Mayor of Guildford.

Real Aid

The realignment of British aid policy did not go unchallenged. Charles Elliott, chairman of the independent group on British aid, and Sir Peter Preston, were the principal speakers at a seminar on Real Aid: A Strategy for Britain on 30 September 1982. This seminar at the Overseas Development Institute, was chaired by David Henderson, professor of political economy at University College, London.

The Archbishop of Canterbury, Robert Runcie, at a conference organised by the commission for international justice and peace in November 1982, expressed the view that it was wrong that aid funds should be used to help British industry and noted that ODA was phasing out support for the Centre for World Development in Education. He looked forward to the day when overseas development might become an important issue at election time, as in the Netherlands. Politicians and professionals working in the aid field may have underestimated the moral appeal of overseas development amongst the British public.

Chapter 12.

HELPING THE POOR IN INDIA

In travelling to and from the Far East, I had transited at Bombay airport on several occasions during re-fuelling stops, and viewed the videos of India's architectural heritage (Konark, Khajuraho). For many years, I had felt that a development specialist should have experience of India. Much to my delight I was given an early opportunity to become part of the group of advisers associated with the India desk, responsible for the Ministry's largest bilateral aid programme. A rural development mission was to visit India in order to launch a much expanded programme of assistance in this sector. Peter Stutley kindly put my name forward, and I met Bob Kiernan, desk officer for India. Bob was from Yorkshire, and combined shrewd common sense with a great capacity for explaining the background to all the projects for which he was responsible in India.

India is not a country that fails to leave an impression. Many are overwhelmed by its very real poverty, especially visible in urban areas, less visible but more pervasive in rural areas. Population pressure and urban slums are very soon apparent to the first time visitor to Calcutta or Bombay. First time visitors are quickly aware of the cacophony of urban sounds, the vivid colours of women's garments, the special smells, grand buildings, and wonderful landscapes. Former US Ambassador Galbraith described India as a "functioning anarchy". Even now, as I return to India each year, there is a period of adjustment, as I come to terms with the unique features of Indian society, the poverty, the heat, the pollution, and the dust. Many of those I meet are concerned about poverty, but do not have any magic solutions or quick fixes. Some Indians try in various ways to bring benefits to their fellow citizens, through sponsoring children's education, while intellectuals debate alternative pathways for growth and development in the columns of the Economic and Political Weekly.

Natural Resources Mission

Our first mission to India was led by the desk officer Bob Kiernan with the enthusiastic support of Professor Hugh Bunting. Hugh held a Ministry financed chair of overseas development at Reading University. He was often referred to as the human dynamo, on account of his ability to write and talk good sense at considerable speed and length. John Davie for animal health and Ken Anthony for agricultural research completed the team. We set off on a three weeks mission in November 1977, soon after Indira Gandhi had lost the election to Morarji Desai. Our projects in India were as diverse as the interests of the several specialist NR advisers. Following talks with the British High Commission and British Council and officials of the Government of India in Delhi, we embarked on Indian Airlines flights to various parts of India. I accompanied John Davie to meetings on cattle herd improvement with the Tamil Nadu dairy board in Hosur, Ken Anthony to ICRISAT in Hyderabad, and Ken and Hugh to Indore in Madhya Pradesh.

One of our strengths as a bilateral aid agency was the technical back-stopping expertise we had in the renewable natural resources field, a heritage of our colonial past. One of my suggestions to Bob Kiernan was that a directory of this expertise should be compiled and given to the Indian authorities. Eventually such a directory was compiled with the help of Tim Denning.

In those days, BA flights to India from London re-fuelled in the Gulf, or sometimes in Teheran. Civil servants of middle rank (principals) would travel business class, while professors and under secretaries would travel first class. With the approval of the desk officer, lesser mortals could be upgraded to first class so that consultations could take place during the journey. Our VC 10 carried a happy group of advisers back to London in December 1977. We had accomplished an extensive travel itinerary. With Hugh Bunting I had met MS Swaminathan, permanent secretary for agriculture, in Krishi Bhavan. We had good ideas for building a substantial natural resources programme in India.

In January 1978, Jim Callaghan made an official visit to India to pay his respects to the new Prime Minister Morarji Desai. One outcome of these talks was a commitment on the part of the UK Government to deliver assistance for rural development in India. Two months later I was India bound again.

The Indo-British Fertiliser Education Project

The UK had previous involvement in conjunction with FAO and FCI in three smaller fertiliser education projects in Uttar Pradesh and Madhya Pradesh. The total amount of fertiliser shipped for these projects did not exceed 10,000 tons. The project proposal presented to ODA in February 1978 entailed shipping fertiliser worth £30 mn (some 200,000 tons) over a three year period. The fertiliser would be consigned to the Fertiliser Corporation of India (FCI) which would sell the fertiliser to Indian farmers through its normal distribution channels. The proceeds of the fertiliser sales would accrue to the general revenue account of GOI, and would be used to finance a fertiliser education programme benefiting farmers in 35,000 villages in nine states.

Our appraisal of this project took nearly two years before a financing decision was made, but I believe the time spent was worthwhile and we ended up with a manageable, and ultimately successful, poverty focused project. During the appraisal period FCI split up, and the project was taken over by the part that became the Hindustan Fertiliser Corporation (HFC), looking after eastern India. HFC evidently had its own commercial objectives to encourage fertilizer consumption but it also served our developmental objectives in reaching out to farmers in remote parts of rural India.

Thus Mike Watson, agricultural adviser, and I were despatched on a two week appraisal mission in February 1978. After discussions in Delhi with the Government of India, Mike and I travelled to Calcutta to meet the management of the HFC. In three days of visits to villages, we were given an oversight of an ongoing Indo-German fertiliser education project benefiting farmers in a thousand villages in West Bengal. Dr Bandyopadhyay was the enthusiastic and knowledgeable project leader. It was proposed that the main features of the Indo-German project would be replicated in the Indo-British Fertilizer Education Programme (IBFEP) spread over West Bengal, Assam, Madhya Pradesh, Uttar Pradesh, Bihar, and Orissa. In these six states, the Green Revolution was lagging behind the spectacular progress achieved in the Punjab and Haryana. Mike Watson and I were quite impressed by what we saw. Villagers were genuinely appreciative of the work of the field demonstrators. We observed good demonstration plots. Small farmers were participating. Group extension activities and soil testing involved large numbers of farmers. Higher yields were being obtained. Field demonstrators had helped to make available inputs other than fertilizers. The interim evaluation by the National Council for Applied Economic Research (NCAER) was generally positive in its findings.

However, my initial reaction to the project was cautious. We had been given to understand that the project would follow the same principle of earlier UK and FAO supported fertiliser projects, whereby two-thirds of the revenues raised would be put into a fund for village level investments complementary to increased fertilizer use. We found in our appraisal mission that there were many opportunities for this kind of investment. Surface water storage tanks, drainage, land levelling, shallow tube wells, feeder roads, and storage sheds, were all candidates. Particularly impressive was the work of PADI within one fertiliser project in Gorakhpur in which shallow tube wells were introduced into poor haridjan villages.

In a wrap up meeting in Delhi with Mr S M Kelkar of the Ministry of Chemicals and Fertilizers, I made some suggestions for reshaping the project. I felt that the project build up was overly ambitious, not to say unrealistic, since it implied a very rapid expansion of staff numbers, rates of recruitment, and training. I was also concerned that the project did not address directly issues of access to credit for marginal farmers (for which I suggested a rural development fund). However, FCI said that they were not a credit agency and they were reluctant to get tied up with other Government agencies, whose administrative procedures were slow and cumbersome in relation to their own. A further concern was that there should be co-ordination with other extension programmes, notably those assisted by the World Bank.

Following discussions with Bob Kiernan in London, we suggested a phased programme of expansion over seven years, which would cost some £ 10 mn, rather than the £ 30 mn project originally envisaged. By March 1978 Bob Ainscow had already signalled his in-principle approval of the project on the basis of its potential to fulfill the aims of the 1975 White Paper More

Help for the Poorest. Because of uncertainties regarding the availability of UK fertiliser for export, the ODA sought the agreement of the GOI that the UK contribution to the project should be financed from local cost aid. Since the source of the aid was to be the portion of RTA funds which had been reserved for direct assistance to the poorer income groups, the project would give priority to small farmers.

The World Bank had expressed concern that the fertilizer education campaign might compete with their own efforts to revitalise the regular extension services of the States, along the lines of the Benor train and visit approach. Benor's philosophy was to encourage improved husbandry practises before other inputs are used, whereas the FCI envisaged their field demonstrators being the handmaidens of the farmers, helping them to obtain all the inputs they need to adopt the new technology within certain selected villages. We held a number of meetings with the World Bank office in Delhi in order to iron out our differences of view. In the view of some sceptics, the *t and v* approach (as it was called) became the *train and vanish* approach.

Dr S K Dhua, a Bengali and a graduate of Cambridge University, was the general manager of the Hindustan Fertiliser Corporation. Many times I climbed the stairs to the HFC office on Chowringhee in Calcutta for exchanges with Dr Dhua and his colleagues. When in Delhi I would consult with Dr Saxena, one of Dr Dhua's deputies, in order to gain his perspectives on the project. Initially Dr Dhua wanted to appoint Dr Bandyopadhyay as project manager, but I felt that he had plenty to do in supervising the Indo-German project in West Bengal. Eventually Dr Dhua appointed Dr Das as IBFEP project manager. He proved to be an excellent choice, and quickly won the appreciation of the ODA advisers for his professional competence and low-key managerial style. My questioning and probing may have caused Dr Dhua some sleepless nights, but eventually I was able to recommend to Bob Kiernan that we should go ahead with the project.

This followed a meeting with Dr Dhua in Calcutta in November 1979 during the course of an ARDC appraisal mission. Some of the ARDC evaluation studies I had read pointed to the need for a project like IBFEP, so as to encourage farmers to make the most of irrigation investment.

The project would help to overcome some of the deficiencies of the state agricultural services and help farmers who were recent beneficiaries of irrigation investment to move rapidly to a new farm income plateau. Several of the ARDC evaluation and monitoring studies referred to delays in realising the full benefits of irrigation because of limited use of complementary inputs like fertilisers and pesticides, and lack of extension advice. The train and visit approach which had been plugged so hard by Benor in India was being questioned by GOI officials and even by World Bank staff. As the GOI had expressed its willingness to use RTA finance for the project, I therefore proposed to the desk officer Bob Kiernan that we should take the proposal to the projects and evaluation committee.

By February 1980, ODA officials were able to inform the GOI in bilateral aid talks that we were satisfied that the project had technical merit, it was economically worthwhile, and that it would bring direct benefit to small farmers ie the rural poor. Further, the project would do much to assist a large number of farmers to reap the full benefits of minor irrigation investment, while the project would contribute directly to increased food supplies for both rural and urban consumers. We considered that the Hindustan Fertilizer Corporation had the managerial competence and administrative network to carry out the project in collaboration with the State authorities in West Bengal, Uttar Pradesh, Madhya Pradesh, Bihar, Assam, and Orissa. However, in order for the project to achieve its objectives, the number of districts to be covered by the project and the rate of development should be limited in the initial phases, with a gradual build up to target levels. It was also agreed that the project would be monitored by AERDC of Reading University, and technical support would be provided as necessary from COPR and LRDC. The field demonstrators should be resident in the key villages. Accordingly I prepared a Projects Committee submission, and computed an internal rate of return based upon the project's ability to speed up the uptake of the new farm technology mix of high yielding varieties, irrigation, and fertilizer use. On 1 May 1980, Bob Porter and his colleagues on the Projects Committee were happy to give the project their approval.

The basis of the fertiliser education campaign was an agricultural graduate resident in a key village of a cluster of 10 villages. He had a catalytic role in linking farmers with the suppliers of inputs, principally fertiliser, but also pesticides, seeds, power, water and credit. His duties included working out crop improvement plans for farmers incorporating fertiliser recommendations based upon soil analysis carried out in mobile soil laboratories. Crop demonstrations were carried out in all villages within a cluster, and extension activities supported by literature and films were arranged periodically.

One of my principal concerns was that the project beneficiaries should include smaller farmers, so that the subsidies which were given for fertiliser use in the initial years would not be creamed off by richer farmers. To help check on this and other matters, we engaged Howard Jones of the Agricultural Extension and Rural Development Centre at Reading University. He supervised the agricultural economists Charles and Helen Stutley who were based in Bihar and did sterling work there.

Mike Watson, and his successors as agricultural adviser for Asia (Peter Weare, Tony Peers, and John Goldsack) and I made regular monitoring visits of our own. The Project Management under the capable leadership of Dr Das arranged long journeys often through remote countryside. It was very satisfying to see how well the farmers responded to the fertiliser demonstrations. After a positive evaluation, IBFEP went into a second phase. An article on IBFEP was published in the Journal of Agricultural Administration.

One measure of IBFEP's success was the extent to which others sought to muscle in on what was generally perceived to be a successful project very much in line with our stated Aid objectives. The senior management of the British Council office in Calcutta, many of whose junior staff provided very helpful support to us, used the project to showcase their own engagement in addressing poverty in rural India. Having seen photos in HFC headquarters of various Council dignitaries being taken to IBFEP villages, I allowed myself a wry smile when I saw the name of the Council's representative in Calcutta in the New Year Honours list for services to rural India.

The Second Aid Mission to India

By May 1978, it was time for a follow up aid mission to India, this time led by the head of Asia Department, Bob Ainscow. Bob was a serious, hard working, and dedicated civil servant, whom Bob Kiernan once described as a "trendy lefty". Bob Ainscow was much disturbed when our Boeing 747 was struck by lightning over the Alps en route to Delhi. He seemed to attribute it to a failure on the part of BA management. After an anxious few minutes, the captain assured us all was well. The highlight of this visit was a meeting with Mr Srinivasan, Member of the Planning Commission, in the impressive Government buildings designed by Lutyens. He was a charming person who said "Where have you (the Brits) been? Welcome back!".

India had its own justifiable pride, maintaining that with its own well trained expertise, it did not need technical assistance from the UK rammed down its throat. Nonetheless, Peter Stutley was able to place a UK agricultural economist into the Indore dryland research project. I did my bit by slotting UK monitors into IBFEP, and in association with NABARD's agricultural lending programme, an agricultural economist based at Coimbatore in Tamil Nadu.

The British High Commission

Our mission was guided by the aid section of the British High Commission in New Delhi. Veronica Beckett was in charge, assisted by Alex Sutherland, both very much foreign office types. Veronica gave us a useful lead on a project for fertilizer extension. Playing tennis, she had met the Joint Secretary of Minerals and Petroleum. His department was responsible for the state owned Hindustan Fertilizer Corporation.

In the course of time, Veronica Beckett was succeeded by Michael Jay, who passed the baton to Vincent Maclean, who went on to head up the Development Division in Bangkok. Vincent was succeeded by Christopher Raleigh. Brian Thomson was appointed economic adviser, and in September 1983, Indu Nair joined the aid section as senior development officer.

Michael Jay was a hugely successful first secretary (Aid) in India. At that time, Michael was still a member of ODA, but later moved across to the FCO where he went on to become permanent secretary. He and his wife Sylvia, who took up a post with the British Council, were very popular with the Indian staff. They lived outside the British Embassy compound and entertained regularly. Once they returned to London, Sylvia became ODA desk officer for India. Together with Tony Peers and Indu Nair, we carried out the mid-term review of IBFEP in 1984. Later that year when Dr Dhua was visiting London, the Jays invited him and me for dinner.

ODA's capacity to identify rural projects in India had been subject to criticism by the Select Committee for Overseas Development in 1979. The High Commissioner in Delhi was strongly opposed to any kind of development division in his embassy, which meant that technical advice always had to come from London.

Our relations with the aid section in the British High Commission in Delhi were almost always cordial. However, there was one occasion when Bob Kiernan, more or less at my instigation I must admit, managed to cause some flutterings. The aid section had always taken pride in its relations with Dr Kurien, the redoubtable managing director of the milk cooperative in Gujarat. He had devised a rigorous system for the collection of milk from buffaloes and cows, which had brought valuable incomes to many poor and landless people. The scheme, known as Operation Flood, was largely funded in the early years by large donations of surplus European milk powder. Needless to say, Operation Flood had its critics as well as its advocates.

Michael Jay had sent a useful and detailed note following a visit to Gujarat suggesting that we looked favourably on a proposal to set up a system of routine health care for humans, to match the excellent veterinary services set up for the milk animals. Bob Kiernan sent a telex reply to Michael Jay thanking him in the briefest possible way for his report, but making it clear that he would not be in any position to make a decision until a mission of professional advisers had taken place. Bob Kiernan may have rather enjoyed this exchange, but it was left to Peter Weare and myself to journey to Gujarat to meet Dr Kurien and carry out the so-called professional appraisal of the proposal. As neither of us was a health expert, we felt a little small in meeting Michael Jay and his colleagues in Delhi when we understood (without any particular word being spoken) that some sensitivities had been offended.

Agricultural Credit

In 1979 another string was added to my India bow: agricultural credit. The Agriculture Refinancing Development Corporation (ARDC), an apex financing institution based in Bombay, channeled funds through the cooperative banking system for small scale investments made by poor farmers and landless people.

For some years the World Bank had been giving soft loans to the ARDC. These funds were channeled through the branch network of the land cooperative banks to large numbers of small and medium sized farmers. ODA was invited to participate in this programme. Accordingly Bert Youngjohns, the cooperatives adviser, and I were despatched to join a World Bank monitoring mission. Ray Headworth was the mission leader, who had worked earlier with Barclays in Uganda. Ray was quite proud of the project. However, he was concerned about the growing number of *over dues*. This issue dominated a lot of our discussions over the next years.

In those days, I had still to adjust fully to India, and I did not enjoy arriving in Calcutta in the early morning, after an overnight flight from London, and spending a full working day in the headquarters of some of the land development banks in Calcutta. This was not the best start for me with this project, or with Ray, but as time went by I participated in a number of missions with a succession of World Bank project leaders. Gert Stern was a former "white farmer" from Kenya who succeeded Ray. Jacob Intrator, an Israeli, was next, and finally I worked with Gert Van Santen, my former colleague from Indonesia days. Each team leader had his particular style. After Bert Youngjohns' retirement, I became ODA's lead adviser on ARDC. With the annual budget process of aid disbursement, ARDC (and its successor NABARD) was a useful means, from a pragmatic point of view, of fast disbursing any left over funds at the end of the year in the name of poverty alleviation.

ARDC had its headquarters in Bombay, and it was customary for the World Bank team to pitch its tent at the comfortable and world famous Taj Hotel opposite the Gateway of India. Typically, we would meet up there, have an initial round of discussions with headquarters staff, and then the project leader would assign us in twos and threes to visit different states. During the appraisal of ARDC IV (the World Bank's largest ever loan of $ 350 mn), my team was sent to Aurangabad in Maharashtra, and then to Ahmedabad in Gujarat. On another mission, we visited Madras and Tamil Nadu. Once the field trips were completed, we would return to Bombay for a wrap up meeting with ARDC management. We would then journey to Delhi to hold discussions with the national authorities in the Ministry of Finance where I would brief my High Commission colleagues.

MV Gadgil was the general manager responsible for ARDC's in-house evaluation studies. These studies were professional pieces of work reflecting the competence of Dr Gadgil and his team. They also gave me independent and corroborating evidence in favour of ODA support to IBFEP. The studies provided the evidence that we needed that the funds channeled through ARDC were actually affecting events on the ground, and in particular benefiting the poor. Most of my colleagues on the review missions were concerned with the financial data provided by the participating land cooperative and private banks. I was more concerned to track down the investments being made by individual farmers through the branch networks at the end of the line. This is why I would insist on field visits to loan beneficiaries whenever we went to branches. Particularly intriguing was the issue of the causes of "over dues", and I sought to involve UK researchers so as to strengthen ARDC's capacity in this area. One of our NRSS students was commissioned to undertake research in collaboration with Tamil Nadu agricultural university on the matter of *over dues* in Tamil Nadu.

One scenario for the causes of over dues began with the question of whether the funds allocated were in fact used for the investment intended, or were they diverted into other uses (school fees, consumption needs). If they were used for the purpose intended, was the investment fruitful? Many dug wells, for example, were abandoned before water was reached. Perhaps, a band of rock could not be penetrated by normal manpower. Or a buffalo was purchased which turned out to be barren, or sickly. If the investment was fruitful, did it yield the anticipated returns? Some wells might be successful in terms of reaching water, but electricity outages might mean that the farmer could not pump the water to his crops (many farmers would irrigate at night when the electricity was on). Others might have opted for diesel engine pumps but could not obtain the diesel to run the pumps. Thus some defaulters could be considered *unwilling* due to their inability to realise the full returns on their investment. An intermediary category were those who made some loan repayments but were not up to date, who were labeled partial defaulters. *Willing* defaulters were those who had realised the returns expected from the investment but had not chosen to repay the loan. Unfortunately for ARDC, in many states there were strong political influences brought to bear in the administration of agricultural credit. A not uncommon election slogan by political parties was a pledge to write off agricultural debt, hardly making life easy for the ARDC officials and their participating banks.

In order to shed light on these issues, I organised a seminar in ODA in March 1983. Michael Lipton was in the chair, and Judith Heyer opened the discussion. One point of view, led by Dale Adams of Ohio State, was that subsidised credit led to an excess demand situation, allowing more powerful groups in rural society to corner the market. Low interest rates reduce the incentive to save, depriving financial institutions of domestic savings. The opposite view was that the type of investment for which medium term credit was being used like minor irrigation had underpinned much of the growth of the Indian agricultural sector. Informal credit was not available for such purposes. Village money lenders were only interested in the short term end of the market. The seminar found that the evidence in support of the Dale Adams efficiency propositions was not conclusive. On balance, it appeared that credit was a constraint on growth. The elasticity of supply of private credit was low, while institutions are reluctant to provide credit to small farmers because of the high costs of doing so. Subsidies do invite diversion of credit to the rich and powerful. Continuing aid in support of rural credit is justified providing institutions charge rates of interest sufficient to enable them to remain viable and take steps to ensure loans reach the intended target group.

Mike Barber was a specialist in irrigation. At home in Ireland, he was a keen horseman and hunter. On missions to India, he was a hard core professional on whom Ray Headworth depended and whom I came to respect. As a lot of ARDC funding was being used for groundwater irrigation (dug wells in hard rock areas, tube wells in the flood plains) it was important to be sure that the investment was not leading to mining of the water resource. Mike was adept at making these assessments. He had all the professional knowledge combined with enormous stamina to work in difficult circumstances, and a great capacity to draft the technical annexes upon which so much of the ARDC financing depended.

Sant Dass was Managing Director when ARDC became NABARD. He was a gentle person who had to withstand the rather strong admonitions from young Bank staffers who had been charged by their seniors in Washington to bring pressure to bear for reforms. Sant Dass' predecessor was made of much sterner stuff and used to put the World Bankers in their place without much ado. Sant Dass invited us one evening to have dinner with his charming family in Bombay. Even allowing for the overall scarcity of good housing in Bombay I was struck by the modesty of his apartment for a person dealing with crores of rupees on a daily basis. Despite tales of rampant corruption in India, many in the civil service and other public institutions like NABARD seek to preserve integrity and high standards of service.

Dry Land Farming at Indore

The Indore dry land farming project commanded a lot of attention from NR advisers in ODA, as it was the only project where we had a TCO team on the ground. This project situated on the Malwa plateau in Madhya Pradesh had been identified some years earlier by Ralph Melville, a former CNRA. The project got underway in 1976. Dr G P Verma was the manager, assisted by the UK team leader, Francis Shaxson, and Peter Long, animal draught specialist. The aim of the project was to improve the productivity of rainfed food cropping while conserving the black cotton soils which were subject to severe erosion during the intense monsoon rains.

Dr G P Verma set much store in winning the confidence of farmers in view of previous imposed solutions to land and water management which had undesirable consequences. His analysis of past rainfall data enabled the project to give useful advice to farmers as to when they should plant the *kharif* crop. Encouraging early planting reduced the risks of pest and disease attack, and increased the chance of a quick turn around for *rabi* planting. Short duration sorghum or soya bean varieties planted in kharif on black soils gave a better chance for the farmer of being able to obtain from the same piece of land a rabi crop of wheat or green gram. By providing hybrid seeds and other inputs (initially at subsidised prices to overcome farmers' aversion to risk), cropping intensity increased from 108 per cent to 140 per cent within the project area. Francis Shaxson and Peter Long identified measures to prevent soil wash which leads to gulley erosion, through broad based bunds. Storm drains, grassed waterways and gabions helped to improve the natural drainage system while reducing soil erosion.

The agricultural economist, Trevor Sweetman, made a valuable contribution to the work of the team in analysing farmer constraints, using a farming systems approach. Trevor had been working for DG Development in the European Commission before joining ODA as a TCO. Judith Heyer and Ian Carruthers visited Indore to give professional backstopping to Trevor. I also encouraged links with the economics department of ICRISAT. Indore was one of the few projects in India with resident TCOs, and the British High Commission in Delhi took a close interest in the welfare of these Brits living in a fairly remote part of India. In those days TCOs and their wives found it quite tough to stay in rural India for extended periods.

In September 1978, I visited India at the request of Bob Kiernan to consider with the Indian authorities the future of UK involvement in dryland farming. During a meeting in Delhi with Dr MS Swaminathan, Director-General of the Indian Council of Agricultural Research, I encouraged him to visit Indore for an ICAR/JNKVV meeting to review the project findings, and consider the needs of a second phase. Many in the UK were keen to sustain this foothold in Indian agriculture. Hugh Bunting, Tony Smyth of LRDC, Bob Bell of NIAE, Professor Hudson and Charles Abernethy of the Hydraulics Research Station in Wallingford, and I all made strenuous efforts, without much immediate success. Dr GP Verma left the project in 1979 to become Dean of Agriculture in Ratlam and the TA team withdrew from Indore at the end of 1979.

All was not lost however. In October 1983 I joined discussions in Washington between the World Bank and the Government of India on a new project concerning watershed development in rain-fed areas. It was agreed that British institutions like LRDC, HRS, NCAE and NIAE would provide technical support, building upon existing twinning arrangements such as those between LRDC and NBSS in Nagpur and between NIAE and CIAE at Bhopal.

An evaluation of the Indore project was carried out in 1982 by Edward Clay and Norman Clark of IDS Sussex, working in association with a former Director of the Research Centre for Arid Land Agriculture in Rajasthan, R P Singh. One significant difficulty encountered by the project was that for administrative purposes it belonged to the agricultural university in Jabalpur (Jawaharlal Nehru Krishi Vishwa Vidyalaya) some hours away in the centre of Madhya Pradesh. Another administrative lesson was that it would have been easier had the TA inputs been subcontracted through an institution like LRDC. A more important question in my view was how representative was the project site of dry land farming areas at large. For example, how much additional irrigation investment took place in the project area during the first phase of the project. How significant was the proximity of the project area to the large urban market for milk in Indore city.

Large Dams

Through ARDC I gained some knowledge and experience of minor irrigation schemes involving tube wells and dug wells. I was fortunate to gain some insights into the larger irrigation schemes involving high dams. In May 1979, I joined the senior engineering advisor, Terry Pike, on visits to the Damanganga (Narmada) and Tehri dams. We were asked to appraise a proposal for the provision of land moving machinery from British manufacturers. Clearly this was a project motivated by commercial as well as developmental considerations. Terry and I had to assess the technical and economic viability of the power and irrigation schemes, within the context of GOI's irrigation development plans. We were also asked to assess the cost-effectiveness of alternative methods of construction, including consideration of capital versus labour intensive techniques, as well as the competence of the institutions concerned to operate and maintain the equipment.

The Tehri dam on the Bhagirathi river north of Rishikesh was a ten year project to construct at a height of 260 metres one of the largest rock filled dams in the world. The benefits were estimated to include 1,000 megawatts of power, drinking water for 7 million people, and irrigation water for 270,000 hectares of land. The dam would moderate flooding in the Gangetic plain. Disbenefits would accrue to those 100,000 persons displaced by the flooding of Tehri town and the surrounding areas. There had been much dispute concerning the compensation package offered to those displaced. There was also the risk that the dam, in an earthquake zone, might collapse and bring disaster to those downstream, as happened when the Panshet dam near Pune collapsed in 1961.

We found that at Tehri, large machines would help to meet the tight deadlines associated with the building of the coffer dam, when construction has to be completed during a single dry season. We noted at the earth-filled dam at Damanganga that the masonry central section was being constructed by labour-intensive methods. When we visited, this enormous earth-fill dam was already under construction, and thousands of labourers were carrying material in head-loads.

The Narmada dam had its fair share of controversy. The Narmada river rises in Madhya Pradesh and flows through Maharashtra and Gujarat states before reaching the Arabian Sea. The immediate employment effects of the dam were very impressive, but there were many wider issues including the division of the water among states, the displacement of people, and the impact of the project on the environment and other livelihoods, including fishermen. India's five year plan for this period envisaged that irrigation would expand from 55 mn hectares to 72 mn hectares, of which 8 mn hectares would come from irrigation schemes, with the balance from minor schemes and tube wells. We concluded that large earthmoving equipment was necessary if the Government was to meet its irrigation targets. Having received assurances from the Indian authorities on the adequacy of compensation for the displaced, and on the design of the dams in relation to the risks from earthquakes, Terry Pike and I gave our visa to the project to supply earth-moving equipment. Others might judge that our appraisal of the project in the course of a ten day visit was a little superficial, but at least we reached the sites and met most of the people directly concerned. It is interesting to speculate whether we could have sustained a case *against* the supply of the equipment in the days following the elections which brought Margaret Thatcher into Downing Street in that month of May 1979.

The World Bank later gave substantial support to the Narmada scheme, in terms of a dam and power project, and a water delivery and drainage project. There was success in helping the GOI to bring about a comprehensive basin development and management plan based upon water allocations among the states of Gujarat, Madhya Pradesh, Maharashtra and Rajasthan. However, public concern about the environmental and resettlement aspects of the project led to an independent review. It was found that the needs of tribals whose land was to be inundated, and those who would lose lands to irrigation canals were not properly addressed. Following the report, the World Bank cancelled the remainder of the loan at the request of the GOI.

Social Forestry in Karnataka and Tea in Assam

On a less controversial note, Ron Kemp and I joined World Bank staff in appraising a social forestry project in Karnataka in 1984. This project (I was pleased to see from subsequent evaluation reports) was successful in meeting its objectives.

Earlier Ken Anthony and I made a visit to Tocklai in Assam in July 1979. It was the monsoon season and the Brahmaputra was in flood as the Indian Airlines 737 wended its way up the river from Calcutta to Jorhat. The research station at Tocklai was redolent of the past, and included a nine-hole golf course which I was able to play with some borrowed clubs. From Jorhat we returned to Calcutta and then flew to Bagdogra and drove up the hill to the tea research station at Kurseong en route to Darjeeling, a fascinating town with a population of Nepalese and Tibetans. At dawn we rose in order to see the sun rise over Mount Everest from Tiger point. Tea is an important crop in India for domestic consumption and export, so we were happy to find a strong research effort which we could support.

Travelling in India

As time went by, I became regarded (mistakenly) as some kind of "India expert" within ODA, perhaps on account of the frequency of my visits to that country and the lengthy reports that followed each mission. The regular monitoring visits for IBFEP, which took us to Orissa, Uttar Pradesh, Bihar, Madhya Pradesh, and West Bengal, usually occurred (at Tony Peers' suggestion) in the month of February, when there was pleasant sunshine in Eastern India compared with the cold of winter in the UK. These missions were matched by frequent ARDC missions, which took me to Tamil Nadu, Gujarat, Karnataka, and West Bengal. Somehow the World Bank staff were less sensitive to climate, and often these missions were scheduled for the less appealing times of the year in May, June, July and August (high summer in England and heat and monsoon time in India).

Missions to India were often exciting, invariably exhausting, and frequently memorable. At the end of the mission I would look forward to a comfortable return flight to London. On one occasion I was booked for a non-stop return flight to London on Japan Airlines. Due to exhaustion or stupidity, I misread my air ticket (converting 20.00 hours into 10.00 pm) and turned up at Delhi airport just as the JAL flight was departing. Some eight hours later I left Delhi airport on the infamous PanAm 001 round-the-world flight. This flight stopped in Karachi and Frankfurt before depositing me at Heathrow some 12 hours later than originally scheduled. On another occasion in July 1979 I spent more than twelve hours at Delhi airport waiting for a flight to Indore. The plane (an Avro) was due to leave Delhi at 7.00 am but was suffering some technical problems, and the flight was eventually cancelled at dusk. I abandoned my trip to Indore on that occasion. The Jays invited me to dinner and arranged for Sue McHugh to visit Indore later in my stead.

On another occasion, Hugh Bunting (who was made of sterner stuff than me), Mike Watson, and I travelled by taxi from Bombay to Indore, as the flight was overbooked. Hugh Bunting tried all his powers of persuasion to get us on board the Indian Airlines flight, but to no avail. The journey by taxi took 12 hours, and I was suffering from a cold. It was May, when daytime temperatures were well into the 40s. As we started to climb the Ghats, engine problems developed in the ancient Ambassador taxi. The driver buried himself under the bonnet and wedged a matchstick in such a way as to allow us to continue. I was relieved that this put a break on our speed since I have never been very keen on travelling by car on the highways in India. The citizens of India have their own particular rules of the road, based seemingly on a strong belief in pre-destination.

These missions to India gave me considerable professional satisfaction. I took seriously ODA's policy of *More Help for the Poorest*, and without being naïve, I think we made some difference, even if at the end of the day it is impossible with official aid to reach the poorest of the poor in a country like India with its rigid social stratification in rural areas. One of the attractions of NABARD was the possibility of lending to the landless through loans for animals or the establishment of minor enterprises, even if these loans did not always command the best repayment rates.

Chapter 13.

PAKISTAN, BANGLADESH AND NEPAL

While I spent a lot of time on India, I also became involved in other countries in Asia, notably in Pakistan, but also Nepal and Bangladesh. Together with Mike Watson, I visited Pakistan on a number of occasions in connection with ODA's support to the Left Bank Outfall Drain, the SCARP (Salinity Control and Rehabilitation) Projects, a water-harvesting project in Baluchistan, and a mid-term review of Bob Bell's land levelling projects. During the course of these missions I visited Quetta, Islamabad, Lahore, Hyderabad, and Karachi, and travelled extensively in Punjab and Baluchistan provinces. Later on I visited Peshawar.

Pakistan

Pakistan has a very different feel from India, even if the people share a common ethnicity. However, their characters have more in common than their differences, and both cultures share a warmth of welcome and hospitality, which is not so common in western societies. The Islamic character of the country is quite marked, compared say to Indonesia, even if Muslims are as numerous in India. Pakistan is run by engineers and the military. India is run by economists and politicians. The Indian army keep themselves to themselves, within their own special cantonments, with good housing, golf courses, and medical services, and have no political role. Thanks to Nehru, India is a secular state but where religion is never far from the surface, be it Hinduism, Sikhism, Jainism, Islam, or Christianity.

Whereas in India my inputs may have been significant for decision making, I felt that in Pakistan my influence was less. Very often it seemed that advisers were being asked to give their stamp of approval for project proposals that were already agreed in principle for political reasons. However I was able to focus attention on some issues in large scale irrigation and drainage development, as well as those relating to aid supplied machinery and its impact on employment. In India I became familiar with small scale irrigation via agricultural credit. In Pakistan I became acquainted with the large scale canal irrigation schemes for which the World Bank was a principal financier. These schemes were put forward by the Water and Power Development Authority (WAPDA), often on the basis of British consultancy studies.

WAPDA, with its headquarters in Lahore, was a centre for Pakistan engineers, who commanded enormous respect in the country, and with lending agencies like the World Bank. Despite my best efforts, I was unable to place an agricultural economist in WAPDA. Like many good engineers, they saw little utility for an economics input. However, we managed to place an agricultural economist at the Kamalia sugar factory for one summer, and I arranged for short term assignments for an agricultural economist in Sind, as well as in Baluchistan.

Sind Province is an important zone in Pakistan for food and cotton production, which relies on irrigation from canals from the Indus. Over time, many of the irrigated areas have become saline as a result of allowing the water table to rise too close to the surface. A number of World Bank financed salinity control and reclamation (SCARP) projects have been implemented in order to improve the soils through drainage, and thereby arrest the decline in yields.

Land Levelling in Sind

Agricultural economists have lone debated issues relating to the use of tractors in small scale farming. One school of thought argues that tractors lead to better timeliness of operations and hence better yields, and higher cropping intensities. Others argue that tractors displace labour and bullock power, favour the well off, and reduce job opportunities for the poor. It is difficult to generalise about the suitability of mechanised cultivation, as situations vary widely according to the types of crops grown, holding size, and tenurial arrangements.

Sind agriculture is dominated by the traditional landlord *(zamindar)*, tenant *(hari)* system, whereby crop output is shared on a 50:50 basis between zamindar and hari: the former providing land and water, and the latter labour and bullock power. The costs of other inputs are shared equally. The hiring of bulldozers is done by the zamindar, usually without recourse to credit.

The land levelling project in Sind had been initiated by Bob Bell, head of NIAE's overseas department. (Bob had been lecturer in agricultural mechanisation at Wye while I was there as an undergraduate). The project was aimed at increasing the efficiency of irrigation. By ensuring that water was distributed evenly over a field, rather than being several inches deep in one corner, and dry in the opposite corner, there was considerable saving in water. Mike Watson had a good appreciation of this project, which also had a commercial component in finding homes for British bulldozers which were not doing so well in overseas markets.

In November 1982, in the company of Bob Bell from NIAE and Mike Watson (agricultural adviser) we visited seven of the fourteen district workshops that had been established in Sind Province. Some 260 Track Marshalls (70 horse power) had been provided under British aid to Pakistan at a cost of £7 mn. The tractors were maintained and hired out to farmers from these workshops for land levelling, and reclamation work in all the major irrigated areas. Hire charges were set at Rs 76 per hour, far below the estimated real cost of Rs 200 per hour. Coarse levelling was usually followed by a final operation by the farmer using a wheeled tractor, achieving a level of accuracy of about 5 cm (the maximum difference between the highest and lowest spots in the field). Precision land levelling aimed at a 1 cm level of accuracy.

Track Marshall did not have the best reputation in Pakistan because some of the tractors suffered mechanical failure. This British firm was in competition with Fiat, International Harvester, and Russian machines, not least in after sales service and the provision of spare parts. After our review, I made arrangements for Robert Fieldson, an ODA financed agricultural economist at NIAE, to carry out a survey in Sind in 1983 in collaboration with the statistics unit of the Sind provincial government. His results were of interest to the World Bank experts who were working on the left bank outfall drain (LBOD) project.

Land levelling brings two kinds of benefit: a direct yield effect due to the elimination of over-watering and under-watering, and an indirect water saving effect which shows as an increase in cropping intensity. We were informed that 182,000 acres had been levelled by the Track Marshall bulldozers by September 1982, of which 95,000 acres represented new land brought into cultivation and 87,000 acres was land levelled that was already under cultivation. The cropping patterns in this part of Sind were kharif cotton and rabi wheat on the less saline parts of the left bank of the Indus, and kharif rice and rabi wheat on the more saline areas of the right bank. From field observations and discussions with farmers and agricultural research staff, we obtained some estimates of the probable benefits from bulldozer effort for the two main activities of land reclamation and improvements to existing land. The benefits seemed to be greatest in cotton wheat zones, but were less in the rice areas served by non-perennial canals. There had only been nominal increases in bulldozer hire charges and we estimated the subsidy element as more than 50 per cent.

In making a cost-benefit analysis, I was able to demonstrate quite high returns to land levelling, with an economic rate of return of 18 per cent. Because of the subsidy, financial returns were much higher. The main beneficiaries of the subsidy were influential landowners. We observed that most land development was taking place within the canal command areas, rather than in the flood prone riverine areas where additional water supplies from tube wells could be exploited. Most bulldozer activity was concentrated at the top end of the canal systems where new land was being brought into cultivation, thus increasing the demand for canal water. We were not able to assess directly the effects on the availability of canal water for tail-enders, most of whom had serious salinity problems. With the increasing ownership of wheel tractors by *zamindars*, there was a tendency for wage labour to be preferred to tenants or for sharecroppers to have their shares reduced accordingly (usually from 50 to 25 per cent) as tractors replaced bullock power.

In discussions with the government of Pakistan we pointed out that the subsidy, which had increased from 50 to 60 per cent over the previous four years represented a heavy claim on the recurrent budget of the government. Further, the traditional case for subsidising a service did not really apply since financial returns were still attractive at the full cost rate and the benefits were well known to farmers. Moreover, holding rates at artificially low levels very little in excess of the commercial rates for wheel tractors could lead to inefficiency in the use of resources. There was no case in equity for the subsidy as most of the users of the machines were wealthy zamindars. In some rural societies the existence of a subsidy can create a disincentive to the provision of services by other potential suppliers of the service eg private contractors, so that those who do not avail of the service at the subsidised rate are effectively denied access to the service.

Salinity Control

In March 1983 I joined with Mike Watson to monitor progress in implementing SCARP VI, a £ 100 mn project which ODA was co-financing (£ 10.8 mn) with the World Bank. The UK contribution to SCARP VI was £ 6.5 mn for earthmoving equipment and £ 4.3 mn in local costs for canal and drain construction.

We were concerned that the machinery should be regularly serviced and maintained to ensure an adequate working life. We wanted to know if the price at which the machinery was offered for hire reflected the real costs of its provision, so that it did not displace more cost-effective and labour intensive methods of earthmoving, or discourage private sector firms from entering the market. ODA local cost provision was to finance earthmoving activity for the drainage canals of SCARP VI. We observed local contractors engaged in canal and drainage channel construction, using methods which appeared to be cheaper than using the heavy UK equipment. Private contractors were employing teams of wheeled 60 hp tractors with rear mounted scapers, shifting earth at rates of less than Rs 200 per 100 cubic feet. More traditional labour intensive methods with donkeys were also used, which raised questions as to whether UK heavy machinery might be displacing rural employment opportunities. However, on balance we were satisfied that UK machinery would only be used for tasks such as wet earth and sludge moving over long hauls for which the other methods are unsuited.

Economists and Engineers

In Pakistan, a country run by the military and engineers, many of my missions were in the company of ODA engineers. In most instances we were able to find common ground, but sometimes Mike Watson as the agricultural adviser and team leader would have to resolve the peace. Economists and engineers tend to see the world differently. Engineers will normally think of the best technical solution to a particular problem, where as economists will ask what is the most cost-effective solution, taking account of the relative scarcities of capital and labour. In India building construction men will typically cut long steel rods into smaller sizes employing a man using a sledge hammer with another man holding a chisel. Engineers may not perceive that this labour intensive method might be more cost effective than using an expensive machine.

The Kuwait Fund

On our way to Baluchistan in May 1982 to appraise irrigation schemes, we called in at Kuwait. Our visit was prompted by the fact that we were to finance the Baluchistan irrigation schemes with the Kuwait Fund and Bob Porter was keen to see a practical expression of the Euro-Arab dialogue. This stopover gave Mike Watson and me a fascinating insight into an alternative aid culture at the Kuwait Fund. All staff would leave their desks for half an hour and come together for a common mid-morning coffee break. In those days the Fund had a relatively small professional staff of 32 seniors and 18 young professionals. The Fund did not favour co-financing because of the complications and delays that can arise when more than one aid donors procedures have to be met. Instead we decided to go for parallel financing. Nespak consultants had been recruited by the Fund to prepare the forty projects to feasibility level. The parallel financing of this project thus gave a concrete expression of aid coordination within the framework of the politically significant Euro-Arab dialogue in the post oil price boom era of the seventies.

Once again our travel plans were thwarted by an oversight. On checking into the hotel we were required to hand in our passports. As we travelled to the airport two days later Mike Watson remembered that we had not collected them. We asked the taxi driver to return immediately to the hotel. Alas, it was 5 pm and the hour of the traffic jam, so we reached the airport just in time to be told that our JAL flight was closed. Through a small barrier we could see passengers being called to join the flight. It was a moment of extreme frustration! We discovered that the next flight to Karachi would leave at 3.00 am the next morning. It was a Kuwait air flight and full of migrant workers. So we spent a boring and restless seven hours at Kuwait airport and duly arrived in Karachi with the dawn. Not a good start to our mission.

Minor Irrigation in Baluchistan

Baluchistan is a remote province in southwest Pakistan, sharing a border with Afghanistan and Iran. Needless to say, it was a place of some strategic significance, even in the eighties. Quetta is only 100 miles southwest of Kandahar in Afghanistan. There is no doubt that our assistance to this strategically situated Province was governed by political considerations. Visits to Baluchistan had their own special excitement. We observed President Zia el Haq reviewing the troops as we arrived at Quetta airport. The headquarters of the Pakistan Staff College is in Quetta, and one evening we received an invitation to dine there. It was quite an eye opener to meet a number of young Pakistan officers, as well as two Brits on secondment from the Staff College at Camberley.

The farming systems of Baluchistan are quite different from Sind. Agriculture in this semi-arid area depends on harvesting the unpredictable and low rainfall (averaging 7 inches a year) which often comes in short bursts, by means of check dams and infiltration galleries. Almond, citrus and apricot orchards are common, and livestock herds follow transhumance systems. Wheat, potatoes, onions and vegetables are common crops.

ODA's small scale irrigation scheme in Baluchistan was one of the UK's development project responses to the political situation. A number of minor irrigation schemes had been identified by consultants, of which the Kuwait Fund had taken their pick. Initially the project was presented to us as the provision of more bulldozers, along the lines of the Sind land levelling project. Once we appraised the project, and visited possible sites for water harvesting schemes in Pishin, Kalat and Loralai districts, it took a different form. It qualified as a rural development project (with a marginal economic rate of return) situated in an under-developed part of Pakistan and hence aimed in a general way at the poorer groups in rural society. The poorest groups in Baluchistan are probably the pastoralists and nomads.

The sites depended on bridging natural features in valley heads between arid rugged mountains, identified by the engineers of Baluchistan. We visited a number of these sites and thus became familiar with the basics of infiltration galleys, check dams, karezes, wells, and the like. At one remote site, the senior engineer, a Pathan, told me in an aside that his grandfather had been beheaded by the British. We continued our discussions while I reflected as to whether he would have liked to balance up the slate. The scenery in this part of Pakistan is of immense dry landscapes backed by mountain ranges. Driving along empty roads one occasionally comes across heavily fortified dwellings occupied no doubt by the local warlord. People in this region carry guns as routine. Osama bin Laden would have felt very much at home in this landscape.

In carrying out an economic analysis for two typical schemes at Sitani (reservoir) and Amach (delay action dam) in Kalat district, I obtained rates of return of about 12 per cent. Much depended on assumptions about crop yields and siltation rates affecting the life of the investments. Other variables (or imponderables) were the estimated costs of the dam (depending on site), frequency of rainfall, volume of water collected, the area of the catchment, the area to be commanded, the farmer response to the new opportunities, and rainfall frequencies. The project was approved by the PEC in July 1982.

On another occasion in May 1983, we passed by the Sukkur barrage, an impressive construction controlling the waters of the Indus, and close to the prison where the former Prime Minister Bhutto was executed in 1979.

The Kamalia sugar factory near Faisalbad (where Jim Moran spent a few months during his studentship) was a good example of a turnkey project delivered by Tate and Lyle. While a good project from a technical point of view, I asked about the consequences of introducing capital intensive handling and harvesting procedures for rural employment opportunities for poor people. My concern was not to encourage premature or inappropriate mechanisation in cane harvesting, handling or processing which is labour displacing in a densely populated part of Pakistan. Bullock cart operations are an important income earning opportunity for the rural poor, notably in Maharashtra in India.

While I made several trips to Pakistan I was only able to visit Bangladesh once.

Fisheries in Bangladesh

Bangladesh (formerly the east wing of Pakistan) was a country I had long wished to visit. Labelled by many observers as a basket case in the 1960s, the country had made remarkable progress since achieving Independence in 1971. However, it was not so easy for London-based advisers to gain access. The Development Division in Bangkok was responsible for ODA aid to Bangladesh. Generally speaking, DevDiv staff do not relish visits from London advisers, as such visits can lead to contradictory advice or "double guessing". As a NR economist I could argue that since like Forestry advisers we had no representation in DevDivs, we were exempt from the general rule. But the Bangladesh desk would not be so inclined to agree my travel costs. So I planned another strategy. I had been given permission by the Economics Service to present a paper at the International Conference of Agricultural Economists in Jakarta, which took as its theme Growth and Equity in Agricultural Development. I then contacted professional chums from my Caribbean visits who were now in post in Bangkok (Paul Tuley) and in Bangladesh (Mick Foster) who assisted my cause, and eventually my visit in August 1982 was approved. Mick as the economist on the spot prepared a very worthwhile itinerary for me. I was careful to clear my findings with Richard Manning, Head of DevDiv in Bangkok, and Paul Tuley immediately after the visit.

Bangladesh is famous for its Grameen Bank (its founder was awarded the Nobel Peace Prize). This Bank seemed able to achieve much greater reach down to poor people than ARDC in India. Small loans were given to women and to landless labourers for the purchase of animals, a rickshaw, or tools for carpentry. There is always a risk in such credit schemes that unsecured funds will be diverted away from the target group, or to consumption rather than investment, resulting in low repayment rates, but the Grameen Bank appeared to be able to overcome these risks.

My impressions of Dacca were of an awful drabness. The number of hand drawn rickshaws competing for business testified to the abject poverty of the people. Life in Bangladesh is a constant struggle for existence, battling the vagaries of the monsoon and cyclones that sweep up the Bay of Bengal, while expatriates tend to cluster in the oases of their clubs.

Inland Fisheries

The Neemgachi inland fisheries project had distinct poverty orientation, although there were problems of organisation and administration. Fishermen are among the poorer groups in society. Growing carp in fish ponds was one way of supplementing their earnings. At the time of my visit in August 1982, the project was just getting off the ground with a new hatchery, training centre, water tower, staff housing, a deep tube well, a bridge and feeder roads all in place. Local and expatriate staff seemed to have the qualities needed to manage and implement a successful project. Given Bangladesh's limited land resources in relation to its population, the project was making use of land of low productivity in alternative use. Derelict tanks were being converted into fishponds of adequate depth using labour intensive methods financed under food for work schemes, thereby creating employment for landless labourers (400 to 500 were employed at any one time).

Fish harvesting normally took place between November and June (outside the monsoon season) when the roads were dry. The Department of Fisheries negotiated a price with a contractor to harvest the fish. Fish could weigh as much as 3 kg. Harvesting was overseen by the chairman of the local village committee. Each group of ponds (there were 528) had a guard who was also responsible for keeping weed growth under control. The tanks depended on monsoon rainfall, so if this was insufficient, yields would be below average. The tubewell could only supplement rainfall within a narrow radius.

Marketing of the fish was critically dependent on the supply of ice, as without ice fish deteriorate within eight hours in hot weather. Without ice, contractors were reluctant to harvest too many fish at any one time as this would increase the risk of spoilage. Frequent harvesting added to costs and reduced yields because of the immature fish captured or damaged. Deep ponds were necessary to ensure that fish could reach maturity before being harvested.

Recorded yields of fish were less than actual yields because of poaching and there was a suspicion of some kind of crop sharing arrangements between project staff and contractors at the time of official harvest. Yields may also have been constrained because fish feed (oilcake, fertilizer) had been diverted to other uses and nets of too fine a mesh meant that immature fish are caught. Inevitably in public sector projects of this kind, the staff had little incentive to maximise the return from fish sales for the benefit of the Treasury. There was a risk that project inputs and outputs would be used to supplement their meagre wages. I suggested that as the most of the ponds were too big to be sold to individuals, some form of cooperative ownership appeared desirable. Evidently there was competition between rice and fish for land. As the number of pumps increased to irrigate rice, so swampy areas where fish traditionally were reared become dry earlier in the year, reducing the potential catch. Other threats were chemical poisoning of fish and flooding.

Deep Water Rice

The Bangladesh rice research institute was already receiving some technical support from British scientists, as well as from IRRI in the Philippines. During my visit, arrangements were made for the posting of one of our young agricultural economists, who had already received training at IRRI. In discussions with the research staff, I queried whether research work on herbicides in a country where labour was so abundant was really justified. It was pointed out that account had to be taken of possible crop damage from hand weeding, as well as the value of weeds to the farmers as animal feed. Because of the several special characteristics which deep water rice has acquired for adaptation to its peculiar environment, and because of the relatively long breeding cycle (once a year as opposed to three for dwarf varieties), it was considered unrealistic to expect major advances in plant breeding work in the short term. As deepwater rice produces a lot of straw I suggested further enquiry into its disposition as between animal feed, fuel, thatch and other end uses.

Our prospective involvement with deep tube wells in Bangladesh (co-financing with the World Bank) raised the dilemma of equity versus growth. There is a substantial literature demonstrating that the benefits of tube well water are often cornered by the more powerful groups in rural society. Commentators on the exploitation of groundwater in Bangladesh have tended to favour shallow tubewells (and even hand pumps which raises important questions about energy balances) in preference to deep tube wells on grounds of equity. Much depends on an adequate system of water distribution so that those closest to the pump do not corner all the benefits. The question of whether to rely on electricity or diesel to power tube wells has to take account of the reliability of electricity supply. In neighbouring West Bengal, some farmers camp out at night to avail of an erratic electricity supply.

Rural Development in Nepal

Nepal, like Bangladesh, is a poor country. Much income derives from remittances sent from Nepalese working abroad, not just in the armed forces, but also in more mundane occupations, such as waiters in Goa. The UK has a special relationship with Nepal through the Gurkhas who over the years have fought so valiantly with the British army. Some aspects of ODA's aid programme to Nepal were specifically targeted at the resettlement of retired Gurkhas.

Scenically, Nepal must be among the most beautiful countries in the world. There are few experiences to compare with trekking in the foothills of the Himalayas against a backdrop of the spectacular peaks. My Wye chum from undergraduate days, Keith Virgo, has been active in recent years in promoting successful village-based trekking tourism in Nepal, and India.

The dark side of Nepal in recent years has been a Maoist rebellion, which *inter alia* diminished the role of the King in ruling the country and put a damper on one of Nepal's most naturally favoured sectors of tourism.

A high population growth rate puts pressure on the natural resource environment, with forestry schemes important for protecting hillsides experiencing high intensity monsoon rainfall. The World Bank was of the view that existing irrigation schemes should be rehabilitated before new ones were built. The need for rehabilitation is due mainly to soil erosion and siltation caused by inappropriate farming practices on steep slopes. Nepal would have been a strong candidate to host the International Center for Research in Agro-Forestry. In fact ICRAF was established in Nairobi, and only latterly has become concerned with problems of watershed management in areas like Nepal.

Kosi Hills

It was by a stroke of good fortune that I was included in the mid-term review of the Kosi Hills Rural Development Programme (Khardep). I was a member of the ODA steering committee for this rural development project. There were only a limited number of places on the review team, and I still feel uncomfortable that my going displaced the desk officer, Michael Allen.

Flying in to Kathmandu from Delhi (on one of the original Boeing 727s acquired by Royal Nepal airlines) was itself something of an adventure, quite apart from the marvellous views of the Himalayas. My prayer that there would be enough visibility to allow us to land safely in the oft-times foggy valley was answered.

Peter Stutley had managed to place quite a number of agricultural economists in Nepal. In Kathmandu, I met up with Malcolm Iles, who worked as an agricultural economist with the agricultural project preparation unit in the Ministry of Agriculture. USAID had given substantial support to this unit which enabled some fifty agricultural economists to receive postgraduate training. Another agricultural economist, Geoff Crooks, was posted at the Lumle agriculture centre, while Jonathan Innes was the Khardep economist, replaced later by Dan Marsh.

The Khardep project area was served by the ODA-funded Dharan-Dhankuta road which linked the *terai* (the plains that continue into India) with the hills. Khardep was described by one ODA undersecretary as a fig leaf to provide development justification for the road. Dharan is a major town in eastern Nepal, not far from Darjeeling as the crow flies, at the foot of the hills and at the edge of the terai. It serves as a major trading centre for the hills region, although situated on the plains. Dharan was an old British army station and recruitment centre for British Gurkhas. The Dhankuta road led into the foothills of the Himalayas. At Dhankuta, any cargo was transferred from trucks to porters. After a year, the road resulted in the doubling in the volume of goods carried in the Kosi Hills. The road itself seemed well constructed, with numerous bends as it ascends into the foothills. Given the high rainfall and terrain, proper drainage is critical for the longevity of a road such as this.

John Dunsmore of the Land Resources Development Centre had a particular interest in Khardep. His wife became engaged in the promotion of women's activities, including the knitting of those colourful caps (*Dhaka Topi*) that all Nepalese politicians wear. The other rural projects in Nepal were the agricultural research centres at Lumle and Pakhribas, and the Gurkha resettlement scheme.

Mike Sexton from SEADD in Bangkok was the team leader for the mid-term review. Another LRDC man, Jenkins, was the TA team leader on the spot. The first evening in Kathmandu we were invited to the famous Yak and Yeti hotel for supper where the beetroot soup borsch was the *specialite de la maison*. The next day we flew to Dharan where we over-nighted in the barracks before setting out along the famous road which wound its way around the foothills as it climbed to Dhankuta. From there we proceeded on foot, with porters carrying our food, drinks and tents on their heads. From time to time we would make way for porters with heavy loads, as we followed the track above a winding river valley. At night we pitched tent and sat around the camp fire in the middle of nowhere. During the day we enjoyed excellent views of Mount Makalu, a peak of some 28,000 feet and the fifth highest mountain in the world. On the third day, some forty km further upstream from the start, we exited the valley from a small landing strip where we boarded a Twin Otter of Royal Nepal airlines. The thrill of taking off from a short airstrip in mountainous country was quite an experience. Given the terrain, it is perhaps not surprising that Nepal has more than its share of air accidents.

The Khardep area covered a range of agro-ecological zones, making it more difficult to apply innovations from agricultural research of the Pakhribas agricultural centre. Slope, altitude, aspect, temperature, soil, water availability, farm size and tenure were some of the factors determining the different ago-ecological zones. Adaptive research for hill agriculture was needed with emphasis on farming systems with the complex interactions between trees, crops and livestock. The agricultural economist had a particular role in defining agro-ecological zones, and identifying small farmer constraints and objectives. There was some evidence that the development of rural water supplies had diverted effort and limited technical manpower away from the design and implementation of irrigation schemes.

The second phase of Khardep had been largely concerned with the construction of essential infrastructure in a large number of sectors, without which a field based extension programme would not be possible. We recommended that Phase III should build on the achievements so far, and concentrate on the strictly limited, but fundamental task of increasing agricultural productivity, combined with a coordinated approach to the natural resources sector in general. In the first instance, the areas for intensive agricultural field programmes should be those covered by agriculture services posts, constructed in Phase II. Main activities would be in the sectors of irrigation, agriculture, livestock, the supply of agricultural inputs, the maintenance of the Agricultural Technical School at Utterpani, the local development sector and communications. The needs of forestry and health would be subsumed under separate projects covering the Kosi Hills.

The review team recognised that it was something of an organisational nightmare for Khardep management to coordinate its actions over several sectors with all the Government departments concerned. The productive heart of the project, namely its objectives for agriculture, had hardly begun, and the scheme had so far been handicapped by its failure to offer any interesting agronomic package to small farmers in the target area. There was hope that the work on maize and wheat varieties that was about to come to fruition would fill this gap, while there was a promise of similar results for rice.

We recommended that increased emphasis be put on the production aspects of the programme, particularly in support of opportunities made possible by improvements in communications. I was a little scathing then about school playing fields taking priority over irrigation schemes. A rural sociologist might have taken a softer view, but I was concerned to find some hard data to justify another phase of Khardep to the PEC. We could make some crude estimates of the benefits arising from the introduction of improved seeds from the Pakhribas and Lumle Agriculture Centres. We also had some figures on irrigation schemes. According to LRDC there were some 43 potential schemes covering 2,000 hectares. Many of these would entail labour intensive construction of terraces (Balinese-style) so as to assist in soil conservation.

The conclusions of the review were in the main positive, but I wonder whether ODA's inputs have had a long term impact on the area. Certainly the handicrafts project, supported valiantly with marketing efforts by Mrs Dunsmore, was innovative. Perhaps the most promising venture would have been trekking holidays for tourists (as promoted later by Keith Virgo), since the scenery in this area is magnificent. High value products like spices and coffee might have found a place in the local farming system, alongside beasts of burden to take some of the weight of the porters' shoulders.

My boss Jim Winpenny was sceptical of our findings, and wrote to me that "if this rural development project (Khardep) is successful it will have a chapter of its own in ODA's annals". He went on to say that hard-bitten ODA officials were becoming conditioned to expect failure from such projects unless there is strong evidence to the contrary. I doubt that my report convinced Jim. Looking back, I find that the prism of an agricultural economist focusing on farming was something of a handicap. A wider view would have recognised the possibilities for trekking tourism.

Both agriculture centres had been going since the late sixties. Their original rationale was to assist the resettlement of returning Gurkha soldiers into their areas of origin. Some Gurkhas were also employed at the centres. The managers of the centres were British colonels from the Gurkha regiment. Both centres had diversified work programmes taking in forestry, livestock, arable, horticultural, pasture and extension elements, while doing a fair amount of training at various levels. These were the only agricultural stations in Nepal's hill areas. Much valuable work had been accomplished in research and testing of new varieties of crops and livestock in hill conditions and in distributing plant and tree stock to farmers, in supplying some inputs, and in pioneering systems of extension for the hill areas.

It was the intention of ODA to hand over the centres to the Nepalese government, with the hope that the less rewarding terms of service that the Government could afford would not undermine their continued activities. A five year transition period was envisaged in 1982.

The Nepalese tea project, which owed something to the Kenya Tea Development Authority approach, had an out grower component attached to the rehabilitation of tea estates with a clear poverty component. We considered the possibility of overcoming the public sector Tea Corporation's debts through the provision of fertilisers and boxes in line with the approach adopted for the Windwards Banana Growers Associations.

Chapter 14.

WEST AFRICA, LATIN AMERICA, AND THE FALKLANDS

Technical assistance (TA) was an important aspect of ODA's development aid. In this chapter I take stock of missions I made in support of TA, which included applied agricultural research projects in Sierra Leone, Bolivia, and the Falklands, TA in support of smallholder rubber planting in Liberia, and TA support to coffee production and diversification in Colombia and Honduras.

West Africa

Having lived in East Africa I was intrigued to see the western side of the continent, which is very different in terms of climate, topography, history, and culture. In the event I had two opportunities to visit in April and December 1980. The first was a review of an ODA funded agricultural research project. The second was a review of an important rural development project co-financed with the World Bank.

As always on overseas missions, I was keen to meet up with ODA agricultural economists and identify new openings for our TCOs and students. In Freetown, I called on Francis Dumbuya, an agricultural economist of some distinction working in the Ministry of Agriculture. Francis had studied at Reading University with Doug Thornton. Two ODA agricultural economists were working with Francis' planning team. The Ministry of Agriculture was housed in an enormous rambling wooden building. In the interests of aid coordination, I called on the EC Delegation where Chris Collins was in charge as Delegate. The Delegation occupied a low modern office building, and the staff gave a reassuring impression of professional competence.

Rice Research in Sierra Leone

The main purpose of the trip was to review the rice research project at Rokupr, part of a network of research stations coordinated by WARDA (West African Rice Development Association). ODA was providing some £500,000 of technical assistance over a five year period (1977-1982) to the Rice Research Station with specialisms in plant breeding, soil science and agronomy. The focus was on increasing the yields of mangrove swamp rice and that grown in the associated grasslands. Mangrove rice accounted for about 12 per cent of Sierra Leone's production and was also significant in Guinea-Bissau, Guinea-Conakry, Gambia, Nigeria and Senegal.

The competence and approach of the team leader, Emlyn Jones, exemplified all the best qualities of an expatriate operating in a remote environment. Notable was the support he gave to his counterpart staff. The project's agricultural economist from Ghana, Dr Kwame Prakah-Asante, kindly agreed to take one of our young students under his wing.

The project had come up with high yielding varieties of mangrove rice, as well as a technique for injecting nitrogen into the special mangrove environment (developed at Silwood Park). Land preparation was done by power tillers. Unfortunately rice prices were at low levels in Sierra Leone at the time as the Government had imported quite a lot of rice from the USA, and food aid from WFP intended to alleviate a drought situation the previous year had arrived late. The over-insurance against food shortages (a development dilemma) had clearly been a disincentive to domestic rice farmers. An IMF team had expressed concern to the Sierra Leone Government about low producer prices for rice and the Ministry of Trade had agreed to limit the number of import licences so as to encourage farmers to sell stocks within the country. The World Bank was pressing the Government to eliminate the high subsidy on fertilisers by 1985, as a loan condition of the third phase of the Eastern Region integrated agricultural development project. Roger Smith and I visited WARDA's headquarters in Monrovia, Liberia in December 1980 and formed a positive impression of the team. WARDA was lobbying to become a member of the donor-favoured CGIAR.

Smallholder rubber in Liberia

The smallholder rubber project in Liberia was another kettle of fish. Here ODA was providing a TA team in support of a project financed by the World Bank and CDC. The team was operating in an economy of extreme instability where Samuel Doe had recently taken command, following a coup in which members of the old guard had been executed on the beach. Liberia is an extraordinary country being a mix of American blacks and indigenous Africans. There were extensive rubber plantations in the south owned by Firestone where expatriates lived a typical plantation-type existence (including a golf course). There were also minerals. The capital Monrovia had one international style hotel perched on the crest of a hill, and one fine Italian restaurant a few metres away. There was one main road going up country. In many respects Liberia is the prototype plantation economy at a very early stage of development. A port, a main road, plantations, a mine, and a capital city. The labour situation in Liberia at the time was complex, characterised by a high rate of urban migration accompanied by apparent labour shortages in rural areas, and open unemployment in Monrovia.

The smallholder rubber project was designed by John Greenwood who had joined the World Bank on leaving North Sumatra. The project was based on the NSSRDP concept of replanting smallholdings with high yielding clonal material. The project had a poverty focus: principal beneficiaries had less than 10 acres of rubber which was worked with family labour. Credit packages were available for replanting and rehabilitation. Crude rubber from the smallholders was sold to the Firestone factory for processing.

Unfortunately the project was not achieving its targets. There had been tensions with the local staff, and the project manager had been fired for misuse of project funds. The World Bank team leader for our review mission was a larger-than-life character, Ridwan Ali, who was supported by a young stagiare from the USA. Ridwan engaged fully with Government in trying to ensure that the project was put back on track.

One evening, we had dinner with the Minister of Agriculture in a restaurant in Monrovia. I had to request one of the Minister's staff to re-position his rifle which was leaning against the back of a chair and pointing at my head. At the end of the mission we had a meeting in the national assembly with Samuel Doe's deputy, during which Ridwan sought (with great emphasis) to remind him of the Government's obligations under the covenants of the project. The meeting had a surrealistic atmosphere. The deputy leader sat with a machine gun across his knees. Each of the doors of the building was guarded by soldiers with AK 47s. We sat in the front row of the otherwise empty hall facing the deputy leader, while Ridwan continued to harangue him. It was clear that the deputy leader was not really focused on what Ridwan was saying to him and gave a very perfunctory response at the end. We then shook hands with him and left. Three weeks later I read that the deputy leader had met his death falling out of a helicopter over the jungle.

The project had major implementation problems. The local project manager had been found unsuitable for the job, delaying project implementation for a year or more (personalities tend to loom large in rural development projects). There is always a need to maintain harmony between funding agencies. Expatriate TCOs were blamed for the failure of the project to achieve targets, which were in any case overly optimistic. The project was later restructured to include a factory, a switch from replanting to rehabilitation. The factory was a concession to retain the interests of the new project manager. Concern focused on the rate of project implementation because the rate of return was very sensitive to delay, at the expense of concern about poverty focus, although this was reinforced by bringing in non-rubber farmer participants. There were problems of encashing cheques, registering tribal land certificates, keeping motor cycles running, convening the steering committee after the coup, of communication (by radio and mail).

The low price paid to farmers for their rubber meant that no additional revenue was being generated for Liberian farmers, or the Liberian government, as a result of project expenditure. Farmers were incurring debts which they could not repay, while the government was spending large amounts of money against the expectation of a distant and uncertain return. The unsatisfactory nature of the marketing and processing arrangements for Liberian rubber, where Firestone exercised a quasi-monopolistic position as price setter, was another reason why the farm gate price was so low. Other worrying factors were the low quality of planting work, unsatisfactory land tenure, an apparent scarcity of labour and the high costs of extension work and collection due to the large size of the project area. The apparent labour shortage was indicated by the difficulties that farmers experienced in retaining tappers and unskilled farm labour, despite the widespread belief that there was large scale unemployment in rural areas. Project operations were also hampered by the difficulties encountered in converting tribal certificates (which give no rights to sale or inheritance of land) into title deeds (which are saleable and inheritable)

Earlier in the mission I had a rather unnerving experience. Staying up country it was common to hear gunfire at night. The UK team leader explained that there was no great cause for concern, as expatriates were not generally the targets of such shootings. However, one Sunday afternoon I was alone writing my report in one of the project's rest houses some distance from the main road. I had a clear view down the track leading to the rest house, and suddenly a soldier carrying a rifle appeared and started walking in my direction. I froze as I watched him approach the house. I had no means of escape. It was clear that he had been drinking. Happily the man's wife and child emerged from the bush and they exchanged greetings. I breathed a sigh of relief.

Somehow, East Africa seemed a much safer place.

Sheep Farming in the Falklands

One of the most exciting of my overseas missions was to the Falklands. This took place in November 1983, eighteen months after the war with Argentina.

Lord Shackleton wrote two reports on the economic development of the islands. His 1976 report was updated in 1982 after the conflict. He observed that

Sheep farming had formed the economic base since the 1870s, and that the few attempts to diversify.... have either failed or been short lived. The challenge was of

producing a sustainable farming scheme within a grassland environment which has been degraded.

The Grasslands Trials Unit was a response to this challenge. Staffed by agricultural scientists it was the brainchild of ODA's Natural Resources Advisory Group. In accordance with Shackleton's recommendations that the GTU should be strengthened, Tony Peers and I were despatched to make an on the spot assessment.

Half the thrill of visiting the Falklands was getting there. In those days the conventional way was by RAF transport, taking a VC 10 to Ascension Island, and then by Hercules to a temporary military airfield at Port Stanley. Because of the vast distance over the south Atlantic, the Hercules had to be refuelled in mid-air by another Hercules. When we were due to travel, the itinerary was made even more interesting because the VC 10s had been grounded. Cracks had been discovered in the wings. Hence the first leg of the journey to Ascension was also by Hercules, with a refuelling stop in Dakar, Senegal. Tony Peers and I travelled by train to Lyneham in Wiltshire where the RAF kept its fleet of Hercules. After a good meal in the RAF canteen, we boarded the Hercules. The seats were not very comfortable for such a long journey, comprising canvas seats slung along the sides of the aircraft. The toilet facilities were fairly basic as well, amounting to little more than a bucket behind a curtain. Rations were standard packs as well. The more enterprising squaddies who had made the journey before came equipped with mattresses so as to stretch out on the rear door which sloped upwards at the rear of the aircraft.

Our first attempt at leaving Lyneham was not successful. The RAF pilots (in their overhauls matched with rather dashing white silk scarves) announced, after revving each of the four engines in turn, that there was a fault in one of them. So we returned to base and slept for a few hours before being awakened for another attempt in another aircraft. This time we were able to take off, and after several hours we arrived at Dakar, where we were able to stretch our legs, before another long flight to Ascension Island. There we had a full English breakfast, before joining another Hercules specially equipped for the mid-air refuelling. I had tried to emulate the squaddies by trying to sleep on the sloping rear of the plane, but gave up because of the extreme cold. We were flying at 18,000 feet, and the outside temperature was several degrees below zero. One has to admire the skill of the pilots for these quite sophisticated manoeuvres carried out at altitude in air, which if not turbulent at that time, was not very stable either. I watched from the cockpit with great fascination as the pipeline with its cone from the refuelling Hercules was eventually brought into contact with the proboscis of our plane. The distance between the two aircraft when coupled could be measured in feet rather than yards. Arriving in Port Stanley after some thirty six hours, we staggered off the plane like zombies.

Sir Rex Hunt, the Governor, and his wife Mavis kindly invited us for drinks. They had a London taxi cab as their official car. Sir Rex was much concerned that the £ 10 mn promised for the rehabilitation of the islands after the war was being consumed by needless advisory visits such as ours. "You are part of the £10 million", he said meaningfully, as his wife refilled our glasses. Having travelled so far we felt obliged to do our best to show that this investment was well justified. The two thousand or so people who inhabited the Falklands were a mixed bunch. Some were of Welsh or Scottish ancestry, others came from New Zealand. It was a life of some solitude. The biggest event could be supper at the one hotel in Stanley, the Upland Goose. Things may have changed a lot since the opening of the airport at Mount Pleasant, and the law of the sea which gave prosperity to many on the islands from fishing licenses. The seas around the Falklands are rich in octopus and squid (and perhaps oil), and fisheries revenue has now become a major source of income of much greater value than the wool.

The project that we had come to review was the Grasslands Research Unit. Its basic premise was that improved pasture would help to better the fertility and lambing rates of the sheep flock which numbered some half a million animals, and at that time was the major source of income for the islanders. As an agricultural economist, I had some doubts on this technical approach, since one normally seeks to increase the returns to the scarce factor of production, which in the Falklands was clearly labour. However, based on some coefficients for weaning and lambing rates, I was able to make some projections for the sheep flock for the Falklands which could ensue from the adoption of improved pasture by the farmers.

Travelling around the Falklands was an adventure in itself. Driving overland around the *camp* with John Ferguson the team leader of the Grasslands

Research Unit (whose family kindly provided accommodation for me), we had to avoid areas where mines had still to be removed. Travelling in a small Cessna to Goose Green was quite exciting because of the strength of the winds and the shortness of the airstrips. Once again I had occasion to admire the skill of the pilots.

I retain special memories of this visit. While in Goose Green I visited on my own the spot where Lieutenant Colonel H. Jones won his VC. It was marked by a simple artificial flower in a glass jar. Nearby, where the Argentinian forces had dug their trenches, some old socks and a water bottle were littered on the ground, a stark reminder of their very human presence only a few months earlier. It was a sad but very emotive scene. Even if I had mixed feelings about the action taken by Margaret Thatcher, I was much affected to see at first hand evidence of the bravery of those British troops who had defended these islands. At the same time, I felt a sympathy for the young Argentines who had been consigned by Galtieri to attack the *Islas Malvinas*.

One Sunday afternoon I was wandering along the beach on the Western Island when I encountered a troupe of penguins. These very remarkable birds were absolutely fascinating to observe, and took no notice of me. Another evening we stayed with some farmers in camp, who showed kind hospitality in serving the inevitable mutton pie. I went outside to smoke my pipe and was amazed by a magnificent view of the heavens with an incredibly clear view of myriads of stars. Such is the purity of the atmosphere in the middle of the South Atlantic, far from urban cities and other forms of pollution.

The Governor's Residence in Port Stanley, 1983

Penguins in West Falklands

Coffee in Colombia

In 1979 the ODA was invited by the Colombian authorities to send a team to advise Cenicafe on coffee research, and in particular to help devise a strategy against the threat of coffee rust (*roya*). This followed on a visit in 1978 to UK scientific institutions by a delegation from the *Federacion Nacional de Cafeteros de Colombia*, led by Dr Hugo Valdes.

FNCC had responsibility for the maintenance of coffee production and the welfare of the coffee farmers, most of whom were smallholders. Coffee accounted for sixty per cent of export earnings. Seventy per cent of the population lived in the coffee areas, of which more than a million hectares was under coffee. Rural development incorporating agricultural diversification was seen as a means of reducing the dependence of the economy on coffee and creating employment opportunities.

Given my background in coffee from Tanzania, and my familiarity with the corridors of the International Coffee Organisation in London, I was pleased to be asked to join the mission. After all, Tanzania and Kenya shared the same classification for their exports as *Colombian milds*. The team leader was Brian Robinson, a former director of the coffee research station at Thika in Kenya. John Caygill, a coffee processing expert from the Tropical Products Institute, Peter Oakley, an agricultural extension specialist from Reading University, and Gordon Maliphant, a microbiologist, completed the team.

We spent a couple of days in Bogota in March 1979 before travelling to Manizales. In those days security was not so bad, but we were advised not to wander about at night. Instead I took early morning walks to the Cathedral. In playing golf at the course near Bogota I noted two things. First, the vast distance that my golf ball flew in driving at high altitude. Second, the presence of armed security guards on each tee.

Our Air Colombia Boeing 727 was initially delayed by fog, but eventually we arrived in Manizales to a warm welcome from the director of the coffee research station and his staff. We spent about a week at Chinchina in the department of Caldas, where I was able to use my limited Spanish for professional discussions with the agricultural economist, Dr Bicerra.

We spent another week on field trips in the principal coffee growing areas. Colombia had already achieved significant technical advance with planting *caturra* coffee, a high yielding dwarf cultivar from Brazil, which came into bearing at two or three years, as opposed to the four or five years of Arabica. The director and his family entertained us during the evenings in true Latin American fashion.

We wrote quite a comprehensive report during our stay, which JDB Robinson duly delivered in English with appropriate solemnity to the assembled FNCC authorities in Bogota at the end of our mission. Our main findings were as follows.

The introduction of *Caturra* coffee, a dwarf high yield hybrid, accounted for one quarter of the total area planted. Production potential exceeded exports under the ICO quota which would suggest a further build up of stocks, more than enough to insure against rust to preserve world market shares.

Caturra planting represented an efficient technology which would help Colombia to withstand rust attack, since its high yields could bear the costs of spraying.

Rust would spread throughout the central coffee zone. In the higher altitude belt rust would be controlled on all but the very steep slopes. In the lower climatic belt, rust infection would be very difficult to control because of rainfall intensity.

The plant breeding work at Cenicafe had been highly successful in producing varieties of *Caturra* crossed with Timor hybrid which had total rust resistance. These varieties were ready for commercial planting.

Caturra grown without shade on steep slopes had contributed to environmental problems of soil erosion, water shortages, and water pollution from pulverise.

There had been socio-economic consequences associated with *Caturra* planting and the coffee bonanza which had tended to worsen the distribution of income and land holdings in rural areas.

Diversification efforts were largely focussed on medium and larger farmers, with little impact on land allocated to coffee but some impact in diversifying sources of farm income for coffee farmers by the addition of enterprises such as dairying, flowers, plantain, cassava, cacao, citrus, sugar, honey, chickens, rabbits, and pigs.

Afforestation of the steeper slopes on the upper margins of the coffee zone would bring obvious environmental benefits.

We found the extension service to be well staffed and efficient in terms of implementing the *Caturra revolution*. However, the extension staff were inadequately served by research, had a definite large farm bias, were much involved in credit administration, and weak in advising on soil erosion preventive measures. We recommended an expansion of the *minifundista* credit programme to all departments, an integration of diversification and coffee extension activities, and a target group approach with emphasis on smaller farmers with less than five hectares of traditional coffee.

The British Ambassador invited us for an excellent lunch, and so we left Colombia on a British Caledonian DC 10 with a sense of mission accomplished. At least we had done our best to promote cordial UK-Colombian relations. At best, we had helped Colombia to avoid the threat of coffee rust.

Coffee Diversification in Honduras

Part of my job as NR economist was to recruit and find placements for young agricultural economists to work overseas as TCOs. Many of these postings were in team situations. Occasionally, individuals were working on their own, and needed support.

Phil Bodman, a TCO agricultural economist working with the national coffee authorities (IHCAFE) in Honduras, requested some professional backstopping to identify coffee diversification possibilities, which I was glad to provide. The desk officer amplified the terms of reference for my mission and asked me to appraise a request from the Agrarian Reform Agency (INA) for the provision of £400,000 worth of Landrovers. Accordingly in May 1983, after an initial round of discussions with IHCAFE officials in Tegucigalpa, Phil Bodman and I set off on a tour of the coffee growing regions. The tour happily included San Pedro Sula on the Caribbean coast, and the Mayan temples of Copan. The coffee authorities were eager to identify diversification alternatives for marginal farmers, particularly in the rust prone areas at lower altitudes. We visited some of the larger holdings which were to be sub-divided. Possibilities for diversification included cocoa, bananas, mangoes, pineapples, avocados, and livestock enterprises. Planting tree crops carries the risk posed by high winds, which can destroy several years of investment, as happened in 1998 with hurricane Mitch.

Honduras had the unenviable reputation of a very high murder rate, and the airport at Tegucigalpa had an unfortunate safety record, but we completed our tour unscathed. All in all, a fascinating visit to a central American country sharing a common border with Guatemala which was going through its own problems. En route from Miami, we stopped in Belize where the British air force maintained some fighter jets carefully hidden in their pods.

My last visit to Latin America was in December 1984 in order to participate in a review of the British Tropical Agricultural Mission in Bolivia. BTAM was the brainchild of Gordon Bridger when he was senior economist for Latin America. Gordon had made a strong case for substantial ODA assistance to the mining sector, but had not managed to convince the Minister Judith Hart. Hence ODA aid went to BTAM. The project had trundled along for decades, but no-one quite knew how to bring it to an end. We travelled to La Paz (via Rio de Janeiro), where the airport is sited above the city at an altitude of some 12,000 feet making it the highest international airport in the world. After a couple of days of acclimatisation and briefing by the British embassy in La Paz we flew down to Santa Cruz. Taking off from the four kilometre runway seemed to last an inordinate amount of time.

Farming Systems Research in Bolivia

The BTAM project had the task of developing new farming systems in the campesino. Simon Maxwell had been the farming systems economist there for two years, and achieved a lot whilst encountering some of the normal criticisms that agricultural scientists bestow on agricultural economists. He had sought to steer the project team away from research geared to the larger farmers towards the smaller farmers in the campesino. Important issues concerned the economic and environmental effects of alternative methods of land clearance, and the social impact of mechanisation in relation to labour use. Before leaving I travelled down to Cali in Colombia to meet with agricultural economists at the International Centre for Tropical Agriculture. CIAT has a wide mandate from improving smallholder coffee to pasture management for large scale ranching operations, and was a candidate for CGIAR funding from ODA.

This was my last mission for ODA before joining the European Commission to work in Sudan.

Chapter 15.

BANANAS IN THE WINDWARD ISLANDS

My good fortune in securing overseas trips was further augmented when in January 1979 I was invited to join the team for the mid-term review of the Windwards Islands banana development programme. Peter Stutley graciously agreed to my going. To fly out of the UK in January to Barbados and then visit these four delightful islands was a rare treat indeed, and I enjoyed every minute of it. The mission was led by the desk officer for the Caribbean, Roger Prideaux (a keen cricketer from the west of England). Bob Waddell, agricultural adviser, and Mick Foster, an economist in the Barbados DevDiv, completed the team. To cover the ground in good time, we travelled from Bridgetown in a small chartered plane to Castries in St Lucia, and then to Roseau in Dominica, via Canefield (where unpredictable winds always ensured an exciting landing). After inspecting plantations in the French department of Martinique (for purposes of comparative analysis), we went on to Kingstown in St Vincent, and finally to St George's in Grenada, before returning to Bridgetown.

Barbados en route

My first impressions of Barbados, the island in the sun, were extremely positive, and have remained so ever since. We were accommodated in the Ocean View with comfortable rooms in the old fashioned style, kept in immaculate cleanliness by wonderful old Bajan ladies such as you see in postcards. Breakfast of papaya followed by scrambled eggs, toast and coffee, with bright sunlight after the overcast skies of England, was a real pleasure. Later on we lunched by Bridgetown port at a small place serving flying fish, the national dish.

David Edwards (ex-CDC Indonesia), head of development division, invited us to drinks with him at his residence at Top Rock. Garth Armstrong was the economic adviser, later to be succeeded by David Crapper. We called at the EC delegation whose modest offices in Bridgetown at that time were next to the British Airways office. The head of delegation then was an elderly Dutchman. His agricultural adviser was a keen golfer with a house conveniently located alongside the golf course on the Sandy Lane estate. Development work clearly had its brighter side.

Bananas

The Windward Islands comprise four small islands with populations around the 100,000 mark. Geests, a commercial company with offices in the UK, had introduced bananas to these islands after the second world war. Subsequently, most of the large estates had been sub-divided into smallholdings. Geests maintained a regular weekly shipping line carrying the bananas to Southampton in the UK, and returning with some of the inputs required by the farmers (fertilizers, pesticides, packing material). A price formula had been derived by Geests which essentially made the producer price a residual, once all shipping and marketing costs had been deducted. Winban and the Banana Growers Associations (BGAs) represented the growers and governments in annual negotiations with Geests.

Then as now, bananas were seen as an essential source of income and employment for rural people. Without bananas, there were fears that unemployment and illegal drugs would bring instability to the Windwards, and threaten another vital source of foreign exchange, earnings from tourism.

There were three main concerns to ensuring continued viability of the Windwards banana industry. First, production overall had to be sufficient in volume to keep the regular weekly schedule of banana boats plying to and from the UK port of Southampton. Secondly, production had to be sufficiently efficient to withstand competition from the Latin American producers, who had all the advantages of scale and flat lands in their large plantations owned by Dole and Chiquita.

Thirdly, Windward bananas had to improve in quality if they were to maintain their market share in the United Kingdom. Poor quality was due to poor fruit handling resulting in bruising and early blackening of the fruit. As UK consumers spent more of their income in supermarkets and less from traditional greengrocers or from street barrows, concern about fruit quality became more and more significant. It was believed then that the British housewife had a preference for the Windwards fruit on grounds of cost effectiveness (one small banana each per family member) and sweeter taste. Dollar bananas were of uniform quality, albeit of larger size.

The UK provided a protected market under Commonwealth preference, which was subsequently maintained under the EC banana protocol. As a result, the consumer price for bananas in the UK was significantly higher than in the USA or indeed in Germany. A key question we had to investigate was how much of this price advantage achieved in the market place was actually returned to the grower, and how much was lost on the way, either through too favourable a shipping and marketing contract with Geests or because of additional costs siphoned off by inefficient BGAs or boxing plants.

In the late 1970s farmers sent their fruit stems to boxing plants. Inspection there could result in a loss of as much as 30 per cent in rejected fruit. Further losses in quality as a result of fruit damage could occur from the boxing plant to the wharf as the bananas were trucked over rough roads. Even loading of the banana boxes onto the Geest ships could result in fruit damage, as we observed in witnessing operations in Portsmouth, Dominica.

Banana Development Programme

To help increase the efficiency of the smallholder banana farmers, a Windward Island banana development programme had been prepared by British consultants in the mid-1970s. The WIBDP, costed at £ 5 mn over five years, aimed to improve the welfare of 40,000 small growers. Exports were expected to reach 165,000 tons from yield increases of up to eight tons per acre. Fruit quality was also to improve. The goal was to keep the Windwards in the banana business by increasing the efficiency of production, thus strengthening the chances of being able to compete in international markets. These aims were to be achieved through research and extension. Smaller farmers producing less than 15 tons would be encouraged to increase their uptake of inputs by subsidies which would taper out after a certain period.

The original project proposal included 20 components which made the project difficult for the BGAs to administer. A tapering subsidy linked to an increasing pre-paid input cess added to the complexity. There was no credit component as such within the WIBDP but the BGAs give some farmers short term credit which could be confounded with pre-paid cess. Unfortunately this did not result in a reliable supply system and inputs were frequently unavailable even when growers had the financial means to purchase them. Some of the BGAs (notably St Lucia) had difficulties in keeping their accounts in order, and there was a lack of storage and distribution system.

Other players (including the Americans) showed interest in supporting the banana industry, recognising the risks to economic and political stability should the industry collapse and render many farmers and workers unemployed. The USA was mindful of the threat posed by Cuba, as well as the menace of drugs passing through the Caribbean from Colombia. The American invasion of Grenada took place in October 1983. Miss Eugenia Charles, Prime Minister of Dominica, called upon President Reagan to intervene to prevent another Cuba in the Caribbean. The failure to alert Margaret Thatcher of the invasion plan did not sour the otherwise cordial relations between them, but the British High Commission's lack of intelligence on the matter was surprising.

Winban

Winban was a regional organisation which employed research and extension staff within the four islands and also ordered inputs in bulk, so as to achieve economies of scale in placing large orders. Winban sometimes purchased fertilizer from the Dominican Republic in the interests of cost effectiveness, much to the chagrin of Geests. The delivery of inputs to the farmers and the marketing of output was in the hands of the BGAs.

In accordance with the generous traditions of the Caribbean, the members of the banana review team received a number of invitations from the different interest groups. We had a fine meal at the Green Parrot run by Chef Harry on the hillside overlooking Castries. The Geests team invited us to lunch in Marigot bay, where the Dr Doolittle film had been made. One Sunday, the director of Winban organised the Jolly Roger to take us down to the Pitons. Don McKay, the leader of the TC team supporting Winban, invited us to supper at Monsoon with its verandah overlooking the main square of Castries. Following a busy morning visiting smallholders in the spice island Grenada, Eddie Edwards gave us a picnic lunch in a delightful spot besides a mountain stream.

Of course, these invitations were not given without interest. Geests had a clear commercial interest in the continuation of the banana programme. Winban also wanted to make a favourable impression, as did the TCOs. Clearly there were differences of view between Geests, Winban, and the Banana Growers Associations, each taking its slice of the margins between the consumer price and the returns the grower received. Understandably Winban and the BGAs tended to view the Geest contract with suspicion. Certainly all the risks seemed to be loaded onto the growers who received only what was left of the margin when the others had taken their share. Winban's role was to negotiate the Geest contract on behalf of the growers of the four Windwards. Geests tended to see the BGAs as political organisations employing too many people at boxing plants, and not paying sufficient heed to the technical needs for banana quality. Geests perceived Winban as an unnecessary parastatal.

Needless to say, ODA advisers do not allow their judgements to be influenced by any hospitality received. Any gifts received in the course of an official mission have to be declared if their value was other than nominal.

The review team visited the banana research station in St Lucia. Dr Eddie Edwards, director of Winban research, showed us round. Various trials of varieties, spacing, de-stumping, fertiliser and pesticide application were being undertaken in an efficient manner. Noting the different views about blue diothene and other practises, I recommended the secondment of an agricultural economist to help determine research priorities with potential benefits for smallholder farmers. In due course, Gilbert Addy took up an assignment in the Windwards attached to Winban. I arranged a joint review of Winban research by Hugh Bunting and Simon Maxwell in 1981, and subsequently for Simon to backstop Gilbert Addy.

Blue Diothene

Winban management tended to look to practises on estates in neighbouring Martinique and Guadeloupe as the ideal to which smallholders in the Windwards should strive. As an agricultural economist, I asked whether extension advice should be differentiated between smallholders and estates. This was to become the basis of a strong (but cordial) discussion with Mick Foster during the course of the mid-term review, as we considered the financial and economic benefits of the prescribed Winban package. One of the elements of the package of recommendations was the use of blue diothene (other recommendations included stringing to avoid toppling, chemicals to control nematodes, fertilizer, shoot setting, and other basic husbandry practices). I argued that the reason why farmers were not adopting blue diothene sleeves was because it brought limited financial returns to farmers. Henderson (UWI, Trinidad) in writing on the constraints to the *Adoption of Improved Practices in the Windward Island Industry*, noted that sleeving, while protecting the fruit from rust thrips, tended to soften bananas, thus making them more prone to bruising. From the farmers' point of view it seemed pointless to expend considerable effort and money on sleeving bananas so as to have better quality fruit and then to have such efforts thwarted by rough roads or rugged tracks from field to buying point.

Cynthia Baker writing on the *Economic and Social Aspects of Banana Production in Dominica* in 1975 observed that blue diothene sleeving was used rarely and that farmers were aware of the product but there was a widespread scepticism about its value. Nonetheless, I wonder today whether Winban and Mick Foster may have been right to go for the whole package, given the efforts that extension staff had to put into meeting farmers scattered over hillsides. Was I guilty of farming systems fundamentalism.

St Lucia, St Vincent, Dominica and Grenada

In St Lucia we visited boxing plants run by the BGAs. These plants received stems of bananas carried by farmers from their fields. The bananas were inspected, selected, washed in preservative, and then put in boxes. The labour force at the boxing plants was industrious, and judicious in their selection of bananas, but it was not clear whether or not the handling of the bananas in the plant impacted adversely on banana quality. Our observations of how bananas were loaded into the holds of the Geest ships raised further doubts about whether farmers or rough roads or rough handling were the causes of bruising and loss of fruit quality. During later visits we found that the boxing plants had been replaced by something called "field pack". In this way the boxing plants were circumvented and a lot of casual employment opportunities foregone. Much later, wearing my EC hat, we encouraged individual farmers to build their own small packing sheds.

St Vincent has more of an English ambience compared to the French influence of its neighbour to the north. We stayed at the charming if quaint Cobblestone Inn, after an exciting approach to the airfield while waiting for a thunderstorm to clear. We drove through the Mabouya Valley, where Mick Foster and I continued discussions with the farmers about their perceptions of the recommended package of inputs.

Tony Peers and I were to return to the Caribbean for two further ODA banana reviews. The second mission, which took place in September 1979 was in response to hurricane David which devastated the banana crop in Dominica. Bananas have an advantage over some other tropical fruits, such as limes, avocados, and mangoes, in being able to recover quite quickly from hurricanes which quite often harass the Windwards. During a third mission, thanks to some careful scheduling by Tony Peers, we were able to spend one Sunday afternoon in support of the England cricket team playing the West Indies at the Kensington Oval in Bridgetown.

Personalities

The Caribbean is full of characters, many of them larger than life. Chong Perryman from Dominica, was one such person. A tall and serious man, he was a typical Caribbean mix, his first name suggesting some Chinese ancestry. We held him in high regard, as a person doing a good job as director of Winban under difficult circumstances, recognising the various pressures he had to deal with from inside and outside the industry. He was somewhat reserved. It was a great shock when we learned of his premature death at his own hand during one of our missions. I felt especially sad as he had called me on the telephone the afternoon before asking how our mission was going, and we had exchanged a few cordial sentences without my realising that he was in some kind of distress. How important it is to give encouragement to people working under stress, and not to be seen as the external critic of someone else's endeavours.

A happier anecdote was told by Paul Tuley, agricultural adviser in the Caribbean. One day his predecessor, newly arrived in Barbados, received a visitation from the CNRA in London. Anxious to impress his boss, the adviser invited him to his house for dinner. Unfortunately, in driving the CNRA to his home, he got lost in the myriad lanes that divide the sugar fields of Barbados. Unable to find his house, he returned the CNRA to his hotel unfed. His boss was not amused.

As I wound up my missions to the Windwards and left ODA, little did I know that I was to inherit the *"banana dossier"* fourteen years later as EC head of delegation for Barbados and the Eastern Caribbean. There would be little time for golf.

Chapter 16.

JOINING THE EUROPEAN COMMISSION

In 1984, as a result of a combination of personal circumstances and some degree of professional frustration at the gradual erosion of the influence of agricultural economists in ODA, I decided to apply for a job with the European Commission. As my colleague Johnny Morris informed me, these positions were better paid than those in the UK civil service, and I needed money for the education of my children. Some time earlier, in the 1980s, we had been made aware that the Commission was looking for British candidates with overseas experience. At that time, I did not give the matter serious consideration. However, one of my colleagues among the Natural Resources advisers, Miki Dixon, did make the move, and seemed well satisfied with his new job. Mike Watson had taken leave of absence from ODA in order to take up a well paid TA appointment in Sudan funded by the EC, so as to be able to meet his daughter's school fees at The King's School, Canterbury. He also seemed well pleased with the arrangement.

Accordingly I submitted an application, and was called to interview at the AEC offices in Rue Archimedes in Brussels, just across from the Berlaymont, the Commission's headquarters. The interview panel included the director of AEC, Marc Delauche, his deputy Geoffrey Winstanley, Ingo Feustel, subsequently head of commodity trade in DG Development, and an external economist. The interview lasted about an hour and a half. Although I was reluctant to speak in French, I felt that the meeting had gone well. Some members of the board were impressed by the fact that I was a member of ESCOR, and could speak knowledgeably about its workings. Quite soon afterwards I received a telephone call with an offer of appointment to serve as economic adviser in the EC delegation in Sudan. Having checked that there were no other positions on offer, I duly signed a contract to serve the European Commission in Khartoum.

Relations between the European Community and the African, Caribbean and Pacific States were then governed by the Lomé Convention which provided a framework for trade and development. The first Lomé Convention was agreed in 1975, and I joined the Commission just as the third Lomé Convention was coming into being. The main feature of the relationship was a partnership approach between the EC (as represented by the Commission's delegate on the spot) and the ACP government (as represented by the national authorising officer). For each ACP country there was an agreed amount of ECUs to be allocated for development purposes. In order to give a broad sectoral strategy for the allocation, a programming document (National Indicative Programme) was prepared and agreed between the two parties. Additional resources were available to the ACP country from a wide range of instruments including Stabex and Sysmin, emergency aid, food aid, and assistance for refugees. Development loans were available from the European Investment Bank.

The reduction of poverty became an explicit objective of EC-ACP cooperation in 1985. Lomé III stated that the objectives were to promote and expedite the economic, cultural and social development of the ACP states and improve the living conditions of the poorest sections of the population. Lomé IV introduced a greater emphasis on respect for human rights, democratic principles and the rule of law. The EC's first steps towards conditionality began with the introduction of policy dialogue on National Indicative Programmes. Conditionality was significantly increased with the introduction of the Structural Adjustment Facility and the Framework of Mutual Obligations on the use of Stabex funds (Lomé IV).

I returned to Brussels on the feast of the Epiphany, the same day as Jacques Delors signed on as President of the European Commission. It was a cold day, and the streets were lined with ice. I started a month's *stage* as preparation for my new job in Sudan. In the event, this training period was reduced to two weeks because of the urgency of the situation in Sudan. I had benefited from the kind tuition of Klaus Roh, who had done his best to guide me on the intricacies of the European institutions and their machinery, and the good advice of the excellent desk officer for Sudan, Aslam Aziz. Jan de Kok, who had just vacated the post of economic adviser in Khartoum, gave me a briefing on the delegation set-up the day before I left. The lady in charge of recruitment gave me a warm farewell and told me to do great things in Sudan, but the missing two weeks on EC procedures made for a difficult start in Khartoum.

Chapter 17.

FAMINE IN SUDAN

In the cool desert night of 21 January 1985 I arrived in Khartoum to be welcomed at the airport by my colleagues from the EC delegation. I brought with me several bags (which included a beer making kit purchased from Boots) and a very partial knowledge of the workings of the European institutions and their procedures. The war in the South was once again gaining momentum. Drought and famine threatened lives in the western regions of Kordofan and Darfur, and Sharia law was being rigorously enforced in Khartoum.

Two Revolutions

My stay in Sudan coincided with a period of political turbulence. Two revolutions occurred: one at the beginning and the other at the end of my sojourn. President Nimeiry who came to power initially in 1969 as a socialist, allied himself with the Muslim Brotherhood and declared Sharia Law in 1983. In so doing he alienated the South, effectively abrogating the Addis Ababa agreement which had ended the first civil war. House to house searches for alcohol were conducted in Kkartoum, and great quantities of whisky were poured down the drains. Nimeiry was detained in Egypt on his return from an official visit to the United States in April 1985, and thousands (including my three sons) thronged the streets of Khartoum in jubilation. A transitional military administration took control for an interim period of a year, and subsequently Sadiq al-Mahdi became Prime Minister. Sadiq could never quite decide whether as an Oxford-educated leader he should espouse liberal values, or act as a traditional Muslim like his great grandfather who took on General Gordon in the battle of Omdurman. At the end of the day he fell under the influence of the hard liner Hassan al-Turabi, the leader of the National Islamic

Front. Just before I left Khartoum in July 1989, Sadiq was overthrown in a bloodless army coup led by Omar al-Bashir. That day I drove to the office unaware that anything was amiss, until I noticed a tank on the side of the road. Turning on the radio I heard the sound of martial music.

The second Sudanese civil war started in 1983 as a continuation of the first war of 1955 to 1972. Nearly two million civilians were killed in southern Sudan, and four million were forced to flee their homes. The conflict only ended upon the signing of a peace agreement in January 2005, resulting eventually in the new nation state of South Sudan in 2011.

Sudan at that time (before the separation of South Sudan) was the largest country in Africa. EC funded activities were spread over enormous distances, from rural development in Jebel Marra in the west, to supporting refugees in Kassala in the east, and to forestry in the Imatong mountains in the south. The Nile was navigable for most of its length (I used to windsurf on the White Nile) and there were road and rail links from Khartoum to the Gezira and Port Sudan. However, many of our field trips were by air hiring the Cessnas of Nile Safaris, or occasionally hitching rides on Hercules being used to airlift relief supplies. Most of our travel was without incident, but I recall diversions due to *haboobs* over Khartoum, an engine fire over the Red Sea Hills, and the loss of a Scottish pilot whom we knew well shot down by the SPLA over Aweil.

Responsibilities of the Delegation

The delegation was ruled by Jean-Paul Jesse, a Frenchman who had served in the cabinet of Claude Cheysson, a former commissioner for development. Jean-Paul had served as delegate in Trinidad and Kenya. I learned a lot from Jean-Paul, but he was not an easy task master, and could quite quickly let you know when he was dissatisfied. He managed the delegation by means of weekly meetings with his advisers. During these meetings (conducted in English, much to my relief) significant incoming correspondence would be handed to advisers for action. In this way, Jean-Paul cleared his desk, and agreed the priorities for the work programme for the coming week.

At that time, the position of EC delegate was still somewhat ambivalent, and Jean-Paul Jesse had to be careful in expressing his views when attending the monthly meetings called by the EC Presidency. In the first six months of 1985 the Italians were in charge, and the Italian ambassador took his responsibilities seriously, looking to the EC delegation for positions on dealing with the food crisis. With the Amsterdam Agreement, the role of the delegations evolved with greater attention being given to the political and economic aspects. Eventually delegations achieved full ambassadorial status vis-a-vis their host governments, moving up in the diplomatic list from international organisations towards the position of embassies of sovereign states.

My work as economic adviser was dominated by a series of emergencies: principally by the war in the south and the drought in the west, but we also had to deal with refugees from Ethiopia and Eritrea in the east, and floods in the north. The EC delegation was in the front line, and in the full glare of the world media, we were expected to show the flag and prove ourselves as a European friend to the victims of war and drought. After a somewhat hesitant start, we managed (along with our Member State representatives and their NGOs) to put together a comprehensive programme of relief efforts. The initial breakthrough came with the European air bridge which carried relief supplies from Khartoum to Darfur using Hercules aircraft from the EC Member States. Brian O'Neill, a charismatic young Irishman who came to the Delegation as Emergency Aid adviser, and who helped to save the day for Europe, was the architect of the airbridge.

The EC delegation was sited in Street 13 of New Extension in a pleasant residential building converted into offices. On the ground floor was Nigel Tucker (to be replaced later by Neil Crumbie) as the Administrative Assistant, and the local support staff. On the first floor were the offices of the Head of Delegation and the economic adviser, and the conference room. On the second floor were the engineering advisers and the agricultural advisers.

The functions of EC delegations in those days were determined very much by the framework of the EC-ACP relationship, with priority being given to aid administration under the Agreements. The first Lomé had brought ECU 90 mn to Sudan, and the second Lomé ECU 103 mn. The third Lomé convention was signed in 1984 from which Sudan was allocated ECU 145 mn. The focus was on agriculture and rural development, transport and communications, and education.

At that time, EC aid took several dimensions. Conventional project aid was the domain of the technical advisers. Thus Roelf Smit was in charge of a major rural development project in Darfur, while Otto Muller was responsible for the Nuba Mountains rural development project in south Kordofan and a rice project in Aweil. Joe Bloemarts looked after various road and rail improvement projects, notably the Babanousa railway which provided an important link in the delivery of food aid to the South. Harry Rook was responsible for assistance to Juba airport, Upper Talanga tea, Imatong forestry, Juba University and technical schools. Individual advisers guarded their projects jealously, and did not particularly relish inputs from the economics adviser. The days of a multidisciplinary approach to rural and communications projects had yet to arrive.

In addition to conventional project aid, the delegation was also responsible for fertiliser aid to the Gezira scheme, Stabex, micro-projects, scholarships, NGO co-financing, and food aid. Much of this devolved to my desk as economic adviser. During the 1984-1985 drought and famine crisis the EC provided under emergency food aid tens of thousands of tons of cereals, pulses, and edible oil, in addition to EC food aid chanelled through WFP. The EC played a key role during this period in providing technical assistance first to the Commissioner for Relief and Rehabilitation, and then to the Commissioner for Refugees. Doug McClure was the person with the experience and technical background to accomplish both tasks with a high degree of professional competence.

Lomé III Programming

An important part of the dialogue with the Sudanese authorities on development priorities took place early in 1996 during the programming exercise for Lomé III. Dieter Frisch, our much respected Director-General, led the dialogue with the Minister of Finance, ably assisted by Giorgio Bonacci and Aslam Aziz, also from Brussels. The Delegation played a supporting role. While on home leave I had purchased an Amstrad computer, and my secretary Pelly had thereby acquired skills in word processing. The programming document went through many revisions during the course of the dialogue, and our colleagues from Brussels were amazed that new drafts could be produced so quickly. Pelly quickly became a star, and was rewarded with a walk-on role during the signing ceremony which was broadcast on Sudan's national TV. At the start of the mission a crisis had arisen when Dieter Frisch's suitcase went missing. Eager to demonstrate the Delegation's efficiency to high level visitors, the suitcase in question had been taken by our administrative staff straight from the aircraft's hold to the Director-General's hotel room. Or that was the intention. Unfortunately the chalk inscription on the suitcase written in Arabic had been misread by the bellboy and ended up in another room. A frantic search took place until it was located an hour or so later.

Visitors from Brussels

Visits from officials in Brussels commanded a lot of attention. As Sudan was very much in the world spotlight, we had plenty of visitors including European parliamentarians (led by the formidable Katharina Focke, chair of the committee for development cooperation), the director-general (Dieter Frisch), the commissioner for development (Lorenzo Natali), the head of AEC (Geoffrey Winstanley), and Andre Auclert, deputy director-general for development. Each visit demanded very careful preparation and attention to detail in implementation. Even so, there were some unexpected hiccups.

On one occasion I was responsible for a group of four MEPs who arrived from Chad. My NAO colleague Ali Askouri and I had visited the area a few days earlier to make detailed arrangements for the accommodation and logistics for receiving these distinguished visitors. We met the MEPs according to plan at Al-Geneina, in the extreme west of Darfur, which was hosting a large camp of refugees from the civil war in Chad. The refugees were receiving EC emergency food aid. All went well initially. The MEPs were enthralled to interact with the refugees, and we set off on our chartered Nile Safaris Cessna for the next stop which was the Jebel Marra rural development project. As we flew over the Jebel Marra site we encountered heavy rainfall that had rendered the airstrip inoperable. The pilot then decided to divert to another airstrip about 100 km south in the direction of Nyala. We landed without any problems but in the middle of nowhere. I then had to decide what we should do next. We had no radio communication. Should we hope that the team from Jebel Marra would realise where we had landed and come and collect us. Suppose they did not? There was no accommodation or any facilities at the airstrip. Were we destined to spend the night in the bush? After an hour of uncertainty, and as nightfall was about to descend, a convoy of SCF trucks appeared carrying food for famine relief en route to Al-Fasher. We hitched a ride, and after an hour and a half were happy to see the landrovers of Jebel Marra driving to meet us. It was with a great sense of relief that we sat down to a belated supper that evening at the Jebel Marra guest house.

The visit of Lorenzo Natali in May 1985 was not without incident. This distinguished personality, a vice-president of the Commission and close to Jacques Delors, came to review our performance in responding to the famine. A field trip was planned so that Natali could witness emergency aid delivery in action. This entailed an overnight stop in El Obeid, the capital of Kordofan province. Accordingly, one of my colleagues was despatched to El Obeid to prepare the ground, and in particular to ensure that appropriate accommodation was lined up. He returned with assurances that all would be well. It was my task on this occasion to hold the fort in Khartoum while Jean-Paul and the other advisers accompanied Natali. When I went to the airport to meet the returning party I immediately sensed from their faces that something had gone awry. It turned out that Natali had spent a sleepless night in the guest house in El Obeid. There was no water, no soap, no electricity, no clean sheets, and an abundance of mosquitoes. Afterwards Jean-Paul turned his wrath on my unfortunate colleague in no uncertain terms. I in turn incurred his displeasure when, at the official lunch hosted by the Italian Ambassador next day, my chair collapsed from under me causing an embarrassing disturbance.

Acting Delegate

Jean-Paul decided that as economic adviser, I should be acting delegate in his absence. There was then a six months inter-regnum between Jean Paul's departure and the arrival of his successor Alexander Dijckmeester. Thus I had to represent the EC at official functions and attend the monthly meetings of Ambassadors for quite a period of time. In attending such official functions, I would use the delegate's Mercedes and fly the EC flag (in those days a simple € on a blue background).

On one occasion it was decided that the European Troika would make a démarche to the Prime Minister on the issue of food supplies to the South and in particular to seek permission to make food relief flights to places like Juba, Wau, Malakal, and Aweil. Al-Mahdi dressed in immaculate white *jelabia* and speaking in excellent English listened attentively to our case made by Peter Feith (the Dutch chargé d'affaires), and gave some undertakings on relief flights to the South that were later fulfilled.

Needless to say, the other advisers felt a little piqued that a relative newcomer to the Commission should be granted such an exalted status. I felt some trepidation in dealing with the heads of mission of the Member States. However, the Ambassadors of Greece, France, Denmark, and Germany (and the chargé d'affaires of the Netherlands) were approachable, and we enjoyed attending their receptions. The new Delegate, Alex Dijckmeester (who had established a close working relationship with Prime Minister Museveni in Uganda), decided that the economic adviser should not automatically become acting delegate in his absence. So I had to resume my status as economic adviser, and swallow my pride when my adviser colleagues assumed the role.

Making things happen

Quite soon I discovered that working as an economic adviser in an EC delegation was quite different from being an ODA economic adviser. In London I wrote reports from field visits which were then considered by the administrators who would make decisions which others would then implement. In Khartoum, I found that giving advice to the delegate was not enough. As I came to learn quite quickly, the hallmark of an efficient EC adviser is that he makes things happen. Not all my colleagues in the delegation were of this persuasion, but Roelf Smit was a good example of an adviser who could and did make things happen. Thus when Jean-Paul Jesse wanted sorghum to be purchased for famine relief in 1985, Roelf went off to Gedaref to buy sorghum. A year later I had the confidence to negotiate contracts with Nile Safaris for the transport of the sorghum in old Boeing 707s to Juba.

I learned that the way to make things happen in the EC is through official contracts, of which there are three main kinds: TA, supplies, and works contracts. My initial understanding of contracts was very weak, and I had to learn fast in view of the emergency. Lengthy telexes written in French from Gerard Molinier and Bob Baldwin of the Emergency division of DG VIII would arrive each morning on my desk. My first year in Khartoum was quite tough but I was on a steep learning curve, and in my second year had managed to set up a number of contracts with European NGOs (MSF France, MSF Belgium, MSF Holland, Action International Contre Le Faim, Goal (Ireland), CONCERN (Ireland), SCF (UK) operating close to the unofficial northern-southern border. These NGOs were contracted to provide services and assistance to those displaced by the civil war in the South. Unfortunately, Oxfam was always a bit sniffy about EC aid and my relationship with Mark Duffield, their field director, was far from brilliant.

In working closely with the national authorities, I sat on a number of committees so as to achieve consensus on the utilisation of EC resources. The food aid national administration (FANA) decided on the destination of EC food aid, and as importantly, on the utilisation of food aid counterpart funds. Overtime I built up a good working rapport with the senior staff of FANA, who were fairly strong northerners and supporters of *Sharia*, and with the help of Mekki Osman (himself a northerner) managed to persuade them to use counterpart funds for relief flights to the war affected Christians in the South. In a similar way I established a good rapport with the commissioner for refugees, helped by the admirable Doug McClure, who provided technical assistance having concluded his work with the commissioner for relief and rehabilitation. With the support of the NAO and FANA, we mounted a seminar on a food sector strategy for Sudan, for which Simon Maxwell was the lead speaker.

As economic adviser, I was expected to provide the basic economic reports which later took on an increasingly political tone. I was also responsible for the Newsletter, translated into Arabic by a Sudanese journalist, and the EC-Sudan brochure published in January 1986.

Closing the Juba Office

As conflict escalated in the South, the forestry project in the Imatong mountains, and the Upper Talanga tea project, which Trevor Walker had managed so well, were halted. Harry Rook was our resident adviser in

Juba. It was a task that he relished, and it was with some reluctance that he left Juba when the civil war reached a level of intensity that inhibited his operations and threatened his security. We travelled down to Juba to close the office and bring Harry Rook back to Khartoum in a Nile Safari Cessna. It was a four hour trip each way, and there was only just enough room for Harry and all his belongings.

One of the Juba office's important support functions for the Delegation in Khartoum was the supply of whisky, since the South was not dry (unlike the North which was under Sharia Law). The whisky used to arrive by diplomatic bag, and once the Juba office was closed, we had to turn to alternative sources of supply. In collaboration with some of the EC Embassies we organised a joint order under diplomatic cover from Europe. There would be much anticipation as the consignment's arrival was tracked from Port Sudan to a designated residence in Khartoum. From there it was up to individuals to collect their orders. On one occasion, a Dutch colleague was intercepted by the authorities as he incautiously unloaded cartons just outside his driveway, and had to surrender them. It was decided that his loss should be covered by contributions from those whose supplies had reached safely.

For many Sudanese, including those in charge of protocol, embassy functions were a lifeline to drinks. The normal procedure at an evening outdoor reception was for a soft drinks bar to be set up in a prominent place, while for those in need of something stronger another facility would be established in a darker corner. For those outside the diplomatic circles, home brews were an alternative. The KGB (Khartoum guild of brewers) had a lively following.

Notwithstanding these constraints, the Sudan Club provided a venue for such celebrations as Burns Night, where by some magic, drinks abounded for the participants. Khartoum had a number of clubs for those whose origins lay further afield. The Greek and Syrian clubs were among these. The Sudan club had its origins in colonial times, and some of the clientele and the club staff looked as if they dated back to these times. Membership was limited to those of British and Commonwealth ancestry. Although somewhat down at heel, the club's facilities included a swimming pool and squash courts. It was where I stayed for the first few weeks of my assignment. The menu included such items as mulligatawny soup and shepherds pie, which could be washed down with a cooling glass of karkade.

From Africa to the Pacific

With the overthrow of Sadiq al-Madhi by Omar al-Bashir, my four and a half years of varied experience in Sudan came to an end in July 1989. Having expressed a preference to the authorities in Brussels for my next posting to be in Mauritius, we were duly given our marching orders to proceed to Papua New Guinea!

Chapter 18.

MINES IN PAPUA NEW GUINEA

Papua New Guinea is an amazingly beautiful country, with coral seas and high mountains, rich traditions, and a great variety of languages among its Melanesian people. The coastal Papuans are distinct from those that live in the inaccessible highlands. The first white people to visit parts of the highlands in the 1930s were perceived as ghosts by the local inhabitants. The people of the Sepik river are different from the islanders of East and West New Britain, who in turn are distinct from those who live in New Ireland or Bougainville. Unfortunately, the country's vast tourism potential has yet to be realised because of insecurity, principally in the capital, Port Moresby. PNG has always played an influential role in ACP affairs. Sir John Kaputin was an active Ambassador in Brussels and became Secretary-General of the ACP Secretariat. Rabbie Namaliu, Prime Minister during my stay, was the chief signatory of the Lomé III agreement.

I arrived in Port Moresby early one sunny morning in September 1989 on the Air Niugini airbus. This six hour flight from Singapore crosses Kalimantan and Irian Jaya. Leaving Singapore at night, I really felt that I was heading into the unknown!

Insecurity in Port Moresby

Each Delegation has its distinct style, reflecting the influence of the local staff, most of whom have much longer careers in country than Delegates and Advisers, whom the local staff see come and go. I was briefed on security by Mary Pourhosseini, the Delegation administrative officer. I asked whether it was safe to cross the road from the Travel Lodge to the Delegation offices. She asked me how fast I could run! I had heard a lot about *rascals* in my briefing from Jean-Claude Mellor, my predecessor as economic adviser.

I was fortunate that we only had one personal experience of rascals during our two year stay in Port Moresby, when we were burgled. My engineering adviser colleague John Loftus was less fortunate. Returning one evening to his compound from an official engagement, he found that he had forgotten the *genie* that controlled the portcullis entrance to the compound. A car drew up behind him and blocked his exit. The rascals struck him on the head with a machete, and made off with the car. The following day the car was found crashed with lots of beer cans inside. Fortunately John Loftus' injuries were not serious. Regrettably, he had been driving my office car, an Audi 80. This incident did not deter John from enjoying his stay in PNG. Eventually he served there for nearly six years, much of the time as Acting Delegate.

The EC Delegation

The Delegation was housed in some fine offices overlooking the tropical sea. The rugged hills of Port Moresby make for some stunning views, and we enjoyed some of the best. The office furniture was of a high standard and made from some local timber. Arnold van Niekerk was the head of delegation, having succeeded Goldsmith, the first delegate, in 1988. Arnold had not worked before in the European Commission but had been *"parachuted in"*, as sometimes happened in the early days. Arnold was a hard working individual and a good team leader. He got on well with his colleagues in the diplomatic circle. Unfortunately, his relations with the PNG authorities, and in particular with Robert Igara, who was then head of the Foreign Aid Section (OIDA), were not so good. The relationship had been strained by an individual who wanted a TA contract as assistant to the NAO. Later I was to encounter similar problems in Solomon Islands.

The other members of our expatriate team were John Loftus, engineering adviser, and Charles Goes, responsible for micro-projects. Jaap Van Kemp, a TA from the Netherlands, helped with our agricultural programme. As in the Sudan delegation, the notion of multi-disciplinary team work was not well founded. Individual advisers had a very proprietary attitude to "their projects". Much to my surprise, my engineering colleague prepared the economic analysis for the EDF financing of a Kiribati trawler. Nor was I invited to participate in the appraisal or monitoring of the micro-projects programme.

Visit of the EDF Committee

Soon after I arrived I was given the opportunity to see something of this large and diverse country, as Member States representatives from the EDF committee were scheduled to visit. John Loftus had arranged an exciting programme. We started off in two chartered planes to see a micro-project in the highlands (a vegetable garden). This was attended by a lot of ceremony with a traditional moo-moo (a large feast served on banana leaves, featuring taro and a pig which had been cooked in the ashes of a wood fire). We then inspected a mini-hydro project in Tari (the home of the Huli tribe) before flying on in the evening to West New Britain to view an EC-financed road which had been constructed by French contractors. We were due to visit a CDC oil-palm plantation, but some troubles between labour and management caused this visit to be abandoned. Instead we visited two EC-financed roads leading out of Port Moresby, and a micro-project tourism project at Hissiu along the Papuan coast, where the visitors were entertained by local women performing traditional dances.

Our aid programme to PNG at this juncture focused on communications. There were four major roads projects, supervised by the engineering adviser with the assistance of a British TA. The widely dispersed micro-projects programme incorporated assistance for rural water supplies. Stabex funds were being used in support of oil palm breeding and cocoa rehabilitation. It was my privilege to escort two Guyanese economists who were tasked to carry out an evaluation of the EDF programme. In the course of the evaluation, we visited three beef ranches. Travelling in Papua New Guinea is always something of an adventure, especially in small planes. One ranch was located not far to the east of Port Moresby, a second was in New Ireland province (near the home of the former Prime Minister Julius Chan) and a third was sited near Madang on the north coast. It was difficult to assess how much impact these ranches were having on the local economy, but our evaluators gave the programme at large a positive rating, notwithstanding its diversified and scattered nature. Subsequently, the introduction of country strategy papers gave a much greater emphasis to education at secondary and tertiary levels.

Ramu Sugar

Ingo Feustel was responsible for the sugar protocol in Brussels. Ingo and Impl from DG AGRI came to PNG to assess a request for an export quota under the EC's sugar protocol. No doubt the request had been stimulated by the example of Fiji, which gained very significantly from the much higher sugar price under the protocol. It was my task to accompany Ingo and Impl to the sugar estate. We flew to Lei and then travelled by road up the Ramu valley. Tate and Lyle had been involved with the setting up of the sugarcane plantation and the provision of machinery for its processing. A large herd of beef animals was sustained by the crushed cane and molasses. The Ramu sugar estate was producing about 10,000 tons of sugar annually, hardly enough to meet domestic needs. The climate in the Ramu Valley was not ideal for sugar production as there was not enough sunshine (unlike Kamalia in Pakistan). There was also a problem with a sugar pest. Ingo found a diplomatic solution to PNG's request.

Bougainville

PNG derives a large proportion of its export earnings from copper and gold. Its rich resource base however is not so easy to exploit, because of the remoteness of many of the sites and because of the complexity of land ownership claims in this Melanesian country. Before 1989 the island of Bougainville was still something of a tropical paradise, notwithstanding the activities of the Panguna copper mine managed by CRA (an affiliate of Rio Tinto), which started exports in 1972. Gradually local resentment to the mine built as the environment was spoilt. The first attack by the BRA was to blow up the power line on the road to the copper mine. This was the work of Sam Kauona. Then the houses of workers were burned.

When I visited Bougainville in November 1989 with Tim Curtin from the OIDA office, we were accommodated at the delightful small island resort of Arova. We visited the administrative offices of the Bougainville administration and met the provincial secretary Mel Tegolo and Joseph Kabui his boss. A new housing scheme had just been completed. Everything seemed calm and ready to restart. The next morning, after a delightful swim in the coral waters around the island, a helicopter whisked us from the resort to the main island to view the burned out houses of the mine workers. We topped the mountain and saw the remarkable sight of what was be reputed to be the largest man made pit in the world, the Panguna mine. Flying down the other side of the mountain we observed the mine's tailings which were polluting the environment, and were the proximate cause of the rebellion. Landing on the cusp of the mine, we visited the offices which were still intact with a few people still around. We then drove down the mountainside at some speed, stopping on the way to see the burned out houses from ground level, while hoping not to be attacked by the BRA. We took lunch in the company's canteen, which still fed a number of expatriate workers. The company was keen to use the Sysmin funds for rehabilitating the workers' houses, so as to secure the peace. Quite detailed plans had been drawn up. Later that evening we were invited to supper by Mel Togolo, Provincial Secretary, and his Australian wife. It all seemed very civilised.

Two months later, in January 1990, I returned to Bougainville with Henri Martin, who was responsible for Sysmin funds in Brussels. The situation had changed dramatically. We arrived at the airport in Aropa in the morning in an Air Niugini Fokker 28 to find that the air terminal had been burned down by the rebels. PNG army helicopters were taking off to attack the rebels. We were accommodated in the Devara hotel near Kieta, as the island resort at Arova was off limits. Later that day we were told that the airport had been closed for security reasons. There was no indication as to when it might reopen. Our meetings with Government officials were perfunctory. It seemed clear that the security situation had declined to such a point that there was little prospect of spending Sysmin funds for rebuilding houses, or indeed for anything else in Bougainville. On the third day we were told that the airport authorities would allow a special Air Niugini flight to land. We were relieved to leave Bougainville but much concerned as to what would happen next for the people of North Solomons province.

Porgera and Ok Tedi

Henri Martin's mission required that he obtain a complete overview of the mining sector. Accordingly we flew up to Mount Hagen in one of the DH twin engine props. There we changed planes to a rather battered Twin Otter, which had evidently seen better days as it wended its way through the clouds and the mountains. Along with some highland women and their small children, we landed eventually into the small landing strip of Porgera in Enga province. After touring the mine, which was at an early stage of development, we visited staff housing and the school. This mine was to become one of PNG's richest sources of gold and copper. Landowners' claims and local unrest led to the closure of activities from time to time, while the main road into the mountains from Lae often had to be repaired, as it was difficult to maintain in the high rainfall conditions of the Southern Highlands. Tea and coffee farmers suffered as a result as they were unable to get their produce to the port.

After a comfortable night and day we flew on the next afternoon to Ok Tedi. This was an exciting flight in a small twin engined Cessna. We crossed some inhospitable mountainous terrain. The plane's ceiling altitude was 12,000 feet, while some of the mountains close to our route exceeded this height. There was quite a lot of cloud and, as we came into Ok Tedi, torrential rain. Our two young Australian pilots had the somewhat disconcerting habit of looking out of the window when we broke cloud cover and scrutinising the map on their knees. It was with great relief that I drank a beer in the Ok Tedi guest house in Tabubil that evening.

The Ok Tedi copper mine was much longer established than Porgera and questions were already being asked about its working life. A major issue concerned the disposal of the mine's effluent into the Fly river, and the consequences for the health and well being of the local population. The ore was barged down the river to the port at Kiunga. Attempts to prevent unwanted external effects by building a tailings dam had been thwarted when the dam had collapsed due to the unstable nature of the local geology.

A lateral move

One evening in Port Moresby in 1990, I received a phone call from Hans Carl, who was personal assistant to the director-general Dieter Frisch, inviting me to apply for the post of head of delegation in Solomon Islands based in Honiara. This I duly did, and after hearing that I had been selected for the post, I took up the appointment in time for Solomon Islands thirteenth Independence Day celebrations in July 1991.

Chapter 19.

THE ISLANDS LOST IN TIME

We arrived initially in Honiara from Port Moresby in May 1991 in order to choose a place to stay and meet the local staff. We settled on a house of simple construction (on stilts, Australian style, to make the most of the cooling breezes) and with spectacular views over Iron Bottom sound and the Pacific beyond. One of the major sea battles between the Japanese and Americans in the second world war was fought off Guadalcanal. I returned in July in time to attend Independence Day celebrations on the main arena of Lawson Tama in the presence of the Governor-General, Sir George Lepping. Prime Minister Solomon Mamaloni made a speech. This was followed by a march past by police and navy personnel. At that time, Solomon Islands had no army, although later Solomon Mamaloni established a paramilitary field force when there were border troubles with Bougainville which is only a few miles by sea from Western province.

On being a Head of Delegation

Apart from the professional satisfaction of leading a team, the position of head of delegation meant a white Mercedes with a flag and a driver, a decent house, support staff (a cook, maid and gardener) for help with official entertainment, and the status of being part of the diplomatic circle. On the other side of the coin, the position can be very demanding. It means running an office and leading a professional team, as well as managing the local staff. It means representing the Commission vis-a-vis the host government, and in particular maintaining a harmonious relationship with the national authorising officer. It means hosting the annual Europe Day parties, and organising missions for officials from Brussels. Most of all, it means managing (and being accountable for) the aid programme of the

European Union in the country in question. To do this effectively requires the support and respect of professional colleagues.

For my first posting in Solomons I was fortunate to have the experienced backing of an Irishman, Michael Garvey. Michael's successor, Hubert Martinetz from Gemany, was a skilled craftsman who *inter alia* did a lot to upgrade the office furniture. Two stagiares, Ivo Morawski and then Rossella Soldi (both from Italy), did excellent work. One of the keys to successful EC development cooperation was to build good working relations with the NAO. Christopher Columbus Abe was the Minister of Finance, and to begin with we got on well together.

Solomon Islands are sometimes referred to as *The Islands Lost in Time*. The country is remarkable for its scenic beauty, the unsophisticated warmth of its Melanesian (and Polynesian) population, and its rich natural resources, notably in forestry, and fisheries. Historically, the country had little contact with the outside world until the mid-1800s. Early explorers like Mendana from Spain in 1568 and La Perouse from France in 1788 did not survive for long. Inter-island head hunting expeditions were common, and foreign visitors did not often receive a warm welcome. After a number of false starts, Christian missions were established. The practice of recruiting indentured labour to work in the sugar estates in Queensland, known as black birding, was outlawed by the time most of the islands had come under British protection in 1893. While the population is today about half a million, the land and sea areas combined occupy quite a large slice of the world's surface. It is a country at an early stage of development, with a focus on agriculture. A large oil palm estate in Guadalcanal was owned and managed by CDC. Widespread small plantations growing coconuts and cocoa are scattered through out the islands. Fish is an important part of the diet, and an export earner.

Forestry Issues

Unfortunately, the development of natural resources has been problematic. Too often landowners have been induced (for a few cases of beer) to sign away their forest resources to foreign logging companies from neighbouring south east Asia. The result has been indiscriminate logging and devastation of the environment. Flying over the Morovo lagoon, an ecological paradise and major tourist attraction, it was disturbing to observe the tell-tale discolouration of its waters by sediment coming from logged areas. Mindful of what I had seen in the Philippines, Indonesia, and Papua New Guinea, and in order to bring greater recognition of the scale of the problem to the attention of policy makers, we commissioned a study of the forestry sector, building on earlier work done by the British. Unfortunately, it was always going to be difficult to convince politicians to adopt conservative policies in relation to forestry, and we made little headway, despite concerted attempts to gain the attention of the European Parliament.

Rural Development

EC assistance focused on programmes in the rural sector, each with a technical assistant (TA) in support of a Solomon Islands manager. Rural training centres were assisted by Sue Mackie (VSO), fisheries by Michael Batty, rural transport by Peter Drummond, rural health by Dr Soares from France and Joe Bola from Fiji. A smallholder development programme, with emphasis on coconuts and cocoa, was assisted by David Bick, Giles West and Mark Whitton. We gave support to the Development Bank (DBSI) in the person of Vincent Yee from Fiji. We had finance to upgrade the airport, as well as for a housing scheme in Honiara. David Abbott and David Baker worked with the Ministry of Finance in support of the NAO office.

From Stabex resources we financed re-afforestation in Viru, labour intensive road works in rural areas, wharves and jetties, and smallholder out grower schemes linked to the CDC oil palm estate. In sum, it was a large and diverse programme, and it kept me fully occupied while providing a lot of professional satisfaction. I travelled a lot among the islands with members of the NAO team in order to ensure that things were running as smoothly as possible, and to identify new opportunities for assistance.

My first months were very exhilarating as I toured the islands to become familiar with our extensive rural development programme. Unlike the Japanese, who tend to focus on high visibility projects close to the capital, the bulk of our efforts were dispersed throughout the several islands that make up Solomon Islands. Early on, Michael Garvey took me by plane to Western province to see the recently constructed Munda-Noro road, and the associated water supply works for the town of Noro. We visited the commercially successful tuna factory, Solomon Taiyo, employing scores of women. This enterprise was then under Japanese ownership and management, with a fleet of concrete pole and line fishing boats. I soon became fond of canned chilli tuna as a lunchtime snack.

Shortly afterwards we travelled by boat to Isabel island to view the fisheries centre at Tatamba with Snyder Rini, who came from the Morovo lagoon and was then permanent secretary in the Ministry of Finance, and deputy NAO. We were accompanied by the editor of The Courier, Simon Horner. The fisheries centre was managed by a mature VSO who was doing an excellent job in encouraging local fishermen to catch red snappers, which were then shipped to Honiara and onwards by air to export markets in the Pacific as far away as Hawaii. New kinds of fishing tackle had been introduced, as well as an FAO sailing boat. Key components were ice machines and the diesel engines to power them.

One of the EC's more successful development activities was the rural transport project, managed by Peter Drummond in close collaboration with the permanent secretary in the Ministry of Transport. Given the geography of Solomon Islands, inter-island sea transport was crucial for trade and development. The maintenance and development of wharves and jetties became a key objective, alongside the provision of feeder roads and river crossings in certain key locations. In collaboration with Tom Krawczyk of ILO, we supported labour intensive road construction in Guadalcanal and Isabel provinces. In order to transport heavy equipment for more significant works, the project acquired an ancient landing craft MV Vitu which proved its worth inter alia in facilitating the building of a road to Lake Tegano in Rennell Island, and assisting in Cyclone Nina rehabilitation works in Rennell and in Temotu.

Rural Training Centres

One of the projects that I helped to launch was in support of rural training centres, most of which were managed by one or other of the many churches spread throughout the islands. An Australian, Brother Peter, made the suggestion that the EC could become involved, and I am happy that we did. The purpose of the project was to transfer vocational skills to young people in order to improve self sufficiency in rural areas and to create job opportunities. In appraising the proposal I visited several training centres in Guadalcanal, Makira, and Western provinces, and was impressed by the commitment and achievements of the staff and trainees, notwithstanding very modest resources. It was not difficult to convince my colleagues in Brussels of the merits of the proposed project. Much later I was pleased to read an evaluation of the first phase carried out in 1998 which concluded that it had been a highly relevant project which had achieved many positive results. There were more than 40 success stories where RTC graduates had obtained loans, were running income generating activities, and repaying their loans.

Malaita

Another project was much more problematic, at least in the launching stage. The Malaita Integrated Rural Development Project (MIRDP) was the main thrust of the Lomé III indicative programme, and it was my task to bring it into being. Initial discussions about the project in Auki with the premier of Malaita, David Oeta, and his provincial secretary, Fred Fono, were extremely cordial. However, as time went by, their patience wore a little thin. It was another rich learning experience for me. The allocations of funds within the national indicative programme is only the first step of a lengthy process. A financing proposal has to be prepared, and approved by the EDF committee. Then tenders have to be prepared and bids received and evaluated for the machinery and equipment. Even to prepare the financing proposal, it was decided by Brussels that consultants had to be shortlisted, and their proposals evaluated. When the consultants eventually arrived, it was some weeks before their field work was concluded. Their report identified the need for roads and wharves needed to link up existing cropped areas to shipping in South Malaita, and new roads to open up three areas of agricultural potential in North Malaita. In order to finalise the proposal for the EDF committee, I gathered together a small task force of TAs. In strengthening the economic justification of the project, I made estimates of the benefits that would accrue to offset the costs of the road infrastructure. Such benefits would largely arise from expansion in the area of smallholder cocoa, consequent upon higher farm gate prices for the product.

When my colleagues in Brussels began to query the financing proposal, I became quite agitated. A mission was immediately arranged for a visit to Malaita by Robert Carreau, the agricultural adviser in Brussels. As a Frenchman with experience of West Africa, Robert conceived such projects in terms of settlement schemes. I had an uphill task to convince him of the power of the market to bring about an expansion of smallholder cocoa production, along with extension and proper pruning, combined with the distribution of seedlings. In order to bring the desk officer on board, I arranged a helicopter tour of Malaita for Peter Craig McQuaide so he could see for himself the location of smallholder cocoa production, and envisage the benefits that would accrue from an improved road network. Following these visits, the project sailed through the EDF committee.

The EC programme was largely run with the assistance of TAs, for reasons of management and accountability. Solomon Islanders in charge of projects would be put under pressure to hire relatives, and disburse funds for non-project purposes. Of course, relying on TAs raises issues of sustainability when the TAs departed. Obviously, the principle of training counterparts was one that we aspired to, with TAs working themselves out of a job, but in practice this does not always happen. When it comes to managing finance, local project staff are subject to enormous pressures to favour individuals from family or tribal groupings.

Misunderstandings

With the size of the EC aid programme to Solomon Islands, and recalling Jean-Paul's instructions to give a high profile to EC activities, I decided to start a newsletter. This was initially well received, but quite soon ran into a problem. In one edition I reported on an independent evaluation that had been carried out into an earlier programme of EC support under the previous government of Ezekiel Alebua. The evaluation effectively cleared the Alebua government of any misuse of funds. Perhaps understandably, this riled Solomon Mamaloni, who felt that the previous government had been let off. In the event, Mamaloni declined to be interviewed by Simon Horner for the Courier magazine, despite some fairly strong pressing from my office. So on two counts I lost favour with Mamaloni. A more experienced person would have played his cards more carefully, and kept a lower profile.

Regional Fisheries

The Solomon Islands delegation had responsibility for regional fisheries programmes. The Forum Fisheries Agency, based in Honiara, had an important mandate to safeguard the interests of the Pacific islands in receiving fair returns from foreign fleets (mainly Pacific rim countries) fishing for tuna. The EC gave financial support for work on maritime boundaries delimitation, inter-island satellite stations for tracking fishing fleets, and a regional conference centre. Sir Peter Kenilorea (Solomon Islands), Andrew Wright (Australia), and Phillip Muller (Samoa) were some of the influential personalities at FFA who were dedicated to ensuring that the Pacific Islands received the full benefits from their fisheries resources as defined by the UN law of the sea. Despite their efforts, and even with the monitoring support of the New Zealand air force, and more recently, satellite technology, poaching remains a problem, as it is difficult to find vessels in the vast tracts of the Pacific. The South Pacific Commission (SPC) had valuable complementary programmes in assessing the extent of the tuna resource in the Pacific, using tuna tagging techniques to determine populations. Under Lomé III, the EC gave continuing financial support to this programme, and in 1993 I visited Nouméa to sign a financing agreement with the Director-General of SPC. The main aim of the project was to determine whether the dramatic increase in purse seine activity had affected the stocks of yellowfin and skipjack tuna in the south Pacific.

The Diplomatic Corps

In those days, the diplomatic corps included the UK high commissioner (Ray Jones), the Australian high commissioner (Ruth Pearce, Rob Flynn), the PNG high commissioner (Frank Miro, Joseph Assaigo), the New Zealand high commissioner (Bernard Hillier, Tia Barrett), and the chargé d'affaires of Japan (Noburu Kawagishi). We enjoyed cordial relations with all these colleagues, and shared political news and development information over monthly lunches, and during numerous cocktail parties. Occasionally there were elements of competition, as well as collaboration, over projects. While we benefited from Japanese finance for ice plants supporting EC fisheries projects, the Japanese benefited from our infrastructure work in Noro. On the other hand I had to agree to exchange financing the airport terminal for the airport runway, as the Japanese put pressure on the Minister (Victor Ngele) to give them the higher visibility terminal project. The USA promoted democracy by providing a fine new parliament building. The UK was our development partner "in residence", and we coordinated our aid efforts with Ray Jones and his staff, especially in rural health and forestry, while keeping in close touch with New Zealand on matters to do with agricultural extension.

The Ambassador of Taiwan was the dean of the diplomatic corps, but stood alone as the other embassies all recognised the People's Republic of China. The relatively large diplomatic presence reflected the significance of natural resources in forestry (ROC) and fisheries (Japan) with which Solomon Islands was endowed, its aid worthiness as a poor country, and its strategic importance within the Pacific.

The Moti Affair

In PNG, the relationship between the head of delegation and the national authorities was soured by the actions of a technical assistant. So too in Solomon Islands, what started off as a very good relationship with the Minister of Finance, was spoilt by a technical assistant who took on tasks way beyond his terms of reference. I was to learn an important (if painful) lesson.

One fine day in 1993, I received a courtesy call from Julian Moti, a Fijian. He seemed a very plausible individual, with a law degree and excellent references from one of Australia's private universities. Some weeks later Christopher Abe requested that we take on Julian as a TA in support of his office. Accordingly terms of reference were drafted, and after discussing the proposal with Peter Craig McQuaide, desk officer for Solomon Islands who happened to be on mission from Brussels, we decided to go ahead (I must acknowledge that Peter was less convinced of the merits of this than was I). All went well initially, but then I found that Julian had become engaged in the long drawn out struggle between the Ministry of Finance and the Central Bank. While I had great regard for Minister Abe, I also had considerable respect for the governor of the central bank, whose annual reports were soundly reasoned and gave an objective picture of the state of the Solomon Islands economy. One morning I read newspaper headlines that Julian Moti (an EC financed TA) was instigating a court case against the central bank on behalf of the Minister of Finance. This was clearly not something with which we wished to be associated. I unilaterally abrogated Julian Moti's TA contract on the grounds that he had gone far beyond his terms of reference. I was then subject to threatening phone calls from Christopher Abe. Later I was summoned by the permanent secretary of Foreign Affairs, Wilson Ifunao, to be informed that the Prime Minister wished me to leave the country. Only after some speedy high level intervention from Brussels was I saved from the ignominy of being declared *persona non grata*. I am grateful to the director-general Philippe Soubestre and his assistant Jim Moran for their crucial support during this saga. Roelf Brenner, division chief in Brussels, kindly made a special detour to meet Christopher Abe in an attempt to resolve matters.

For a few months I kept a low profile. There was a change of government in May 1993, and Francis Billy Hilly became Prime Minister. It was like a breath of fresh air. My family and I accompanied Billy Hilly on a memorable boat trip from Gizo to Ranongga to open EC-financed health centres in his home island. The Australians and the donor community at large backed Billy Hilly in taking a tough line on forestry concessions. But the logging companies used their influence to bring about a vote of no confidence in Parliament. Thus, after only eighteen months, Solomon Mamaloni and Christopher Abe returned to government. As time went by, I was able to rebuild the dialogue with permanent secretaries Snyder Rini and Manasseh Sogavare. Relations with Christopher Abe were eventually restored. He generously hosted a farewell dinner for us when my four years were up. It had been a difficult time, and a rich learning experience for me.

Unfortunately, the seeds of discord had been sown. After I left Solomons, renewed differences over forestry policy caused a rift in the relationship. During a Pacific tour, Philippe Soubestre called by to see Solomon Mamaloni. He was only able to obtain a meeting with the Prime Minister on a Sunday morning. He presented himself as was his custom in a grey suit and tie. Solomon Mamaloni was in sandals, shorts and a T shirt. The meeting did not get off to a good start when Mamaloni asked Soubestre whether he had just come from church. Not long afterwards, Solomon Islands lost its head of delegation post, and thereafter our representative in Honiara reported to the delegation in Port Moresby.

Clouds on the Horizon

Thus my memories of the Happy Isles are mixed. On the positive side, I felt that we had put our best efforts and finance into a viable and widespread development programme that was benefiting large numbers of rural people. However, important issues concerning forestry and good governance were not resolved, despite a lot of advice and diplomatic pressure. But there were even darker storm clouds on the horizon that were to surprise most observers, and which I had to deal with in re-engaging with the Solomons six years later.

With Christopher Abe and Victor Ngele and their spouses in Honiara

With Delegation staff and Technical Assistants in the EC Delegation

Chapter 20.

BARBADOS

Although a small country, Barbados is a thriving democracy with a well developed school system. The island hosts one of the campuses of the University of the West Indies, as well as the Caribbean Tourism Organisation. The Caribbean Development Bank under the prudent leadership of Sir Neville Nicholls has its headquarters there. Historically the economy was based on sugar and rum, with its overtones of a plantocracy and slave labour. High level tourism around Sandy Lane on the west coast has been enhanced as more sugar land has been converted to golf courses.

Credentials

I was nominated as Head of Delegation for Barbados and the Eastern Caribbean in September 1995. After a protracted period of briefing in Brussels we arrived in Bridgetown in November. The Governor General, Dame Edna Barrow, graciously accepted my credentials early in December. Dame Edna had been a member of the Commonwealth Eminent Persons Group vis-a-vis South Africa during that country's transition from apartheid to democracy. The Ambassador of Belgium presented his credentials on the same morning, and we invited him and others from the diplomatic corps for a pre-lunch glass of wine in our new home, the plantation style Highgate House, built in 1740. Sadly, Dame Edna died shortly before Christmas. Her funeral was carried out with great solemnity and dignity in January 1996.

Shortly after our arrival in the Caribbean I was called to attend a meeting of the West Indies Committee in Trinidad which was addressed by Professor Pinheiro, the new Commissioner for Development. This was an opportunity to meet Michael King, Barbados Ambassador to the

European Union. We soon discovered a commonality as former students of St Edmund Hall. Michael displayed an amazing knowledge of cricket, a veritable Wisden personified.

Early in 1996 I set off to become accredited to the other five ACP countries, calling on the Governors-General and Prime Ministers of St Lucia, St Vincent and the Grenadines, St Kitts and Nevis, Antigua, and the President and Prime Minister of the Commonwealth of Dominica. Later I was to repeat the process in Grenada when that country came under our wing, having been relinquished by the Trinidad and Tobago Delegation. I also visited the Governors of the British territories, and their Chief Ministers, of Montserrat, British Virgin Islands, and Anguilla.

The Delegation in Barbados

Philippe Darmuzey had arranged for us to live at Highgate House, which had associations with George Washington and Anthony Eden. We had a good office location, and a strongly staffed Delegation. Among a team of young and energetic advisers were Richard Applebee (UK), economic adviser, who would never take no as an answer from Brussels, Patrice Pillet (France), agricultural adviser, Martin Dihm (Germany), a young economist responsible for regional trade and tourism matters, and Christos Gofas (Greece), a young engineer. Bertram Niles, BBC Correspondent, was our press officer. Matthias Langemeyer (Germany) was an able and helpful *stagiare*.

Denise, our accountant, was daughter of the Chief Justice. Kathleen Hurley from Trinidad was our information officer. Kenrick Husbands was my driver, and very soon became my counsellor, philosopher and family friend. He was our resident poet in the Delegation, and could be relied upon to produce excellent pieces for the Newsletter when occasion demanded, including reports on our Delegation cricket matches. In Antigua we had a sub-office where Hans Okorn was the Resident Adviser, assisted by secretary Ava Edwards. Hans had first line responsibility for EC projects in Antigua, St Kitts and Nevis and the three British dependencies of Montserrat, British Virgin Islands, and Anguilla. Responsibility for overall aid programming and political dialogue remained with our office in Barbados. Dieter Friedrichs was Resident Adviser in Grenada reporting to Eberhart Stahn in Trinidad, and when Dieter left it was decided that Grenada (as part of the Windwards) would come under our wing in Barbados. Glenys Roberts kept the office going as a *bureau de passage*.

Cricket and Development

Francesco Affinito, economic adviser and former desk officer for PNG, kindly gave me a book with this title. Its author reveals how deeply the pride of the Commonwealth Caribbean (whose peoples have strong recollections of slavery) was boosted by the prowess of the West Indies cricket teams which toured England and Australia in the fifties. Much of their success could be attributed to three distinguished Barbadian (*Bajan*) batsmen, the three Ws: Worrell, Walcott and Weekes. Two of the Ws had strong links with our office. Lana (my secretary) was the only daughter of West Indian cricketer Frank Worrell. She was married to Michael Walcott, son of Sir Clyde Walcott. Sadly, Lana suffered a brain tumour and died in 1998. Marva (Richard Applebee's secretary) was the wife of David Holford, another test cricketer, who as manager took the West Indies team to India.

Philippe Darmuzey had given a Challenge Cup which was competed for on an annual basis against the British High Commission. In our first cricket match during my tenure of office we lost the Cup and I was determined that we should get it back before I left, which we duly did. Our Delegation team had a strong Highgate House element: Wilmont our gardener bowled, as did Wally our security guard, while our cook's partner Chandler also played. These three Bajans led by our captain Eric provided the strength to compensate for the lack of experience of some of our Greek and German players. For our final match in 1999, I made sure that we fielded the strongest team possible by calling in Glenys' husband and young son from Grenada. We had a special collection in the Delegation to pay for their airfares.

Head of Delegation

By the time I arrived in Barbados, the role of the Head of Delegation had expanded quite a lot with the Maastricht Treaty and the Common Foreign and Security Policy. I was fortunate to succeed Philippe Darmuzey who had built excellent relations with our client Governments and with the local staff. In Barbados, Indu and I attended two or three official engagements each week, and frequently hosted dinners or receptions. Among the embassies in Barbados were the USA, UK, Canada, Australia, Brazil, Colombia, Guatemala, and Venezuela. The Cuban ambassador was the dean. The monthly diplomatic lunches were lively occasions.

Ten Days in May

Some times things could get particularly hectic. I recall in particular the first ten days of May 1998 when Ministers and Officials from the 15 European Member States and 71 countries of the ACP group gathered in Barbados for a ACP-EU Council of Ministers meeting. Clare Short chaired the meeting. While Barbados as the host government had responsibility for hosting the event, we in the Delegation necessarily had a strong supporting role, not least in ensuring that our Commission colleagues were well looked after. At the close of the meeting, the Delegation hosted a Europe Day reception at the PomMarine Hotel. Billie Miller, Deputy Prime Minister, was the principal guest and Commissioner Jaoa de Deus Pinheiro entreated the guests to enjoy themselves.

On Managing a Delegation

The key to managing the Barbados Delegation were weekly meetings, at which Advisers shared their experiences and we planned ahead in the light of forthcoming events. Special meetings with the local staff took place when birthdays were celebrated. For such occasions I was grateful for the large conference room in the Fort St James building, overlooking the Careenage. With the inclusion of social development advisers from the UK in our team, and additional staff from Brussels, this building became too small for our needs. Following some intelligence given by Billie Miller, in early 1999 our Delegation moved to a splendid historic building. Mervue House is situated close to the EU's flagship project in Barbados, the Hospitality Training Institute at the PomMarine hotel.

UK Ministers

EU heads of delegation were invited to an UK-Caribbean summit which took place in Bahamas in February 1998. Robin Cook was in the chair and gave Jim Moran and me the floor to talk about the future of bananas in the Caribbean. With director Francesco Granell, we had exchanges with Baroness Scotland. Billie Miller and Robin Cook had a lively exchange on the issue of ships carrying nuclear waste en route through the Caribbean, which Billie Miller saw as a potential threat to the tourism industry. Earlier on Malcom Rifkind as secretary of state for Foreign Affairs came to Barbados on an official visit. We briefed him on our efforts to revitalise the smallholder banana industry in the Windward Islands. He observed that the UK had successfully passed the baton for financial and technical support to the EU.

Two other meetings with Ministers were distinctly less cordial. Returning to Barbados from St Vincent one evening I ran into Jack Cunningham (cabinet minister in Blair's Government) in the VIP lounge at Grantley Adams airport. He was waiting for a return flight to London. He had visited St Lucia at the invitation of Prime Minister Kenny Anthony, and attacked me for not releasing Stabex funds quickly enough. I was taken aback as we had already set in train measures to speed the release of Stabex funds. Cunningham subsequently mellowed and spoke nostalgically about Newcastle United. It was perhaps ironic that on my way to Grenada for the CDB meeting in May 1998 and the signing of the St Vincent FMO which brought in targeted budgetary support for Stabex funds, I was waylaid by the UK Minister for International Development, George Foulkes. The meeting which took place in the VIP lounge of Barbados airport had been arranged by the High Commission with no special agenda. I had expected that we would discuss the difficult situation in Montserrat, following further volcanic eruptions and EU plans for the new airport there, but it turned out that George Foulkes wished to lambast me for failing to release Stabex monies in good time. I gave Mr Foulkes copies of our Newsletters which explained the steps that had already been taken for the speedy release of Stabex resources. I also mentioned that I was accountable to the European Commission and the Court of Auditors for the effective utilisation of these funds, and it was not just a question of writing cheques.

Montserrat

In July 1995 the Soufriere volcano erupted and discharged ash and pyroclastic flows down several sides of the mountain. No-one suffered injury at that time, and I attended the EC-OCT meeting in the capital Plymouth in November of that year. It was a heartening occasion well chaired by Chief Minister Reuben Meade, and Francesco Granell from the Commission. The participants did not seem overly concerned, and our Twin Otter flight from Antigua landed without incident at Bramble airport (named after the first Chief Minister) on the eastern side of the island, within the shadow of the volcano. However, the volcanic eruptions continued and soon Plymouth was covered in several metres of ash.

My colleague from the Commission Yves concerned with OCT matters, Hans and I visited again in 1996. We inspected the rice cleaning operation which enabled Montserrat to earn some much needed revenues from rice exports to the EU. We also assessed how EC emergency aid could be harnessed to help those displaced. On this occasion we were still able to fly in and out of Bramble airport. The governor Frank Savage took us on a Land Rover tour of the affected areas in the south west, including Plymouth and its port. The devastation was like a scene from Dante's inferno. Frank kept in radio contact with the observatory, as the volcano was giving off periodic bursts of ash cloud. Having seen the situation on the ground, Frank had kindly arranged for us to see the volcano at close quarters by means of a helicopter. The pilot had thoughtfully removed the door from my side of the aircraft so that I could feel the heat from the glowing rocks as we flew around the peak. It was quite an adventure, which I managed to capture on video.

Sadly, several people lost their lives when a pyroclastic flow occurred in July 1997. After this event, the evacuation zone was extended further to encompass about two-thirds of the south of the island. Bramble airport was out of bounds. Hans Okorn, Franco Affinito and I next visited the island in 1998, this time by helicopter. EU emergency funds had been used to build housing for the displaced in the north, and we were considering how we might co-finance with the British a new port and airfield. In the event, I believe the UK funded the lot after Clare Short had been criticised for not paying enough attention to the plight of the Montserratians.

Illegal Drugs

Geographically, the Caribbean lies between the United States in the north and South America. A principal market for illegal drugs produced in South America (notably Colombia) is the USA. Thus much of this trade passes through the Caribbean by one transport mode or another. There are abandoned airports in some of the islands that could be used for transit, and of course yachting thrives.

An important meeting to enhance coordination among agencies in combatting drug trafficking was held in Bridgetown in May 1996, which led to the Barbados Plan of Action. Commissioner Anita Gradin attended this meeting for the European Commission, and joined our Europe Day celebration at Highgate House. Subsequently, a regional EC drugs office was opened in Bridgetown with a TA, Michel Amiot, in charge. Franco Affinito represented the Delegation at the frequent inter-agency meetings held under the auspices of Caricom.

Leaving Barbados

For my farewell on 27 August 1999, Kenrick Husbands kindly wrote the following:

Eighteen years aboard this ship
Six captains did I tend;
But him I served upon this trip
I would serve him once again.

Upon the deck in '95,
A new but thoughtful captain joined the crew;
Through rain and shine we all survived
With just the loss of two.

Though he himself had fallen,
He quickly rose and took his stand;
For the journey to be taken
Required the captain in command.

And so from port to port he journeyed,
Each trip with special care,
And in his case he ever carried,
The missions of Lomé

To NAOs and statesmen,
Governors of these isles,
The working class and field men –
All logged within his files.

On and on, through night and day,
Duty led him from the start,
Forging links along the way,
Building bridges to his heart.

But just before his journey ended
In goodwill to his crew
He steered the ship from James Fort
To the placid waters of Mervue.

And now we bid farewell today
To our Captain, Boss and friend,
With hope he'll sail along our way
Before his sailing days shall end.

My dealings with the Prime Minister of Barbados were mainly of an official kind, for signatures of the National Indicative Programme, and project opening ceremonies. However, following a farewell courtesy call to his office, Owen Arthur was kind enough to issue a press release saying *"If your approach to the discharging of your duties was to be followed by everyone we would gallop ahead"*.

I am afraid that not everyone in the Windwards shared this sentiment.

Chapter 21.

STABEX AND BANANAS

There were two major professional challenges during my time in the Caribbean. The first concerned our role in helping to sustain the smallholder banana industry in the Windward Islands. Bananas has been a source of employment and income for significant parts of the population of these islands, and failure could mean political disturbances. The industry had been nurtured by EU financial and technical support (succeeding the British support I have mentioned earlier) and by preferential access to the EU market.

The second challenge was management and delivery of the large Stabex flows that had accrued to the Windwards in compensation for years of relatively low export prices. The Stabex instrument had been controversial and I felt a sense of responsibility to ensure that these funds were spent in as developmentally sound a manner as any other monies coming from the EDF.

WTO and the EC Banana Market

For many years, the Windwards along with other ACP producers of bananas received preferential treatment in the European market, by means of guaranteed access for specified quantities (a hang over of the former Commonwealth preference). The market was protected by an external tariff which Latin American producers had to pay. The Caribbean producers are mainly smallholder producers that are unable to compete in a free market against the plantations owned by Dole, Del Monte and Chiquita which could reap economies of scale. The Windwards had some plantations in the river valleys of St Lucia, but these had been subdivided into smallholdings with Independence. Geest had always been significant for the Windwards, providing the weekly shipping service of banana boats to the UK.

The WTO decided in September 1997 that the EU's banana regime did not conform with WTO rules. The decision was in response to a panel established by the WTO at the request of the United States, Ecuador, Guatemala, Honduras and Mexico. Accordingly the European Commission in January 1998 came up with a modification to its regulations, including a change in import licensing arrangements and a freer sharing out of the tariff quota to all ACP suppliers. The Commission also proposed to provide financial and technical assistance to traditional ACP suppliers to increase their competitiveness.

The US Challenge

The challenge from the United States came as a surprise to us all since President Clinton had declared when he visited Barbados in May 1997 that the United States would not trample on the fragile economies of the Windward Islands. When I questioned the US Ambassador to Barbados, Jeanette Hyde (from North Carolina), on this I found her response quite unsympathetic to the plight of the smallholder producers, taking a position at the other end of the spectrum to that of Glenys Kinnock.

We felt that if the US had held off until the expiry of the EU banana regime in 2002 we would have had a much longer transition period. With the possibility of another less favourable banana regime it was going to be more difficult to bring about the efficiency gains that we needed to achieve in the Windward Islands. As David Rudder of Trinidad expressed it in his Calypso Banana Song, the USA had let the Windwards down under commercial pressures from Dole and Chiquita.

Well Uncle Sammy used to visit the Church of Banana
He used to go to church with a girl named Grenada
And then he went to church with a girl named Dominica
He used to bow down to one St Vincent
Then he used to go and pray to one called St Lucia

He say he loved the way they preached in the Caribbean chapter
But one day Uncle Sammy he went South America
And he bounced up a girl she name was Chiquita
Chiquita Dole is her name and she got plenty power
Them West Indian girls get vexed and the whole thing turned sour.

Banana Dilemmas

Glenys Kinnock, who later chaired the European Parliament's Development Committee, made an unannounced visit to the Windwards at the instigation of the OECS Ambassador to Brussels Edwin Laurent. When our counterparts in the Windwards informed us of the mission, in the interests of inter-institutional coordination I telephoned the Kinnocks in London and spoke to her husband Neil who was celebrating Tony Blair's election victory, which had taken place that day. Martin Dihm was duly despatched to Dominica to shadow her mission. Eventually I caught up with Glenys and her party in St Vincent and arranged a breakfast briefing to inform her and her colleague Wynn of how we in the Commission were supporting the banana industry and attempting to reform it. Glenys was not totally convinced by our case. She did not see things in the same light (she had seen the impact of the closure of the coal mines in South Wales). We sat in on her meetings with the Prime Minister and others as she expressed her understandable concern about the plight of the two-hectare woman with five children to feed and clothe. As an economist, it is difficult sometimes to deal with dilemmas like this, but I think Owen Arthur, Prime Minister of Barbados, got it right when he said to the West India Committee in London in 1995 that change is coming and it is coming fast and we had better prepare for it, rather than adopt an ostrich in the sand attitude. After this visit to the Windwards, Glenys proposed a new budget line in support of ACP producers of bananas, which was duly approved by the European Parliament. It was ironic that when I returned to Brussels from Barbados, one of my first tasks was to implement this well-intentioned but procedurally complex programme.

Banana Policy Dialogue

When I was involved in my ODA days with Windward bananas our discussions took place at technical level, with the directors of Agriculture and the head of Winban (Chong Perryman) and Eddie Edwards (head of Winban research). Now the dialogue shifted to the political level.

As part and parcel of delivering financial and technical assistance to the Windwards banana industry, we held a number of meetings at Prime Ministerial level in order to strengthen and encourage political will. Difficult decisions were needed for the industry to survive in an increasingly competitive world market situation. To use a marine analogy, the captain had to jettison some weaker passengers if the crew of the Windwards banana boat was to survive in increasingly stormy and turbulent WTO waters. To help those who were to leave the boat we offered a number of lifebelts so that they could survive. Thus Stabex resources were allocated between increasing efficiency of banana production and quality improvements, and the provision of social safety nets.

The first of these dialogues took place in Kingstown (dubbed Kingstown I) a couple of months before my arrival in 1995. The next dialogue which I attended along with Brian Thomson from the Barbados DevDiv took place in Castries in 1997. Prime Minister Vernon Lewis was a good interlocutor. I started the meeting by introducing my team in cricketing terms. Brian was the slow left armer. John Ferguson was the wicket keeper. I was the opening batsman. This drew a smile from the Prime Minister, a cousin of Sir Arthur Lewis (one of two Nobel Prize winners from St Lucia).

Castries II was a wider dialogue and took place in January 1998 when Francesco Granell, Director for the Caribbean, led for the Commission. The Castries II accord made provision for the continuing reform of the Windward Islands banana industry in the light of the decision of the World Trade Organisation to decertify the European banana regime. It recognised the importance of improving efficiency in the marketing arrangements and at farm level, and of eliminating debt from the growers associations.

At a news conference in Castries in January 1998 we pointed out that from an efficiency point of view we had to invest our banana-linked funds in those who are going to stay in the industry long term. Hence we had to identify who was likely to stay in and who was not. That was not an easy task, either technically or socially. Who wants to tell a poor farmer that her bananas can no longer be accepted by the export market? But this message is easier to convey if there is a programme of support enabling the farmer and her family to find new employment and farm income earning opportunities. To help identify the last type of programme we had taken on board two social development advisers paid for by DFID.

Banana Recovery Plan

In 1998 a banana recovery plan prepared by banana industry officials was launched at a press conference in Barbados. A Memorandum of Understanding (Castries III) was signed to give effect to its implementation. One goal of the plan was to increase industry export production back to 220,000 tons from levels of about 130,000 tons.

The Prime Minister of St Lucia, Kenny Anthony, endorsed the plan, including the privatisation of the St Lucia Banana Growers Association. Significantly he said that he wanted to de-politicise the banana industry for the very first time, while endorsing the Certified Farmers Programme with direct links to supermarkets in the UK. The new environment would require a farmer that was aggressive and competitive. Those who are unable to keep up with those requirements would be displaced. However, he expected that the vast majority of our farmers would be able to satisfy the criteria. He also recognised the importance of irrigation, while acknowledging that it was not easy to identify sources of water for the major valleys. He concluded by saying that:

"Obviously there are still problems to be resolved but farmers understand that there is an entirely new environment. There is still a very long way to go. It is not going to be painless but ultimately we will have a banana industry that is leaner, that will have a greater output per acre, higher yields per acre, and overall I am extremely confident about the future of the industry".

Speeding up Stabex Flows to the Banana Exporters

For many years the Prime Ministers of the Windward Islands had appreciated the volume of Stabex funds they have been awarded in compensation for declines in export earnings from bananas. Some ECU

150 mn had been provided in the mid-1990s from Stabex, which was a huge sum for these small islands. On the other hand they had expressed concern about its slow delivery. Sir James Mitchell, Prime Minister of St Vincent, was fond of telling me that Stabex funds would still be sitting in bank accounts in Brussels when the banana industry would have collapsed. On another occasion Orsalia Kalantzopoulos, director of the Caribbean for the World Bank, came to our office in Bridgetown and offered to take over the management of the Stabex funds on our behalf. I declined her kind offer.

Stabex Committees

My first approach to the sensible management of Stabex funds was twofold. The creation of Stabex committees chaired by the NAO (in a similar manner to the Stabex Committee in Solomon Islands). The Stabex committees were to be supported by Management and Coordination Units.

This system worked extremely well in St Vincent where Karl John and John Townend grasped the concept and put it into effect, with the blessing of Laura Anthony-Browne, an excellent NAO. The system also worked well in St Lucia with the support of Bernard La Corbiniere as NAO, Rodinald Soomer, and Vincent Peters.

It took some time to take off in Dominica where it had to mesh with an existing mechanism for managing EDF funds run by Cary Harris, who went on to become Permanent Secretary of Finance. The system was beginning to take shape in Grenada, where the volume of Stabex resources was much less.

The terms of reference of the Stabex committees were initially based upon those we had derived in Solomon Islands and which had worked successfully. However the project approach (except in St Vincent) seemed to be too slow in relation to the magnitude of the funds involved.

Irrigation in St Vincent

In 1997 a proposal was formulated by the EDF Project Management Coordination Unit in St Vincent for a fast track irrigation project. The Unit was ably led by Karl John, a very experienced Vincentian, supported by a capable UK economist John Townend. The scheme involved the irrigation of some 400 acres (200 farm families) in the Langley Park and Rabacca Farms area. The project was inspired by the farm of Victor Hadley, where yields of 27 tons of bananas per irrigated acre were being obtained. Trial plots under smallholder conditions using Stabex 1993 funds were already yielding 15 tons of bananas per acre in their first crop year. Irrigation had to be accompanied by precise fertiliser application, management of suckers, and pest and disease control. On returning to St Vincent in 2000 for a training seminar, I had the pleasure of revisiting this area to see that things had turned out well and in accordance with our original expectations. It was disappointing that similar schemes on a relatively large scale could not have been prepared and implemented so quickly for St Lucia and Dominica.

Targeted Budgetary Support

During a mission to Brussels in the summer of 1996 I discussed the problem of Stabex delivery with colleagues in Brussels, including economists of the Structural Adjustment Unit. Two missions from Brussels ensued. As a result, following the Castries II meeting in January 1998, a new approach to Stabex delivery was started. Under targeted budgetary support, Governments received Stabex funds in support of specified expenditures within their public sector investment programmes, notably for training and education as a means of facilitating the transition to new activities, and as a means of addressing poverty. At the same time, the Stabex committees continued to function using a proportion of the funds to be committed under the traditional project approach. The Stabex Committees, chaired by the National Authorising Officer in each country were empowered to make project financing decisions up to ECU 2 mn without reference to Brussels. Projects had already been approved in the fields of raising banana productivity and quality, agricultural diversification, general economic diversification, and poverty alleviation. The Stabex committees approved a venture capital fund to assist the private sector in Dominica and activities sponsored by the Ministry of Community Development for poverty reduction in St Lucia.

The Castries II Accord and a separate memorandum of understanding concerning the utilisation of Stabex transfers were signed by Prime Ministers Kenny Anthony of St Lucia, Edison James of Dominica, Sir James Mitchell of St Vincent and the Grenadines, and Dr Keith Mitchell of Grenada, along with Francesco Granell of the Commission, Helene Dubois, Ambassador of France to the OECS countries, Brian Thomson of the British Development Division in the Caribbean, UNDP, and a representative of the Caribbean Development Bank.

Dr Kenny Anthony said when he signed the Stabex FMO in April 1998:

We are breaking new ground here not just for the Caribbean, but for the ACP group as a whole. Targeted budgetary support could well become a new instrument of aid delivery for the next Convention.

Back to Brussels

As my time in Barbados drew to a close I received an invitation from Director Hamburger to join him in Brussels as his Adviser. After several years in Delegations I was happy to accept the opportunity to work in the headquarters of the European Commission. The new posting was to bring me back to earth with a bump.

Chapter 22.

WORKING IN BRUSSELS

The Commissioners of the European Union are appointed by the Member States. Nowadays, the European Parliament has a say in their confirmation. Most Commissioners will have had experience in national governments. When I came to Brussels in September 1999, Romano Prodi (Italy) was the President of the Commission, Chris Patten was responsible for External Affairs, Neil Kinnock for Administration, Pascal Lamy (France) for Trade, and Poul Nielson (Denmark) for Development.

The earlier Commissioners for Development from 1958 to 1985 had all come from France, including the formidable figures of Claude Cheysson and Edgard Pisani. Their influence meant that French had become the *lingua franca* of the Directorate-General for Development. Notwithstanding a two weeks refresher course at my own expense in Avignon, I struggled to speak French. All my colleagues had good French and at least one other language other than their own. The Director-General at this time was Philip Lowe, an Englishman, who had the remarkable skill of starting off a discourse in English and without hesitation, switching into perfect French.

During my years with the Commission, there were opportunities to meet successive Development Commissioners. Lorenzo Natali came on mission to Sudan in 1985, Manuel Marin I met in Papua New Guinea and Miami, and I arranged two missions for Joao de Deus Pinheiro in the Caribbean. Needless to say, each Commissioner had his own style. Poul Nielson was no exception. He spoke frankly to the assembled Heads of Delegation in Brussels urging them to move into *the premier league of aid donors and deliver the pizza.*

Delivering the Pizza

As I discovered in my first year in Brussels, delivering the pizza within the framework of the European bureaucracy was no easy task. Assigned responsibility for bringing the Banana Budget Line into being, I soon found out that the matter of inter-service consultation could be laborious and frustrating. One individual in AIDCO was particularly stubborn in giving his visa, and caused me many sleepless nights.

Another cause of concern during my first year was that the status of Advisers within the Commission was being questioned by Neil Kinnock. My own work schedule was somewhat fragmentary, and I felt underemployed after the excitement of commanding my own Delegation in the Caribbean. It was with considerable relief that I learned from Athanassios Theodorakis (acting Director-General) towards the end of 2000 that I was to be given responsibility for the Pacific.

The Pacific Unit

Sadly, the very day that I took up the Pacific post in Brussels in January 2001, we received news from Port Moresby of the untimely demise of Richard Applebee, a good friend and colleague. His funeral on the outskirts of Brussels was attended by so many that the church was overflowing, a moving testament to his popularity, and the esteem that everybody had for Richard.

We were a strong European team in the Pacific Unit. Bas Van Helden (Netherlands) looked after Solomon Islands and Vanuatu, Dieter Friedrichs (Germany) was responsible for Fiji, Kiribati, Tonga, and Samoa, Augustine Oyowe (Belgium) followed events in Papua New Guinea, Tine Schmale (Netherlands) kept a watchful eye on the new ACP members (Micronesia, Palau, Marshall Islands, and East Timor), and Francesco Affinito (UK) covered regional matters. Later on Sergio Piazzardi (Italy) joined our team. Jo (Georgette Miserque) from Belgium and Colette Demogue from France gave us excellent secretarial support, and we benefited from the assistance of *stagiares* from Denmark, Germany, and the UK.

Experienced people in the Delegations included Frans Baan at the helm in Suva, Anthony Crasner in charge in Port Moresby, Hendrik Smets in Honiara, and Costas Tsillioganis in Port Vila. Our Unit kept in close touch with the Pacific ambassadors resident in Brussels, especially those from PNG, Fiji, and Solomon Islands. Regular exchanges took place with staff from the Australian and New Zealand embassies over matters to do with conflict resolution. In the course of our work we attended European Council meetings, and liaised with MEPs, notably Glenys Kinnock, who was then chair of the Development Committee.

Travelling to the Pacific from Brussels inevitably takes a long time, and sometimes a mission would take us around the world. Initially we had planned a visit to the Pacific for Commissioner Nielson in 2001, but this had to be postponed until 2002 because of civil disturbances in Papua New Guinea. In the event, a fuller itinerary could be accomplished, starting in Samoa, stopping briefly in Tonga, and then to Fiji. From there we flew to New Zealand to meet with their development Minister in Wellington, and then on to Canberra for discussions with AusAid. The next stop was Port Moresby, with a side trip to Bougainville, before taking a chartered jet to Micronesia. On the way home, I stopped off in Manila for meetings with the Asian Development Bank.

Our Mandate

The Unit's Mission statement gives an indication of our responsibilities.

In line with the overall objectives of the Directorate-General for Development, which are to contribute to the elimination of poverty through the promotion of sustainable development and the integration of developing countries into the world economy, the Unit is responsible (in close cooperation with, and in support of, the Delegations) for the management and co-ordination of all relations with the ACP countries in the Pacific, and (with Relex) for East Timor as a new member of the group, as well as with the regional institutions, notably the Forum Secretariat, the Secretariat of the Pacific Community, and the other agencies of the Council for the Regional Organisations of the Pacific.

In terms of political relations, the Unit is responsible for monitoring evolving political situations and events, and ensuring appropriate political dialogue with the leadership of the Pacific countries, regional entities, and other players, in accordance with the provisions of the Cotonou Agreement, and in consultation with the Member States, with a view to the effective use of EC coooperation instruments in support of human rights, democracy, the rule of law, good governance, conflict prevention, and peace consolidation.

In terms of development cooperation, the Unit is responsible for the programming and monitoring of EDF and Budget resources to the Pacific ACP countries and the Pacific region, ensuring regular reviews (including the Mid-Term Reviews) and proper dialogue with the national and regional authorities and non-state actors, as well as coordination with the EU Member States and other donors, including Australia and New Zealand.

In terms of economic relations, the Unit has the responsibility to ensure coherence among the EU's policies which impact on development (eg trade, fisheries, forestry, harmful tax) taking due account of Council and Parliament resolutions, so as to ensure that the longer term development objectives of the Pacific ACP countries are safeguarded. In relation to trade, the Unit has, within the context of the negotiations for Economic Partnership Agreements (EPAs), a particular responsibility (in liaison with DEV 01 and DG Trade) to assist the region's efforts for regional economic integration and integration into the world economy.

The Pacific Unit also maintains a watching brief with DEV D/1 on the EU's relations with the OCTs in the Pacific, and in cooperation with RELEX H/5, follows events in West Papua (Indonesia).

Thus the work of the Pacific Unit went beyond conventional development assistance and the preparation of country strategy papers, to more fundamental issues to do with conflict resolution and democracy. One of the challenges was to harness budget resources commanded by others in the Commission in support of peace building in the Pacific.

Chapter 23.

CONFLICTS IN THE PACIFIC

When I arrived at the Pacific Unit in January 2001, there had been two coups during the previous year: in Fiji and Solomon Islands. The situation in Bougainville was becoming calmer after several years of civil war. We were confronted with three countries in which elections were to be held to restore legitimacy to Government, and in which peace building efforts were needed to overcome tensions.

These were the challenges we faced. Our instruments were the Cotonou Agreement, embodying the commitment to political dialogue, and the stick of appropriate measures under Article 96, along with the carrot of EDF funds that we were about to programme. At this time we were instructed to produce country strategy papers which would indicate the principal focal sectors for the deployment of EDF funds, taking into account the particular circumstances of each country, including needs for conflict prevention and peace building. In PNG and Solomons, we also had substantial uncommitted Stabex funds left over from Lomé. We had the possibility of accessing resources from EU budget lines, which are controlled by other DGs in the Commission (Relex and AIDCO). Later on, we found finance for a seminar *Insecurity and Conflicts in the Pacific Region* which was held in Brussels on 30 June 2003. Sonja Siegmund, our stagiare at the time, did an excellent job in organising this seminar, and writing up the proceedings.

In this chapter, I have only attempted an outline of some very complex and fast moving events, primarily to illustrate how trying and time consuming a peace process can be. The importance of close collaboration with other partners (including those in DG Relex who command budget lines in support of conflict prevention) is evident.

Dealing with Conflict in PNG

My first experience of conflict in the Pacific was when a Delegation team visited Bougainville in November 1989. We were commissioned to identify worthwhile uses for € 30 mn of Sysmin funds which might help to prevent the escalation of tensions following the closure of the Panguna mine. A few weeks earlier Sam Kauona had blown up the power line to the mine. Many of the workers' houses were torched.

The Panguna mine started in 1972, and became the largest opencast mine in the world. Coming upon it in a helicopter from Arovo island where we were billeted, the mine was an amazing sight. The gigantic dredgers were idle at the bottom of the vast pit, and the offices empty of personnel. We drove speedily down the hill, inspecting burned out houses on the way.

The mine was the cause of considerable ecological damage, as we saw from the tailings trail as we flew over the island. The landowners made claims for compensation, which the PNG government refused, notwithstanding the considerable foreign exchange earnings from the export of gold and copper. Ten years of jungle warfare ensued, leading to tragic loss of life. Eventually, thanks to the mediation of the New Zealand government, a ceasefire was agreed in 1997, and a peace agreement was signed the following year.

During the dialogue with the national authorities about the programming of new EDF resources in 2001, we considered how to deliver a peace dividend for Bougainville. By this time, the peace process for Bougainville, led by the UN, New Zealand and Australia, was well entrenched. Bougainville had lost out earlier in the allocation of Sysmin funds, which the crisis had generated through loss of export earnings. Stabex funds were already being used for substantial agriculture programmes in Bougainville. The political dialogue continued in Nadi in August 2002 with Director Friedrich Hamburger, and again when Commissioner Nielson visited PNG in October 2002. In Port Moresby he spoke with the Prime Minister, and in Bougainville met Ministers of Government and Father John Momis. The dialogue continued in Auckland in August 2003 with Director General Koos Richelle and the Minister for Foreign Affairs Rabbie Namaliu, and subsequently in Port Moresby.

The Pacific Unit was keen to get EU involvement in the PNG elections which took place in 2002. After negotiating with colleagues in DG Relex, who controlled the funds, we succeeded in getting PNG on the priority list. An exploratory Electoral Observation Mission went to PNG in January 2002. However, this mission concluded that the situation was too dangerous for EU election observers to participate, a view that was readily endorsed by the European Council.

When in 2002 I returned to Bougainville with Commissioner Nielson, this tragic conflict had virtually ended, and the process of collecting weapons under UN auspices was underway. A new constitution for a separate Bougainville province was being prepared. It was especially interesting to meet Sam Kauona, one of the BRA leaders, who had returned after taking time out for further studies in New Zealand. Francis Ona was still holed up in the no-go area of the Panguna mine.

Although the EC was not able to support the UN efforts directly in the weapons collections process, as requested by Ambassador Sinclair, some significant amounts of Stabex funds were invested in cocoa rehabilitation and rural roads, as well as for vocational training, with a special focus on ex-combatants. So all in all we made a significant contribution to the peace process in Bougainville.

The impact of this conflict on the people of Bougainville and on the PNG economy at large is difficult to underestimate. When copper prices have increased, there has been renewed talk of re-opening the mine, which is estimated to have one of the richest deposits of copper and gold in the world.

Dealing with Conflict in Solomon Islands

When after four years in Solomon Islands (once dubbed the Happy Isles) I left Honiara in July 1995, I had little premonition of the violent conflicts to come. That is not to say that I was unaware of tensions between people from Malaita and Guadalcanal. Indeed, much of our efforts had focused on the launching of the Malaita Integrated Rural Development Programme (MIRDP) which was intended to open up new opportunities for Malaitans in their own island. An expansion of cocoa production sparked by an improved road system would reduce their need to migrate to Guadalcanal for jobs. The fact that this programme absorbed the bulk of the National Indicative Programme (NIP) was itself tacit recognition of the need for Malaitans to feel part of Solomon Islands, not least in the distribution of aid resources. In this sense, the MIRDP can be seen as an early attempt at conflict prevention. Clearly, it was not enough.

From 1998 onwards the Isatabu Freedom Movement (IFM) started attacks on Malaitans living in Guadalcanal, and some 20,000 people returned to Malaita in 1999. In response, the Malaita Eagle Force (MEF) was formed, and took control of Honiara, ousting the Prime Minister. The overthrow of the Bart Ulufa'alu Government (himself a Malaitan) took place on 5 June 2000 while MEPs Glenys Kinnock and John Corrie were in Honiara. Their attempts at reconciliation took place in a highly charged situation, before they escaped in a small plane to PNG arranged by our Delegation colleagues in Port Moresby.

Manasseh Sogavare from Choiseul was subsequently elected Prime Minister by Parliament by the end of June 2000. In October, the Townsville Peace Agreement was signed by both parties, with commitments to hand over weapons.

We had agreed in talks with the Minister of Finance and NAO (Kemakeza) in Brussels in August 2001 a €12 mn Emergency Rehabilitation programme *inter alia* to give support to the national elections and to Solomon Islands students attending regional universities (USP, UPNG). Assistance to rural training centres and micro-projects under the NIP continued meanwhile. These were activities bringing direct benefit to rural communities.

Tony Crasner (head of delegation in PNG) and I held discussions with Prime Minister Manasseh Sogavare in Honiara in November 2001, at the time when Jimmy Rasta and his MEF gang were still roaming the streets of Honiara. This dialogue did not amount to very much. Manasseh seemed pre-occupied and I sensed that his term as PM was about to end with the forthcoming elections.

One of our achievements was a significant contribution from NIP funds towards the costs of the December 2001 elections. It was a race against time to convince the Brussels bureaucracy to approve the financing, but the desk officer Bas van Helden won the day. Unfortunately, we were not able to field an observer mission, but the Commonwealth did. Snyder Rini from Morovo was returned as an MP and became Deputy Prime Minister and Minister of Finance in Kemakeza's government. Kemakeza came from Savo island, and hence was considered a neutral party in relation to the conflict.

After the elections in December 2001, it soon became apparent that the matter of compensation payments to the two sides in the conflict was not being properly handled by the new government. We had little confidence in the fiscal policies being pursued by the Ministry of Finance which seemed ever willing to grant tax exemptions to importers and exporters alike. We decided that under these circumstances the substantial Stabex balances would be frozen. Commissioner Nielson accordingly wrote to Prime Minister Kemakeza in 2002, explaining the circumstances under which we would be able to release these monies. The conditions included a soundly based development programme to be presented to the donor community which had the approval of the BWIs, and the adoption of policies leading to the sustainable exploitation of fisheries and forestry resources. The bulk of Stabex funds were to remain frozen until we were confident that they would only be used for developmental purposes.

In May 2002, Tony Crasner, the British high commissioner and I met with Prime Minister Allan Kemakeza in Honiara. It was a somewhat surrealistic occasion. Three Australian and New Zealand advisers, who knew very little of Cotonou, seemed to want to conduct the dialogue on behalf of the Prime Minister.

Friedrich Hamburger led a more meaningful exchange with Kemakeza in Nadi in August 2002, in the margins of the Pacific Forum. Deputy Prime Minister Snyder Rini, who was in Nadi at the time, declined the invitation to join us. On this occasion, we promised to respond positively to Kemakeza's request for a British Police Commissioner, and subsequently managed to convince our colleagues elsewhere in the Commission to agree to this unusual but significant TA posting. Dialogue continued in Auckland, during the Pacific Forum with Director General Koos

Richelle in 2003, and again when Commissioner Nielson visited Honiara in February 2004.

In June 2003, the Regional Assistance Mission to Solomons Islands (RAMSI) came into being. This was an Australian and New Zealand led initiative to help stabilise the political and economic situation. Allan Kemakeza formally requested the assistance, and then Parliament ratified the request in July, tacitly acknowledging the complete breakdown in governance. Some two thousand security personnel were involved in the initial stages, as well as civil servants to help restore management of the economy. The EU financed Police Commissioner helped to pave the way for RAMSI. After some reflection, we came to acknowledge this extreme form of intervention as necessary in the circumstances, even if it smacked of neo-colonialism. In the event, RAMSI has continued operations in Solomon Islands for the last ten years, in its quest to restore stability.

Dealing with Conflict in Fiji

Politics in Fiji is dominated by the interface between the indigenous Fijians and the Indo-Fijian community. The latter are descendants of indentured labour brought in for the sugar industry by the British in the nineteenth century. Many became sugar farmers in their own right, on land leased from indigenous Fijians. Rental payments for sugar land have often become a cause of conflict.

The twists and turns of Fijian politics over the last two decades are too complex to be recounted here. Suffice to note that in 1987 the government under indigenous Fijian leadership (but with several Indo-Fijian ministers) was overthrown by colonel Rabuka. In 1999 Mahendra Chaudhry became the country's first Indo-Fijian Prime Minister. On 19 May 2000 Chaudhry and his cabinet were taken captive in the Fiji Parliament by George Speight, a Fijian nationalist, with the tacit support of Rabuka.

The European Council was alerted of the coup by reports from the UK High Commissioner in Suva, and a statement was made by the Presidency on the same day. The European Parliament was informed by MEPs Glenys Kinnock and John Corrie, who played a key part in raising the Fiji issue in the EU institutions, following their dramatic escape from Solomon Islands.

Glenys Kinnock ensured that the matter was raised during the ACP-EU Joint Assembly. Fiji was expelled from the Commonwealth in June 2000. Qarase, an indigenous Fijian, was appointed Prime Minister in July.

Political dialogue took place in Brussels with Minister Tavola under the Swedish Presidency, which I continued in Suva in December 2001. Director Hamburger took up the baton in Nadi in August 2002 during the Forum. Subsequently, Commissioner Nielson visited Fiji in October 2002 and held discussions with the new Prime Minister Qarase, and separately with Chaudhry. Koos Richelle continued the dialogue in Auckland in August 2003. Glenys Kinnock visited Fiji again during this period, in her capacity as co-chair of the ACP-EU Joint Assembly. She was briefed by the Pacific Unit before her mission, and again by the European Commission Head of Delegation in Fiji. During the political dialogue we reminded the Fijian political leaders that their failure to resolve their tensions were delaying critical reforms of the sugar industry which boded ill for the future of the Fijian economy and for long term relations between the different communities.

Elections were held in August 2001. We tried to obtain funds to support the election process and to mount an election observation mission (EOM). Despite my best efforts, the EOM proved impossible to finance, as the list of countries which would receive election support or electoral missions had already been determined by my colleagues in Relex, and I was unable to convince them to show flexibility. Nor was there a willingness to reallocate NIP funds for this purpose. I was taken to task by the Council for our failure. Fortunately, one MEP was able to be in Fiji to monitor the elections and along with Sir John Kaputin on the ACP side, join with the UN and Commonwealth teams.

We had better success with colleagues in Relex responsible for other budget lines. A conflict prevention mission (financed by the rapid response mechanism) took place in 2001. Furthermore, Fiji was chosen as one of 30 focus countries for the European Initiative for Democracy and Human Rights (EIDHR). Some € 3 mn was made available to suitable local organisations and institutions. In the meantime, support to Rev Yakabi's Citizens Constitutional Forum continued from the NGO budget line.

Initially we suspended all ongoing EDF projects financed under the National Indicative Programme, including work on Suva's rubbish dump, the Rewa bridge, and a sewerage system, all activities that had high visibility in Fiji. A block was put on the release of ninth EDF funds. In line with Article 96, we had to define the conditions under which aid would be resumed: the holding of free and fair elections, and the formation of a legitimate Government. The EU representatives in Suva were understandably impatient for the sanctions to be lifted. For them, it was frustrating not to be able to advance projects that were already underway and which had been frozen. In fact, after the elections of 2001 were generally recognised as being free and fair, we decided in 2002 to unfreeze the 8th EDF funds, while delaying the signature of the ninth EDF until there was clear evidence as to the legitimacy of the Government formed by Qarase.

It should be emphasised that the threat of suspending Fiji's participation from the sugar protocol was not invoked, as it was realised that this could have such a devastating effect on the economy and on all Fijians that it would make matters much worse rather than better. Other countries rather quickly removed their sanctions. Australia was the first, and eventually the Commonwealth gave tacit recognition by allowing Fiji to participate in CHOGM in Brisbane in 2002. Our own sanctions continued until November 2003, as we awaited the verdict of the Courts on the legitimacy of the Qarase Government. Member States in Council were of different views as to how long the sanctions should be retained.

Our NIP funds under the ninth EDF were targeted at primary school education in rural areas, hoping thereby to improve relations between communities in the longer term through positive interactions at schools based on a constructive curriculum.

In sum, we applied appropriate measures in the case of Fiji, but the leverage was not so great as if we had used the sugar protocol. We acted in line with other partners, but took longer than them to remove completely the aid sanctions. Political dialogue was frequent and conducted at a high level by the Commission, the Council and the Joint Assembly. There was a clear understanding of our EU position by the Fijians and the other partners, with whom we consulted frequently.

Lessons for Political Dialogue

Political dialogue does not just happen, it has to be worked on and sometimes engineered. One of the responsibilities of the Pacific Unit during this period was to see that political dialogue took place, at an appropriate level, and that appropriate messages were delivered. The Pacific Unit arranged two missions of Commissioner Nielson to the Pacific, as well as making arrangements for senior management in the persons of Friedrich Hamburger and Koos Richelle to lead the Post-Forum dialogue on successive occasions. On both occasions, important bilateral meetings took place with the three countries in crisis, as well as others. This experience suggests that political dialogue in the context of conflict prevention in the Pacific was worthwhile. In writing this I recognise that in the Pacific, the EU voice was not the only voice nor necessarily the most significant. However, our aid weight was considerable, and in coordination with other donors, we helped to make a positive impact on the course of events. There are special occasions for political dialogue, like the Post-Forum dialogue when messages can be delivered direct to the Pacific political leadership in a formal way.

We could perhaps do more to coordinate with the Member States the EU message that we want to put across to our Pacific partners. Some might ask if the EU speaks with three voices during the Post-Forum Dialogue. The EC, UK and France all have separate sessions. To some extent this is overcome by having preliminary meetings before hand. In this area we had come a long way since the Brisbane Post-Forum Dialogue when I accompanied the then Director-General in 1994. There were many more bilateral exchanges in Auckland in 2003.

There are occasions when the opportunity for political dialogue can be seized, or created, for example, by the mission of a commissioner or director-general. There are other occasions when less formal dialogue can take place, and these can contribute to preparing the ground for the more formal occasions. The basis for a good political dialogue is created by informal exchanges beforehand. We tried to maintain regular contact with the Brussels based actors, for example ACP ambassadors, the ACP secretariat, the Presidency and the member states, civil society, Australia and New Zealand, and MEPs, as well as seizing opportunities when Pacific people visit Brussels.

Concerning Support to Elections and Democracy, our record was mixed. We tried and failed in Fiji to support or provide monitors for the elections. The lesson seems to be that a reserve should be created for EOMs for elections which come up at short notice. We supported the elections in PNG but were unable to muster more than an EU exploratory electoral observation mission. We found financial support for the elections in Solomon Islands, but not for monitors.

In many respects, the Joint Assembly works closely along the lines of the Commonwealth with respect to electoral support and observations, and should perhaps coordinate more closely with them. On the other hand, we have provided financial support to institutions favouring democracy in Fiji and PNG. In a formal sense, appropriate measures have only been applied in Fiji. How effective they were in bringing a return (albeit short lived) to viable democracy is a matter for discussion. In Solomon Islands, by freezing Stabex funds, we sought to exert influence in favour of good governance.

In all three countries, EU financial resources within the national indicative programme (NIP) and from budget lines have been used for peace building. The conflict prevention mission of 2001 helped to shape the NIP for Fiji. On the other hand, the recommendation of the seminar of June 2003 was that we should contribute regionally to conflict prevention measures undertaken by the Forum Secretariat. Unfortunately, by that time all the regional resources had already been committed. Again, the lesson of experience suggests that a reserve should be kept at regional level for such contingencies.

There is clearly considerable scope for EU institutions to work together in concert, so that the EU punches its full weight. To some extent this can be achieved by making better use of existing mechanisms (both formal or informal) within the present framework of Cotonou. Other opportunities will arise as the new architecture promised by the EU constitution comes into effect, and brings in its train modifications to the common foreign and security policy.

With war-affected people, Bougainville 2002

With Prime Minister Kemakeza, Honiara 2003

Chapter 24.

DILEMMAS

In this chapter, I have drawn together some of the lessons of experience from my professional life. How do theories about the role of agriculture and the export crop sector in development conform with reality? What are the implications for equity and growth? Which policies can help to promote agricultural development? Which forms of aid delivery are most effective? What are the trade offs during the development process? I examine the performance of the countries where I have worked, and reflect on some issues of developmental significance.

Fashions in development thinking and aid philosophy go through cycles. Sometimes the emphasis switches to the rural sector and the importance of stimulating agriculture. At other times, industrialisation is seen as key, or employment and the informal sector. Today the importance of giving a voice to women and taking care of the environment are widely recognised as priorities.

Agricultural exports and economic growth

When George Tolley and I wrote about agricultural exports and development fifty years ago, theorists referred to the extraction of an agricultural surplus as a means of promoting overall economic development. Employment in agriculture would gradually reduce as workers found higher productivity jobs in other sectors of the economy, as Arthur Lewis foresaw in his famous article *Economic Development with Unlimited Supplies of Labour.* Agriculture was seen as a source of labour and revenue, as well as food, in support of other sectors of the economy. According to staple growth theory, agricultural exports could become a leading sector in overall development of the economy. Backward linkages would stimulate the supply of inputs for the production of the agricultural export, while forward linkages would bring processing of its output. Additionally, the wage and other income generated in the production of the cash export crop would stimulate consumer industries e.g. food, clothing, construction. Smallholder activity and rural infrastructural development e.g roads, wharves, would also ensue.

In colonial times, the British invested in tea plantations in India and Sri Lanka, rubber and oil palm in Malaysia, coffee and sisal in East Africa, sugar in Barbados, Guyana, and Fiji. The Dutch invested in rubber, tea, coffee, sugar and oil palm in Indonesia. The Americans invested in rubber plantations in Liberia and sugar and coconut estates in the Philippines. The French and Belgians established plantations in Africa. In many instances plantation labour was imported, notoriously for sugar cane in the Caribbean, Fiji, and Queensland. Tamils from India went to work on tea estates in Ceylon, while Javanese worked on rubber estates in Malaysia, and people from Senegal on rubber estates in Liberia. These investments were generally helpful in getting export agriculture started, but raised issues relating to growth and equity.

More recently, there have been other kinds of investment outside the colonial context, often in tropical fruits. Consider for example, bananas in the Caribbean by British and French companies, bananas in Central America by US firms, bananas and pineapples in the Philippines by Japanese and US firms. Even temperate vegetables and flowers have become significant sources of foreign exchange for countries like Kenya and Peru.

Country Performances

Looking at the performance of countries where I have lived and worked in the past, the results have been mixed. Kenya has outperformed Tanzania in agricultural exports, with significant success in tea, flowers and vegetables. Indonesia and the Philippines have achieved some growth through agricultural exports, but Sudan, PNG, and Solomon Islands have lost ground due to internal conflicts. All countries save Barbados have experienced large increases in population.

For Tanzania, where I worked for two years in the 1960s, coffee, sisal, cotton and tea were significant agricultural export earners. Some domestic linkages were evident at that time, in processing sisal into twine and sisal bags, but the bulk of production was exported as fibre for processing in Europe. There was one instant coffee factory in Bukoba, but the bulk of coffee went for export as coffee beans.

After several decades, Tanzania remains a predominantly primary producing country, with agriculture accounting for three quarters of employment and a third of economic output. Population has quadrupled from 12 mn in 1968 to 52 mn in 2015.

Agricultural exports have declined or stagnated. Sisal exports peaked at 234 thousand tons in 1964, accounting for one third of agricultural export earnings. Exports fell below 100 thousand tons in 1978, a result of the nationalisation of estates which took place under the Arusha Declaration. Many estates were abandoned due to lack of suitable managers. Declining prices as a result of competition from synthetics in the twine market, and falling soil fertility, also played a part. By 1992 production had dwindled to 24 thousand tons, and has remained at about that level subsequently. Coffee exports fluctuated over the years (due to rainfall variation and the incidence of coffee rust) from 57 thousand tons in 1968 to 61 thousand tons in 2013. Some 450,000 smallholders account for 95 per cent of production.

Neighbouring Kenya, where I lived for two years in the early 1970s, has fared much better. Although coffee exports have declined, tea and horticultural exports have boomed. After several decades, Kenya remains a predominantly primary producing country, with agriculture accounting for 60 per cent of employment and about a third of economic output. Population has quadrupled from 11 mn in 1975 to 47 mn in 2015. Life expectancy at 62, is similar to Tanzania, placing Kenya at 159 in the list of 195 countries for which data are available.

There have been some significant changes in the composition of agricultural exports. Tea and horticulture (mainly cut flowers, pineapples, and runner beans) have overtaken coffee as export earners, each with about one third shares. Tourism has become the other significant earner of foreign exchange. Despite the decrease in coffee exports, coffee production is still a major cash crop in many parts of the central highlands of Kenya and parts of western Kenya.

Coffee exports were at one time Kenya's leading foreign exchange earner, with record production in 1988 of 130,000 tons. Kenya's coffee exports in 1968 amounted to 48 thousand tons, and after increasing to 76,000 tons in 1992 fell back to 49,000 tons in 2013. With falling market prices, some smallholders turned to other crops or sold land for residential use.

Kenya has become the world's leading exporter of black tea, overtaking Sri Lanka, China and India. Tea exports have grown to 500 thousand tons earning $1.5 bn. More than 60 per cent is grown by smallholders.

Kenya's horticultural exports are another success story, becoming a major earner of foreign exchange. More than half the exports are produced by smallholders. Between 1974 and 2000 the value of horticultural exports quadrupled. Cut flowers are grown many by large estates, whereas fruits (pineapple) and vegetables also involve smallholders. Sisal exports amounted to 25 thousand tons in 2013, more or less at par with the much diminished exports of Tanzania.

For Indonesia, where I lived for four years in the 1970s, rubber, oil palm, and copra were significant agricultural export earners. Some linkages were evident at that time, in producing crumb rubber, and fractionating palm kernel oil. Cloves were produced domestically, largely for the *kretek* cigarette industry.

Indonesia remains a significant primary producing country, with agriculture accounting for 35 per cent of employment in 2012, compared with 56 per cent in 1990. Population has almost doubled in forty years to 256 mn in 2015. Per capita income has grown from $365 in 1972, to $733 in 1988 (double that of Tanzania's), and $1,810 in 2013. On this score, Indonesia ranks 134 in the list of countries. Life expectancy at 71 places Indonesia at 115 in the list of 195 countries for which data are available.

In the Philippines, where I worked for two years in the 1970s, copra was a significant agricultural export earner. Some linkages were evident at that time, in domestic production of coconut oil. After several decades, the Philippines remains a significant primary producing country, with agriculture accounting for 32 per cent of employment in 2012. Population has more than doubled in forty years to 102 mn in 2015.

Sudan, where I lived for four years in the 1980s, remains a significant primary producing country, with agriculture accounting for the bulk of employment. Population has more than doubled in thirty years to 40 mn in 2015 (excluding South Sudan which became an independent country in 2011). Unsurprisingly, in a country affected by civil war, tribal conflicts and droughts, per capita income has grown slowly. Life expectancy at 62 places Sudan at 156 in the list of 195 countries for which data are available.

Papua New Guinea, where I worked for two years in the 1980s, remains a significant primary producing country, with agriculture accounting for two thirds of employment. Population has almost doubled in twenty five years to 7.6 mn in 2015. In a country affected by civil war (Bougainville), and with considerable mineral wealth, per capita income has grown gradually. On this score, PNG ranks 149 (just below India) in the list of countries. Life expectancy at 62 (similar to Sudan) places PNG at 156 in the list of 195 countries for which data are available.

Solomon Islands, where I lived for four years in the 1990s, remains a predominantly primary producing country, with agriculture accounting for the bulk of employment. Population has almost doubled in twenty five years to 584,000 in 2015. In a country affected by civil war since 2000, per capita income has declined. On this score, Solomons ranks 148 (just above PNG) in the list of countries. Life expectancy at 68 (similar to the Philippines) places Solomons at 134 in the list of 195 countries for which data are available.

Barbados, where I lived for four years in the second half of the 1990s, has a diversified economy, with agriculture no longer accounting for a significant percentage of economic output. Population density is high at 669 per square kilometre, and numbers have grown slowly to 287 thousand in 2015. Per capita income increased to about $ 15,000 in 2015. On this score, Barbados ranks 53 in the list of countries. Life expectancy at 75 places Barbados at 65 in the list of 195 countries for which data are available.

Plantation Crops vs Food Crops

In the development literature, allegations have been made that plantations displace food crop production, and perpetuate a colonial system of exploitation with appropriation of a surplus for the benefit of rich countries. Prior to independence, processing of output was generally carried out in the metropolitan country, thereby inhibiting the important forward linkage for development of the domestic economy. Thus copra was exported instead of coconut oil, sisal fibre instead of twine or carpets, sheet rubber instead of rubber tyres, coffee beans rather than instant coffee.

Plantation agriculture is a good way to stimulate growth at an early stage of a country's development, as it brings with it backward linkages in the form of useful infrastructure, ports, roads, dispensaries, primary schools in remote areas, and forward linkages in terms of processing facilities eg Solomon Islands' oil palm and coconut estates. But few countries have managed to prosper only on the basis of agricultural exports. Sooner or later, the drift from rural areas to the towns occurs as countries develop their manufacturing and/or service sectors as Arthus Lewis' classic text *Economic Development with Unlimited Supplies of Labour* makes clear.

Tourism and Development

Small island economies like St Lucia (Arthur Lewis' birth place) cannot expect to achieve sustained growth on the basis of banana exports to Europe, but, in the absence of mineral wealth, have to exploit their comparative advantage in tourism. Tourism can be a leading sector, or it can be a useful adjunct to growth. Tanzania in its socialist days, notwithstanding its remarkable game reserves and pristine beaches, exhibited a marked distaste for foreign visitors, while its neighbour Kenya was much quicker to realise the economic and employment benefits from tourism. Financial services have also been popular in small island developing states (SIDS), but some have incurred the censure of the OECD's Financial Action Task Force or appeared on its Harmful Tax List.

Equity versus Growth

At the end of the day, it is apparent that thwarting basic economic principles of markets and entrepreneurship does not work. Tanzania's experiment with socialism under *Ujamaa* and the *Arusha declaration*, notwithstanding the appealing arguments of Nyerere, was not successful from a productive point of view. However, there were improvements in education and health in rural areas. India's decades of slow growth may be attributed in part to the belief of Nehru in the importance of state ownership, and restrictions on trade. Five Year Development Plans determining (Soviet-style) national investment in state owned industries were all the rage in countries like India and Tanzania, with little evident benefits to the poor or the rich.

On the other hand, the pendulum can swing too far in the other direction. The Washington consensus of the 1990s was associated with the advent of the banker Clausen to the presidency of the World Bank. Anne Krueger was appointed chief economist in place of Hollis Chenery. She reinstated the importance of market forces (prices matter) in promoting development and implied a diminished role for government. Aid effectiveness appeared to be greatest in countries which were open to trade and foreign investment, and allowed markets to function. The notion that a rising tide lifts all boats seemed to be borne out by economists like David Dollar. Most economic commentators today concur that the cake has to grow if the poor are to benefit.

But the post-Washington consensus associated with economists like Joseph Stiglitz (a successor to Anne Krueger as chief economist at the World Bank) contend that market forces alone are insufficient to promote development, citing the example of the tiger economies of East Asia where governments played a key role in bringing about enhanced rates of growth. I am reminded of the structuralist vs monetarist discussions of my student days in the USA.

The development literature is replete with articles advocating equity-based growth. Historical experience seems to indicate that there are few examples of this happening, and the poor have to wait for trickle-down effects. Is it then inevitable that in the process of achieving self-sustained growth that some classes of society have to carry the burden with little reward for themselves? One recalls the children working in mines during Britain's industrial revolution, and the landless poor working long hours for pitiful wages on construction sites in India.

The debate continues, in India and elsewhere, as to whether there are paths that combine greater equity through social investment with growth, as an alternative to trickle down. The fruits of *Shining India's* growth have yet to impact on the vast numbers of rural poor, even if the rapidly growing middle class is enjoying a life style hardly imaginable thirty years ago.

Countries which ignore equity considerations during the process of development face the risk of political instability, which can sour the investment climate and seriously impede growth. It is very difficult to deliver development aid in times of conflict, as experiences in Sudan and Bougainville illustrate. Lack of good governance results in short-termism on the part of the political elite, and can introduce the virus of corruption in both the private and public sectors.

Agricultural Policies for Growth

I now turn to policies that impact on agricultural development. As part of development policy, agriculture price policy has often been used negatively to keep food and raw materials cheap for the growing industrial sector. In some situations, low product prices for farmers are compensated by subsidies on inputs like fertiliser and credit, as in India.

Other countries have deliberately taxed agricultural exports in order to raise revenue to fund infrastructure or expenditures in the social sectors. Malaysia is a country that encouraged its agricultural exports of rubber and oil palm, with the backing of first class agricultural research, as a springboard for more general economic development. The Rubber Research Institute meetings in Kuala Lumpur (which I attended in 1975) are a fine illustration of how the innovations from plant breeding achieved by competent scientists can win the support of a vibrant plantation sector. Research by plant breeders in Colombia enabled farmers to withstand the threat of coffee rust.

Many critics of African development have pointed to cash crops such as cotton being grown at the expense of food crops like millet or sorghum, leading to loss of food self sufficiency. Whilst working in Kenya, I argued in favour of hybrid maize on the basis that its higher yields enabled a farmer with a limited acreage to meet family food requirements from a smaller area, thus freeing land for the cultivation of cash crops. In Tanzania, the mixed farming (coffee, bananas, dairy cows) practiced by the *Wachagga* people on the slopes of Mt Kilimanjaro, similar in many ways to the smallholder farmers in Nyeri district of Kenya, are prime examples of how farming can yield a healthy cash income sufficient to pay for school fees and other essentials. Planners in third world countries should not disadvantage their agricultural export sector by nationalisation (sisal in Tanzania) or by excessive taxation (cocoa by the West African Marketing Boards). Instead, they should seek to render it internationally competitive in the long term by investing in agricultural research. Agricultural exports are an important source of foreign exchange earnings and should not be taxed so highly that investment in new varieties or maintenance is discouraged.

Forms of Aid

Political parties in the UK have usually argued for a substantial aid programme based on three main pillars, humanitarian, commercial, and political. The first of these is sometimes called the moral argument, recognising our responsibility as a multi-faith society to help those less fortunate than ourselves. But for some tax payers this is not enough, and so the case is made that there are commercial benefits from aid. Thus in the early days of official aid, commodity aid took the form of shipments of fertiliser or tractors eg to India or Pakistan, goods which had been manufactured in the UK and paid for from the aid budget. Aid was tied to the purchase of UK goods and services. The latter could include consultancies to undertake feasibility studies for large projects, or the provision of technical cooperation to overcome skilled manpower constraints in the recipient countries. A refinement of the commercial case is that aid leading to development would lead to enhanced trade prospects for UK exporters.

Food aid is a form of commodity aid that was a convenient mechanism for disposing of food surpluses in the USA and the EU. The development literature is replete with the merits and demerits of food aid. Those who oppose food aid cite the deleterious effects on domestic production through lowering prices to farmers in the recipient country.

One of the pluses of commodity aid for donors is that it creates counterpart funds, which can applied to meet the local costs of development projects, as was the case for some of the earlier fertiliser shipments to India which helped to finance wells for poor villages. In Sudan, we were able to use food aid counterpart funds for the transport of food to those in greatest need.

The political case takes account of foreign policy considerations. The Cold War gave rise to a spate of development aid to Africa and the subcontinent, often linked with military assistance, to retain allegiances to the USA or the USSR. Some of these transfers earned development aid a bad name, with suspicions that funds were being transferred into Swiss bank accounts, rather than being applied to genuine development.

Aid can be a lever to secure votes in the UN. In the Pacific, aid rivalry was intense between the Republic of China and the People's Republic of China.

Project versus Programme Aid

Traditionally, official aid was delivered in the form of discrete projects, with each item of expenditure identified. Donors could visit and inspect projects within a given locality, and speak to project beneficiaries. Project aid gave aid donors a sense of accountability as well as visibility. It was the World Bank under McNamara that made initial forays away from project aid towards programme aid, accompanied by sectoral plans and policies. The rationale for this shift was that agricultural projects were deemed to be undermined by factors like inappropriate pricing policies. So sectoral policy dialogue became key, and this would be accompanied by loans and technical assistance for the sector at large. This was very much the approach we adopted with the Windwards banana industry when I was based in the Caribbean.

The next step, following the oil price boom and the debt crisis, was to structural adjustment lending, or balance of payments support, in which the dialogue was extended to the macro-economy, and the term conditionality became current. By 1978 ODA was building up a pipeline of project aid, but at the same time earmarking other funds for balance of payments support or programme aid for Ghana, Sudan, Zambia and Jamaica. The funds could be used to purchase British goods in situations where shortage of foreign exchange would otherwise preclude the import of spare parts. Such programme aid was normally delivered in the context of a country's stabilisation programme, agreed with the IMF. By 1983, as a result of the debt crisis, many developing countries were locked into policy agreements with the IMF and/or World Bank structural adjustment loans. At the macro-level, there was a revival of interest in export earnings as part of structural adjustment.

This is how we approached the utilisation of Stabex funds in St Lucia, having found that the project approach on its own was slowing up disbursement. Critics of this approach referred to cheque book aid, akin to budgetary support in colonial dependencies. Of course, such forms of lending did much to boost commitments and disbursements. In order to strengthen conditionality, loans would be made in tranches, with each tranche being dependent upon the achievement of specified macro-economic targets, such as a progressive reduction in budget deficits. In following this approach, the World Bank moved closer to the agenda of the IMF.

Rural development and smallholders

Prior to the new wave of rural development thinking in the 1970s, World Bank lending for agriculture was predominantly in the plantation sector. When Montague Yudelman was given charge of agricultural lending by McNamara, the emphasis switched to smallholders. For some export crops like coffee, large scale plantations have no great advantages of scale over smallholders, as processing can be done as well by smallholders as by estates. For some other crops such as tea, oil palm, and sugar, access to a large scale processing facility is critical. In such cases, the way forward for balanced growth is to encourage smallholders as out-growers. Spreading the benefits of agricultural export earnings by encouraging nucleus estates to bring in smallholders (CDC tea in Kenya, oil palm in Indonesia and Solomon Islands, sugar in the Philippines and India), brings benefits in terms of employment and income distribution in the process of development. Historically, smallholders were often discouraged by plantation owners, for fears of losing scarce labour, or of adverse effects on product quality. But more enlightened attitudes prevailed in Kenya with the Swynnerton Plan, the encouragement of rubber smallholders in Malaysia, and of tea out-growers by CDC in East Africa. On the other hand, some economists have argued that multilateral funding of aid projects to stimulate tea and coffee production will diminish overall returns to producers, because of price inelastic demand for these commodities.

It was in Nairobi in September 1973, that World Bank President McNamara gave a hugely influential speech, prioritising rural development as a means of tacking absolute poverty in the Third World. He set an ambitious goal of increasing production from 100 million smallholders by 5 per cent a year. In pursuit of this goal, he promised a large increase in aid commitments to the rural sector. Project investments included irrigation, rural credit, perennial crops, agricultural processing and area development projects. One of the largest projects was $ 350 mn for agricultural credit (ARDC IV) in India, which I was involved in appraising ten years later.

There was a mushrooming of integrated rural development projects financed by the World Bank and other donors, mostly in Africa. Unfortunately, many of these projects did not succeed, notably in Nigeria. The primary reason is that the good intentions of assisting smallholder farmers to improve productivity could not be realised, for want of worthwhile innovations. Sound agricultural research has to precede extension efforts, and research takes time. Sadly, many research stations in Africa had become moribund following Independence. It is a moot question as to what might have happened to developing country agriculture if the funds poured into rural development projects in the seventies and the eighties had been applied to agricultural research.

Not all agricultural development projects were failures. Those that focused on a single commodity like rubber that could benefit from improved clonal material, or involved smallholder tea out-growers, had the makings of success. The EC-sponsored Nuba Mountains and Jebel Marra projects in Sudan made some worthwhile impact on smallholder farmers, with increased animal draught and improved food crop varieties. In Asia, investment in irrigation and drainage was largely successful, and underpinned the Green Revolution. In Africa, where land was more abundant, but irrigation systems less developed (with the notable exception of the Gezira scheme in Sudan) success often came by enabling smallholders to expand the rainfed area under cultivation with ox drawn ploughs, rather than increasing yields per acre. Returns to labour rather than to land are more critical in Africa than Asia.

The introduction of tractors into small scale farming has often been controversial, whether in the context of *ujamaa* villages in Tanzania, land levelling in Pakistan, or for opening up new land in Bolivia. If tractors displace bullock power, does the improved timeliness of operations result in higher crop yields and free land that would otherwise be used to provide animal feed?

Technical Assistance in Rural Development

Many of the rural development projects funded in the 1980s required expatriate teams to manage the projects, and live in remote areas. The formula for staffing such projects raises interesting issues. The costs of the expatriate TA teams (salaries, housing, leave tickets) usually amount to large sums which can seem disproportionate to total project costs. Jealousies with poorly paid local staff can easily arise, and compound management difficulties.

Thus the NSSRDP in Indonesia was reached by a four hour car drive from Medan. The three expatriates (with their spouses) were housed in purpose built houses on the project compound, and no doubt were paid quite large salaries by the World Bank in compensation for the remoteness of their posting. For wives who had lived on rubber plantations in Malaysia, it might not have seemed such a hardship, but for the wife of one of the TA team who came from middle America, it must have seemed rather isolated.

I encountered many such TA teams in different parts of the world, and found that it is often quite difficult for the spouses of the TA staff who may feel isolated. Such individuals require a certain resilience, and belief in what the project or research is about. I think of such expatriate teams in smallholder rubber in Liberia, in WAPDA rice projects in Sierra Leone, in Jebel Marra and Nuba Mountains in Sudan, our friends the Baums in Ifakara in Tanzania, the Moocks in Kenya, and the Sweetmans in Indore. For such people, visitors from the outside world are usually welcome, as they bring news of the motherland. People like myself, who were always based in capital cities, lacked this kind of special experience.

It is worth recalling that in those days (as so vividly recalled in some of Somerset Maugham's short stories) most communication with the outside world and the family back home was by letter, which might take one or two weeks to arrive. Telephone calls where they were possible were prohibitively expensive. Telex machines did not exist, let alone mobile phones or e-mails!

Agricultural Extension

In the chapter on India I have mentioned the differences of extension approach between the train and visit system, and the farmer education approach. The latter usually is accompanied by a new technology, requiring the careful and timely applications of inputs (water, fertilizer, pesticides, new seeds) in order to increase yields. For the train and visit system to be effective, it too has to have some worthwhile ideas for productivity increases. Agricultural extension systems depend upon a flow of useful messages to deliver to farmers that will have an impact on land or labour productivity, as with IBFEP. Such messages come from sustained agricultural research which lays the basis for understanding the farming systems into which interventions will be introduced. In an ideal world, plant breeders would be able to come up with new varieties where the seed is the package, but this is not usually the case. Other complementary inputs are needed and farmer knowledge has to be augmented. Combatting plant diseases like coffee rust or pests like cocoa moth can be critical to the survival of a valuable export crop industry.

Irrigation

Earlier chapters have noted the very diverse irrigation systems that exist in the Third World, from the vast command schemes in India and Pakistan arising from dams and canals alongside major rivers flowing from the Himalayas, to the long-established terraces of gravity fed rice fields in Java and Bali, to the dug wells of Madhya Pradesh and the check dams and infiltration galleys of Baluchistan. Any farmer given a chance will favour irrigation over rain fed farming, and in high rainfall areas will seek to conserve monsoon rains by, for example, building tanks. In the flood plains, pumping underground water by means of tube wells is the norm.

For those farmers dependent on rainfall alone, life is much tougher, and this is where the majority of the rural poor subsist. Many have been pushed by population pressure onto hillsides to practice slash and burn type cultivation, which has the doubly unfortunate effects of destroying forests, and exposing the soil on steep slopes to erosion. The end result is perhaps best shown from experience in the Philippines, where vast tracts of cogon grasslands on otherwise denuded hillsides offer paltry feed to cattle. It is a challenge for agricultural scientists to rehabilitate these lands and bring them into higher productivity use. Some farming systems based upon the planting of the fast growing *Leucaena* species may offer a way forward.

Forestry

Countries like Solomon Islands have been blessed with tropical forests. The valuable hardwood species offer profits to logging companies from East Asia. In an ideal world, these forests would be logged selectively, and at a sustainable rate, and newly planted species would have time to grow to replace those taken out. The prices paid for forest licences and the export tax on logs should reflect accurately world market value.

Unfortunately in Solomon Islands, and in countries like Papua New Guinea, the actual practice of logging by foreign companies is far from the ideal. Given the geography of Solomon Islands, with scattered islands remote from the capital Honiara, it is difficult to inspect and monitor logging operations, even if the political will is present. Our studies revealed (as had the Barnett enquiry in Papua New Guinea) that the overall rate of logging was far in excess of the sustainable rate and that harvesting processes were harmful to natural forest regeneration. Moreover, undervaluation of logs at point of export was rife. Certification schemes have come into being that seek to assure end-users of timber that proper procedures have been followed, and these should be encouraged, but until good governance is in place there is no doubt that such practices will continue. An unfortunate side effect of logging in Solomon Islands is siltation which destroys marine life. Tourism earnings suffer as a result.

Minerals

Countries with mineral wealth should have a head start in development, since the valuable export earnings from selling copper and gold can be invested in infrastructure and education. Quite apart from the so called *Dutch Disease*, with implications for exchange rates and resource movements between sectors, mineral wealth can be a mixed blessing. The exploitation of mineral wealth in third world countries inevitably involves foreign companies which have the technology to discover promising sites, and the enormous capital resources needed for exploration and extraction. In the process of negotiation, three parties are usually involved: the national government, local landowners and the foreign mining company. These negotiations will necessarily be complex. The national government will be concerned that a good share of the revenues accrues to the treasury, the landowners will want a large share of the revenues for local development and as compensation for environmental disturbance and damage, and the foreign company will want a major share to cover the investment costs and risks. Getting the balance right will never be easy. Opposition parties will argue that the Government has acquiesced in a deal too favorable to the mining company; shareholders will tell the mining company that they have given too much away, and local leaders may be accused by their people of ignoring traditional land use rights. The long standing Bougainville crisis is a good example of these dilemmas.

Fisheries

With the ratification of the UN Law of the Sea in 1994, countries like Solomon Islands found that they owned considerable renewable natural resources in the form of tuna migrating in their territorial waters. Tuna can be caught and processed on shore, as was the case in Western province with the help of a Japanese company. Solomon Taiyo used concrete vessels and environmentally-sound pole and line methods of catching. This was indeed a sensible foreign investment opportunity which could well have been replicated more often, not only in Solomon Islands but elsewhere in the Pacific.

However, most of the distant water fishing fleets prefer to remain offshore using long line fishing techniques, and putting the catch in large refrigerated vessels to carry the product back to home bases. A single blue fin tuna can fetch several hundred thousand pounds in the Tokyo fish market. How to ensure that the distant water fishing fleets pay a fair share of the returns from their catch to the owners of the resource: the Solomon Islanders? The notable work of the Forum Fisheries Agency, based in Honiara is explicitly addressed to this issue. Defining maritime boundaries, and organising surveillance over large tracts of ocean using ships, aircraft and satellite technology linked to transponders, all help to minimise poaching.

European Aid

European aid to ACP countries gives greater assurance of continuity, being based on a contractual approach over a five year period (Lomé) or twenty years (Cotonou), with the political dimensions made explicit, rather than an annual aid framework exercise like ODA's.

As a regional entity, the EU favours a regional approach, especially important for example for dealing with issues like Pacific fisheries or Caribbean tourism. European aid offers a wide range of instruments, including humanitarian aid, as well as flexibility with special programmes to address particular problems like the banana budget line. In principle, there is also greater cost effectiveness in aid delivery, owing to wider competition in the supply of goods and services.

The EU structure of a network of delegations at country level allows close dialogue with national authorities. The partnership principle of Lomé and Cotonou is exemplified in the role of the national authorising officer. In practice, the notion of co-management of EC aid may not work so well where governments have weak capacity, and TA is necessary to support the NAO office. Furthermore, over time, the European Commission has become more concerned with conditionality and policy dialogue, with *appropriate measures* appearing in the text of Cotonou when countries depart from democratic principles. European aid offers greater political leverage, when circumstances demand, of 28 Member States acting together. At the same time, scattered aid has given way to concentration on one or two focal sectors in a particular recipient country. An evaluation of EC aid to ACP countries over the period 1985-1995 confirmed a transition from a project based to a policy based approach, with enhanced sectoral dialogue.

On the other hand, European Aid is notorious for its slow delivery mechanisms, due to complex procedures which are time consuming. The process of inter-service consultation is laborious and often frustrating as I discovered in bringing Glenys Kinnock's banana budget line into being.

Part of the reason for delays are the lengthy tender procedures to satisfy Member States that their commercial interests are being safeguarded.

The Stabex and Sysmin schemes are well founded instruments, as far as the theoretical literature is concerned, which focuses on the destabilising consequences of fluctuations in export earnings from primary products. However, there are practical difficulties in programming Stabex and Sysmin resources, as I discovered in the Windwards and Papua New Guinea.

Sources of Conflict

Disputes over land and water lie at the root of many conflicts. Africans resent Europeans for alienating their lands, as in Kenya. In traditional agrarian societies, cultivators are upset when pastoralists allow their cattle to damage crops, as in Darfur. Land designated as wild life parks may be infringed by cattle owners like the Maasai who move their herds around with the seasonal rains. Foresters are concerned when shifting cultivators burn and slash woodland for purposes of cultivation, as in the Philippines.

Tribal people are disturbed when their lands are flooded to create dams, as in the Narmada project in India, and the Victoria dam in Sri Lanka. Transmigrants from Java can affect the livelihoods of traditional hunter-gatherers in Kalimantan. Down-streamers are disturbed when up-streamers divert extra water for irrigation, as between Egypt and Sudan, Pakistan and India. Mines which disfigure the land surface and pollute rivers with their tailings cause grief to landowners, as in Bougainville.

It is self-evident that countries under conflict cannot develop. Instead they regress. Sadly, Solomon Islands since 1996 is a good example. Sudan in the 1980s is another, as is South Sudan today. In such economies, normal aid flows can do little. Relief aid can be used to help save lives, but the principal concern of the global community must be to resolve conflict and restore peace. This is very much the mandate of the United Nations and its development wing UNDP. The World Bank (formerly the International Bank for *Reconstruction* and Development) has been an important global player in aid delivery for decades, but its role as financier of development has been overtaken by private financial flows for several middle income economies. Hence the World Bank's search for an additional role beyond being a development *agency*, as a source of development *knowledge* or development *solutions*. The problems of dealing with fragile economies is drawing the World Bank closer to the United Nations in recognition of the need to overcome conflicts as a precursor of development. They also shared an important agenda in defining the post-2015 development goals, or SDGs.

Wealth and Poverty

There is increasing concern about the concentration of the world's wealth in a very few hands. Piketty has pointed out that as long as the rate of return on capital exceeds the rate of growth of the economy, the income and wealth of the rich will grow faster than the typical income from work. The astonishing statistic researched by Oxfam suggests that the richest 85 individuals in the world have as much wealth as the poorest half of the global population of 3.5 billion.

Some have accumulated wealth by political means, like Marcos of the Philippines and Mobutu of Zaire. Philanthropists like Bill Gates and Warren Buffet have earned their money through innovation and the stock market. Some plutocrats have followed their example and allocated large parts of their fortunes to the needs of the poor in the third world. The worthy objective of tackling poverty underpins much of official aid. However, my experience in India (where most poor people live) indicates how difficult it is to channel official aid to the poorest groups in society. In this context, one must view the World Bank President Jim Kim's aim of eliminating all poverty by 2030 as admirable, but extremely challenging.

Unsustainable hillside farming in the Philippines, 1977

Irrigation canal in Panay, 1977

Hillside farming must be sustainable

Chapter 25.

REFLECTIONS

Looking back to my childhood, I count myself fortunate to have been granted an interesting and fairly comfortable life. Unlike my father, I have never had to put my life on the line in defence of my country. During and after the war we may have been on rations, but I have never suffered any malnutrition. At that time, my mother kept chickens in the back garden. Aunt Mabel from Melbourne used to send us food parcels after the war. Not so long ago, people wondered if India could ever feed itself, while Bangladesh was thought of as a basket case. Amazingly, the green revolution has stimulated the supply side of food production in India, even if the distribution of income is such that too many poor people are stunted, while the middle classes struggle with obesity. Bangladesh has prospered, and even has better human development indices than India.

I am glad that I studied agricultural economics, which gave me some skills and insights useful for working in developing countries. On the other hand, too great a focus on farming in the rural sector tends to limit one's perspective on other aspects of rural livelihoods, as well as for growth prospects in other sectors of the economy. For a long time I was locked into quantitative analysis, when a more people-centred approach might have been better. It took me many years to understand the importance of inter-personal communication, and acquire management skills.

There have been intervals of professional satisfaction, and other times when I lacked confidence. Language skills have never been my *forte*, and I have felt this throughout my adult life, and especially in Brussels where all my colleagues were fluent in two or three languages. I do not regret the science knowledge I acquired at school, but were I to start again, I would try much harder at French.

Generally I would suggest to my grandchildren, once embarked on a course or activity, do not give up, but see it through. Make the most of your academic opportunities. I should have obtained at least an O level at physics, an A level at French, and a distinction in my postgraduate diploma had I applied myself. When I started work on the farm it was some weeks before I overcame homesickness. Similarly, in North Carolina, it was some months before I settled down. In Brussels, it took me nearly a year to adjust to a new office environment.

There have been remarkable advances in technology over the last fifty years. When I first travelled to the USA I went by ocean liner. Nowadays people jet around the world without blinking an eye. Sadly, flying has lost the aura of adventure and romance that I recall from the past. Crowded into narrow seats, and fed poorly, air travellers today are even discouraged from viewing the fascinating terrain that unfolds below. In the sixties in Tanzania, airmail letters were the normal means of communication, taking a minimum of two weeks to obtain a reply. News came from the BBC world service and the Guardian airmail edition. In Sudan in the eighties, we relied on radios to secure a phone patch to Europe via Portishead or Berner radio. It could take hours to get a connection. Nowadays we expect instant communication via Skype, and e-mails wherever we are in the world.

Although I had lived in the southern United States during the time of sit-ins, voter registration, and civil rights marches (and participated in some of these), I was unprepared for the extent of interracial tensions I encountered in Tanzania in the sixties. Perhaps because I worked and lived in a university environment in Kenya, I felt less exposed there, but was nonetheless conscious of some ingrained attitudes towards Africans on the part of white settlers, which I encountered especially in the various clubs that surround Nairobi. In many ways, it was a relief to find in Asia that such tensions are virtually non-existent. In Jakarta, I used to play tennis regularly with my Indonesian colleagues, and curiously, I never felt that kind of tension in our relations with the different peoples of Sudan, be they northerners or southerners. In the Caribbean, the population of African origin has not forgotten slavery, but there are few tensions between the races. Perhaps these differences in attitude were engendered by colonial rather than protectorate status.

Cricket has always been a great leveller among the different races of the Commonwealth. It was great to see the West Indies in their ascendancy, as it is pleasing today to see the multi-racial South African team. At Raleigh, we fielded a Commonwealth team (with representatives from India, Pakistan, Rhodesia, Australia, New Zealand and the UK) in matches against Charlotte, Chapel Hill, Greensboro, Howard University, and the British Embassy in Washington DC. In Barbados, the Delegation team won back the Darmuzey Cup from the British High Commission. *Viva* cricket and development!

Societies have changed, in some respects for the better. I find it remarkable that such positive developments have occurred as the elections of Nelson Mandela and Barack Obama. The records of these two Presidents are not perfect, and nor are the societies which they govern(ed), but it would have been hard to foresee their emergence on the international stage even thirty years ago. On the other hand, the resurgence of religious fundamentalism, and the conflicts which have been spawned, are a major concern for the global community.

It is pleasing that the UK Government has stuck to the goal of delivering official aid at levels close to the UN target. It is encouraging that considerable progress has been made towards the achievement of the MDGs, and that the SDGs have been successfully launched. Poverty has been reduced, girls are being educated, malaria is being tackled, child mortality is declining. It would be wonderful if the example of Bill and Melinda Gates could be followed by other very rich people, rather than flaunting wealth in conspicuous consumption. It remains to be seen whether Jim Kim will succeed in bending the arc of history, but how wonderful it would be if absolute poverty could be eliminated in the next fifteen years.

With Koos Richelle and EC staff at the Pacific Forum, Auckland 2003

The Pacific team in Brussels, 2003

Inspecting pepper vines with Pamudji, Lampung 1974

With NEDA staff in Davao, 1976

Rubber nursery in Kalimantan

With Dr Das of IBFEP inspecting wheat demonstration in Bihar

EU Parliamentarians with refugees in Al-Geneina, 1985

Nicholas Monck at Amboni Sisal Estates, 1968

Governor's residence, Port Stanley 1983

FAO coconuts mission, Menado 1974

With Domingo Raymundo and David Parbery, Panay 1977

With villagers in Maharashtra, 1982

Orphan children under ICRC care, Wau 1989

Inspecting EC Food Aid deliveries, Port Sudan 1989

With Professor Badri and NAO Mekki Osman, Khartoum 1988

Farewell from Kenny Anthony, Prime Minister of St Lucia, 1999

EU Delegation team with the Darmuzey Cup, 1999

Food relief flight arrives in Al-Fasher, 1985

Farewell from the Diplomatic Corps, Barbados 1999

With Ambassador of Cuba, Barbados 1999

Bibliography

Adrien P, *Cricket and Development*, **Basseterre**, 1999

Archives, *including Oral Histories, Project Completion Reports, and Evaluations*, **World Bank**, 2014

Arrowsmith K, *Bush Paths*, **The Pentland Press**, 1991

Asian Development Bank, *Tuna: A Key Economic Resource in the Pacific*, **Manila**, 2001

Badawi F, *Sudan and the European Community*, **Delegation of the Commission of the European Communities, Khartoum**, 1986

Barnett T, *Commission of Enquiry into Aspects of the Forestry Industry*, **Government of Papua New Guinea**, 1989

Boge V, Conflict Potential and Violent Conflicts in the South Pacific, **University of Hamburg**, 2001

Bridger G, *How I Failed to Save the World or Forty Years of Foreign Aid*, **AuthorHouse**, 2008

Bridger G and J T Winpenny, *Planning Development Projects: A Practical Guide to the Choice and Appraisal of Public Sector Investments*, **HMSO**, 1983

Caribbean Group for Cooperation in Economic Development, *Tourism and the Environment in the Caribbean: An Economic Framework*, **Environment Department of the World Bank in collaboration with the European Commission**, 2000

Carruthers I D and G D Gwyer, *Prospects for the Pakistan Tea Industry*, **The Pakistan Development Review**, 1971

Cassen R and Associates, *Does Aid Work?*, **Oxford**, 1986

Chambers R, *Rural Development: Putting the Last First*, **IDS Sussex**, 1983

Communication from the Commission to the European Parliament, *Special Framework of Assistance for Traditional ACP Suppliers of Bananas (Council Regulation 856/1999)*, **Biennial Report from the Commission 2000**, 2001

Coulson A, *Tanzania: A Political Economy*, **Oxford University Press**, 2013

Dollar D and C Burnside, *Aid, Policies and Growth*, **American Economic Review**, 2000

European Centre on Pacific Issues, *Seminar on the Cotonou Agreement and the Conflicts in the Pacific*, **Brussels**, 2004

European Commission, *The Caribbean and the European Union*, **Luxembourg**, 1995

FAO, *Support to Agricultural Planning Indonesia: Project Findings and Recommendations*, **Rome**, 1975

FAO Planning Team, *Agricultural Performance and Programmes in Repelita II*, **Jakarta**, 1973

Fieldson R, *The Demand for Agricultural Economists in Developing Countries*, paper presented to the Agricultural Economists Society Conference, 1981.

Gittinger J P, *Economic Analysis of Agricultural Projects*, **Johns Hopkins**, 1973

Gwyer G D, *Determinants of Long Term Capital Flows to Peru 1950-1965*, PhD thesis, **North Carolina State University**, 1967 (on microfilm at Ann Arbor, Michigan University)

Gwyer G D, *Long and Short Run Elasticities of Sisal Supply*, **East African Economic Review**, 1971

Gwyer G D, *Perennial Crop Supply Response: The Case of Tanzanian Sisal*, **Agrarian Development Study No. 3**, Wye College, University of London, 1971

Gwyer G D, *Agriculture and Unemployment*, **African Development**, 1972

Gwyer G D, *Formal or Informal Commodity Agreements: The Case of Sisal*, **Oxford Agrarian Studies**, 1972

Gwyer G D, *Employment opportunities in Kenya agriculture*, **East Africa Journal**, 1972

Gwyer G D, *Three International Commodity Agreements: The Experience of East Africa*, **Economic Development and Cultural Change**, 1973

Gwyer G D, *Trends in Kenyan Agriculture in Relation to Employment*, **The Journal of Modern African Studies**, 1973

Gwyer G D and P J Avontroodt, *Edible Oils: Supply and Demand*, **Bulletin of Indonesian Economic Studies**, 1974

Gwyer G D, *The Rubber Market: Recent Developments and Future Prospects*, **Menara Perkebunan**, 1975

Gwyer G D, *Demand and Supply Projections for Cloves*, **Bulletin of Indonesian Economic Studies**, 1976

Gwyer G D, *Developing Hillside Farming Systems for the Tropics: the Case of the Philippines*, **Oxford Agrarian Studies**, 1978

Gwyer G, *Herd Simulations in relation to Beef Requirements of the Philippines*, **Oxford Agrarian Studies**, 1979

Gwyer G D (editor), *Beef Investment Planning Manual*, **Overseas Development Administration**, 1980

Gwyer G D, *The Role of Plantations in Development*, **Tropical Agricultural Association Bulletin**, 1982

Gwyer G, *Solomon Islands and the European Community*, **The Courier**, 1992

Gwyer G D, *Barbados-EU Cooperation: Building on Success*, **The Courier**, 1997

Gwyer G D, *Grenada-EU Cooperation: Focus on Infrastructure and Tourism*, **The Courier**, 1997

Gwyer G D, *Stabex Flows to the Windward Islands*, **Caribbean Group for Cooperation in Economic Development**, 1998

Gwyer G D and J C H Morris, *Natural Resources*, **The Evaluation of Aid Projects and Programmes**, ODA, 1983

Hou R N, *The Solomon Islands economy: recent developments and the impact of recent tensions*, **Pacific Economic Bulletin**, 2002

Kengalu A M, *Embargo: The Jeanette Diana Affair*, **Robert Brown and Associates**, 1988

Lea D and T Curtin, *Land, Law and Economic Development*, **Cambridge**, 2010

Lele, Uma *The Design of Rural Development: Lessons from Africa*, **World Bank**,1975

Lewis W A, *Economic Development with Unlimited Supplies of Labour*, **The Manchester School**, 1954

Luce E, *In Spite of the Gods: The Strange Rise of Modern India*, **Doubleday**, 2006

Macmillan H, *Pointing the Way*, **Macmillan**, 1972

Maxwell S (editor), *To Cure All Hunger: Food Policy and Food Security in Sudan*, **London**, 1991

Mellor J, *Toward a Theory of Agricultural Development*, in **Agricultural Development and Economic Growth**, Cornell University Press, 1967

Ministry of Overseas Development, *An Account of the British Aid Programme*, **Text of United Kingdom Memorandum to the Development Assistance Committee of the Organisation for Economic Cooperation and Development**, 1975

Ministry of Overseas Development, *The Changing Emphasis in British Aid Policies: More Help for the Poorest*, **London**, 1975

Morris J C H and G D Gwyer, *UK Experience with Identifying and Implementing Poverty Related Projects*, **ODI Development Review**, 1983

Ranis G and J C H Fei, *A Theory of Economic Development*, **American Economic Review**, 1961

Schultz T, *Transforming Traditional Agriculture*, **New Haven**, 1964

Sharrock G, F C Clift, and G D Gwyer, *Fertilizer Education in Eastern India: The Indo-British Fertilizer Education Project*, **Agricultural Administration**, 1985

Short F, *Policing a Clash of Cultures*, **Kindle**, 2015

Tolley G S and G D Gwyer, *International Trade in Agricultural Products in Relation to Economic Development*, in **Agricultural Development and Economic Growth**, Cornell University Press, 1967

Toye J, *Dilemmas of Development*, **Basil Blackwell**, 1987

Wharton C R, *Subsistence Agriculture and Economic Development*, **Aldine**, 1969